QUARKXPRESS® 4

Advanced Electronic Mechanicals

Revised Edition

AGAINST THE CLOCK
PERFORMANCE SUPPORT & TRAINING SYSTEMS

PRENTICE HALL
Upper Saddle River, NJ 07458

Library of Congress Cataloging-in-Publication Data

QuarkXPress 4.0: advanced electronic mechanicals.
       p.   cm. -- (Against the clock)
  ISBN 0-13-095826-3
   1. QuarkXPress (Computer file). 2. Desktop publishing. I. Series.
Z253.532.Q37Q36 1998
686.2' 2544536 -- dc21

                                                98-34114
                                                  CIP

Acquisitions Editor: *Elizabeth Sugg*
Developmental Editor: *Judy Casillo*
Supervising Manager: *Mary Carnis*
Production Editor: *Denise Brown*
Director of Manufacturing & Production: *Bruce Johnson*
Manufacturing Buyer: *Ed O'Dougherty*
Editorial Assistant: *Brian Hyland*

Formatting/page make-up: *Against The Clock, Inc.*
Printer/Binder: *Banta*
Cover Design: *Joe Sengotta*
Icon Design: *James Braun*
Marketing Manager: *Shannon Simonsen*
Creative Director: *Marianne Frasco*
Sales Director: *Ryan DeGrote*
Director of Marketing: *Debbie Yarnell*

©1998 by Prentice Hall, Inc.
Upper Saddle River, New Jersey 07458

All rights reserved. No part of this book may be
reproduced, in any form or by any means,
without permission in writing from the publisher.

The fonts utilized in this training course are the property of Against The Clock, Inc., and are supplied to the legitimate buyers of the Against The Clock training materials solely for use with the exercises and projects provided in the body of the materials. They may not be used for any other purpose, and under no circumstances can they be transferred to another individual, nor copied, nor distributed by any means whatsoever.

A portion of the images supplied in this book are Copyright © PhotoDisc, Inc., 201 Fourth Ave. Seattle, WA 98121. These images are the sole property of PhotoDisc and are used by Against The Clock with the permission of the owners. They may not be distributed, copied, transferred, or reproduced by any means whatsoever other than for the completion of the exercises and projects contained in this Against The Clock training material.

Against The Clock and the Against The Clock logo are trademarks of Against The Clock, Inc., registered in the United States and elsewhere. References to, and instructional materials provided for, any particular application program, operating system, hardware platform or other commercially available product or products does not represent an endorsement of such product or products by Against The Clock, Inc. or Prentice Hall, Inc.

Adobe, Acrobat, Adobe Illustrator, PageMaker, Photoshop, Adobe Type Manager, and PostScript are trademarks of Adobe Systems Incorporated. Macromedia FreeHand is a registered trademark of Macromedia. QuarkXPress is a registered trademark of Quark, Inc. TrapWise and PressWise are registered trademarks of Luminous Corporation. Microsoft, MS-DOS, Windows, and Windows NT are either registered trademarks or trademarks of Microsoft Corporation.

Other products and company names mentioned herein may be the trademarks of their respective owners.

Printed in the United States of America

10 9 8 7 6 5 4

ISBN 0-13-022966-0

Prentice Hall International (UK) Limited, London
Prentice Hall of Australia Pty. Limited, Sydney
Prentice Hall Canada Inc., Toronto
Prentice Hall Hispanoamericana, S.A., Mexico
Prentice Hall of India Private Limited, New Delhi
Prentice Hall of Japan, Inc., Tokyo
Pearson Education Asia Pte. Ltd., Singapore
Editora Prentice Hall do Brasil, Ltda., Rio de Janeiro

Contents

GETTING STARTED	1
Platform	1
Naming Conventions	1
Key Commands	1
The CD-ROM and Initial Setup Considerations	2
1. INTRODUCTION	5
Assumptions about Current Proficiency	6
What We're Going to Learn	6
2. MANAGING WORKFLOW	9
QuarkXPress Preferences	10
Application Preferences	11
Document Preferences	17
Libraries	27
Templates	30
Managing Images	38
3. STRUCTURING YOUR LAYOUTS	45
Grids + Baseline Grid	46
Using Custom Grids and Template Files	47
Copy and Layout Fitting	59
Kerning and Tracking	59
The Color of Type	63
4. WORKING WITH SHAPES	73
Complex Merging	75
Applying Blends to Merged Objects	80
Advanced Bézier Tool Techniques	86
5. COMPLEX TEXT ELEMENTS	97
Converting Text to Paths	98
Putting Type inside of Character-based Graphics	103
Text on Paths	107
Text on Curved Paths	110
Text on Circles or Ovals	114
Dingbats and Type Paths	116
REVIEW #1	119
6. TEXT AND GRAPHICS LIVING TOGETHER	121
Coloring Text and Text Boxes	122
Runarounds and Clipping Paths	124
Creating Runarounds	127
Adjusting Hyphenation and Justification of Runarounds	130
Kerning and Tracking in Runarounds	133
Alternatives to Automatic Runarounds	141
QuarkXPress 4 Clipping Paths — Avoid	142
Running Text Inside a Picture's Contours	142
Anchored Objects	145
7. ADVANCED STYLES	151
Editorial Priority	152
Building Styles	154
Appending Styles From Another Document	156
Styles and Workflow	161
Creating Character Styles	165

8. Working with Long Documents — 169

The Importance of Consistency — 170
Starting with a Primary Master Document — 170
Books — 174
Lists — 181
Index Creation Prep — 185
The Index Palette — 186

9. Managing Output — 193

Workflow Issues for Printing — 194
Print Dialog Boxes – a Review — 195
Working with Print Styles — 198
Separations — 200
Tiling — 201
Halftoning — 203
Using the PPD Manager — 205
PostScript and QuarkXPress — 205
Creating an Output Request Form — 207
Trapping — 207
Digital Imposition — 209
Output Tips — 209
Contract Proofing — 210

Review #2 — 211

Projects

Gym Ad (Chapter 3) — A-1
Recipe Book (Chapter 5) — B-1
Tropical Suites Brochure (Chapter 6) — C-1
Staying Alive Newsletter (Chapter 7) — D-1
Automation Booklet (Chapter 8) — E-1
GASP Newsletter (Chapter 9) — F-1

Glossary

Index

Preface

Purpose

The Against The Clock series has been developed specifically for those involved in the graphic arts field.

Welcome to the world of electronic design and prepress. Many of our readers are already involved in the industry — in advertising and design companies, in prepress and imaging firms, and in the world of commercial printing and reproduction. Others are preparing for a career somewhere in the profession.

This series of courses will provide you with the necessary skills to work in this fast-paced, exciting, and rapidly expanding business. Many people feel that they can simply purchase a computer, the appropriate software, a laser printer, a ream of paper, and begin designing and producing high-quality printed materials. While this might suffice for a barbecue announcement or a flyer advertising a local hair salon, the real world of four-color printing and professional communication requires a serious commitment.

The Series

The applications presented in the Against The Clock series stand out as the programs of choice in professional graphic arts environments.

We've used a modular design for the Against The Clock series, allowing you to mix and match the drawing, imaging, and page layout applications to exactly suit your specific needs.

Titles available in the Against The Clock series include:

Macintosh: Basic Operations
Windows: Basic Operations
Adobe Illustrator: An Introduction to Digital Illustration
Adobe Illustrator: Advanced Digital Illustration
Freehand: An Introduction to Digital Illustration
Freehand: Advanced Digital Illustration
Adobe PageMaker: An Introduction to Electronic Mechanicals
Adobe PageMaker: Advanced Electronic Mechanicals
QuarkXPress: An Introduction to Electronic Mechanicals
QuarkXPress: Advanced Electronic Mechanicals
Adobe Photoshop: An Introduction to Digital Images
Adobe Photoshop: Advanced Digital Images
File Preparation: The Responsible Electronic Page
Preflight: An Introduction to File Analysis and Repair
TrapWise: Trapping
PressWise: Imposition

How to Use This Workbook

We've designed our courses to be "cross-platform." While many sites use Macintosh computers, there are an increasing number of graphic arts service providers using Intel-based systems running Windows (or Windows NT). The books in this series are applicable to either of these systems.

All applications covered in the Against The Clock series are similar in operation and appearance both on a Macintosh or Windows system. When a particular function differs from machine to machine, we present both.

ICONS AND VISUALS

Pencil icon indicates a comment from an experienced operator. When you see the pencil icon, you'll find corresponding sidebar text that augments or enhances the subject.

Bomb icon indicates a potential problem or difficulty. For instance, a certain technique might lead to pages that prove difficult to output. In other cases, there might be something that a program cannot easily accomplish, so we might present a workaround.

Pointing Finger indicates a hands-on activity — whether a short exercise or complete project. This will be the icon seen most often throughout the course.

Key icon is used to indicate a keyboard equivalent to a menu or dialog box option. Key commands are often faster than using the mouse to select a menu option. Experienced operators often mix keyboard equivalents with menu/dialog box selections to achieve optimum speed.

If you are a Windows user, be certain to refer to the corresponding text or images whenever you see this **Windows** icon. Although there isn't a great deal of difference between these applications on a Macintosh or a Windows system, there are certain instances where there's enough of a difference worth noting.

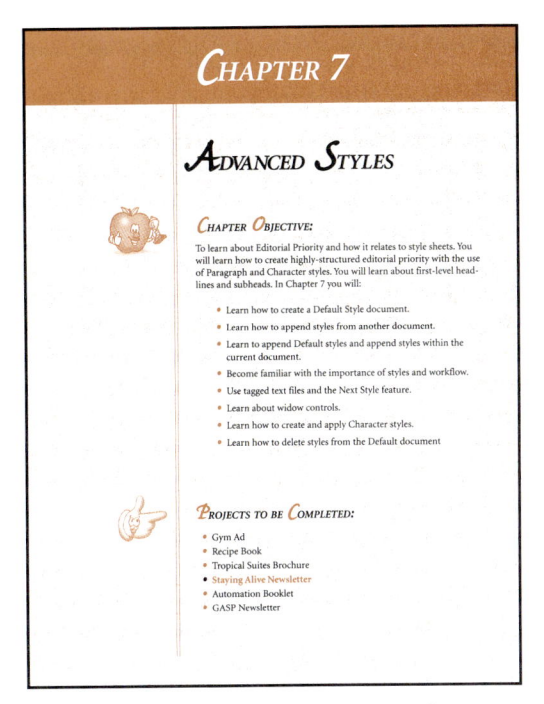

Book Walkthrough

CHAPTER OPENINGS provide the reader with specific objectives.

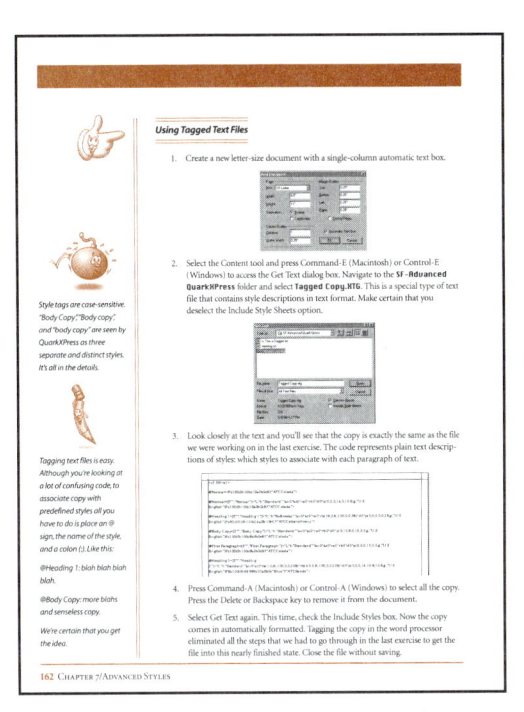

SIDEBARS and HANDS-ON ACTIVITIES supplement concepts presented in the material.

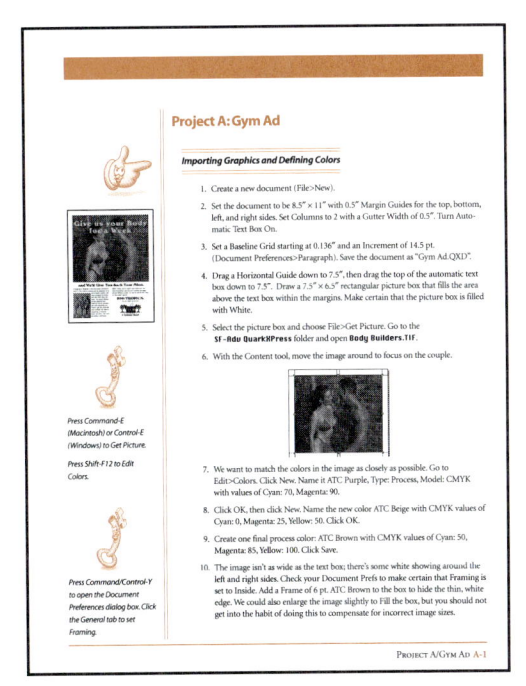

SUPPLEMENTAL PROJECTS offer practice opportunities in addition to the exercises.

PROJECT ASSIGNMENTS will result in finished artwork — with an emphasis on proper file construction methods.

THE PROJECTS YOU WILL WORK ON

The Against The Clock course materials have been constructed with two primary building blocks: exercises and projects. Projects always result in a finished piece of work — digital imagery built from the ground up, utilizing photographic-quality images, vector artwork from Illustration programs, and type elements from the library supplied on your student CD-ROM.

This course, *QuarkXPress 4.0, Advanced Electronic Mechanicals*, uses several projects that you will work on during your learning sessions. You will find the projects that you will have completed by the end of the course displayed on the inside front cover of the book. Here's a brief overview of each:

PROJECT A: GYM AD

The *Gym Ad* requires a solid working knowledge of the various attributes of both text and picture placeholders. The ad design requires the use of multiple columns, a structured grid, and the ability to fit type into the space available. Since most ads are required to fit into predetermined sizes (provided by the publications in which they are to appear), this ad stresses structure and maximizing impact in the space you have avaliable.

PROJECT B: STAYING ALIVE NEWSLETTER

The latest version of QuarkXPress is particularly well-suited to the creation and management of lengthy documents. The *Staying Alive* is a newsletter, and the first of several projects that allow you to practice your skills in managing long documents or publications. As in most of the other assignments, you will be required to balance text and graphic elements together to achieve a professional, structured appearance. Several advanced features are utilized, including text wrap, ranging issues, and the creation and application of drop caps.

PROJECT C: TROPICAL SUITES BROCHURE

QuarkXPress is utilized in many of the nation's leading design and advertising studios, and the *Tropical Suites Brochure* is an example of the type of projects that designers in these environments must produce on a fairly regular basis. This image-intensive sales piece requires the extensive use of styles, and makes use of complex, custom clipping paths and shape runarounds where scanned silhouettes interact with the text of the brochure.

THE PROJECTS YOU WILL WORK ON

PROJECT D: RECIPE BOOK

Using high-quality images from the PhotoDisc collection of commercial-grade visuals, this dramatic layout requires the extensive use of tabular material in the creation of the instructions and ingredient listings. It also uses type along a curved path, a technique offered directly inside of QuarkXPress without the use of an external drawing program. Additionally, the layout utilizes type elements converted into a picture box containing a scanned element.

PROJECT E: AUTOMATION BOOKLET

The *Automation Booklet* requires the construction of a standard set of master pages, visually consistent EPS graphics, and a formal table of contents. As is often the case in these types of projects, heavy use is made of QuarkXPress character and paragraph styles. Upon completing this descriptive booklet and the next project (*The GASP Report*), you will be fully prepared to design, build, and manage complex documents of any size.

PROJECT F: GASP NEWSLETTER

The Gasp Report is the most complex project assignment in the course. A real-world publication aimed at owners and managers of graphic arts service provider companies (imaging firms, commercial printers, web development companies, graphic arts dealers, and others), the *Report* is designed and laid out according to very strict specifications and requirements. Building the entire 16 page publication from scratch will require the use of almost all yours skills — patience and attention to detail among them. The finished product is a professional looking, ready-for-output document that was actually published and distributed. The creation of colored primitives within QuarkXPress are all combined to complete this assignment.

Support Materials

For the Student

On the CD-ROM you will find a complete set of Against The Clock (ATC) fonts, and a collection of data files used to construct the various exercises and projects in this course book.

The ATC fonts are solely for use with the Against The Clock materials. These fonts will be used throughout both the exercises and projects, and are provided in both Macintosh and Windows format.

A variety of student files has been included. These files, necessary to complete both the exercises and projects, are also provided in both Macintosh and Windows formats.

For the Instructor

The Instructor Kit consists of an Instructor's Manual and an Instructor's CD-ROM. It includes various testing and presentation materials in addition to the files that come standard with the student books.

- **Overhead Presentation Materials** are provided to enhance the instructor's presentation of the course. These presentations are prepared using Microsoft PowerPoint and are provided in both "native" PowerPoint format and Acrobat Portable Document Format (PDF).

- **Extra Projects** are provided with the data files. These projects may be used to extend the course or to test the student.

- **A Test Bank of Questions** is included within the Instructor Kit. These questions may be modified, reorganized, and administered throughout the course.

- A **Review** of the material that the student has completed is provided midway through the course, with a **Final Review** at the end.

Acknowledgments

I would like to give thanks to the writers, illustrators, editors, and others who have worked long and hard to complete the Against The Clock series. Foremost among them are Rob McAllister and Michael Barnett, whom I thank for their long nights, early mornings, and their seemingly endless patience.

Thanks also to the dedicated teaching professionals whose comments and expertise contributed to the success of these products, including Renée Prim of Central Piedmont Community College, Ann Page of Marion County Technical Education Center, Thomas Dietre of Arizona State University, Doris Anton of Wichita Area Technical College, and a special thanks to Tara Holod of Allentown Business School.

A big thanks to Judy Casillo, Developmental Editor, and Denise Brown, Production Editor for their guidance, patience, and attention to detail.

A special thanks to my husband for his unswerving support and for living in a publishing studio and warehouse during the three years it took to develop the ATC series of courses.

Ellenn Behoriam, March, 1998

About Against The Clock

Against The Clock (ATC) was founded in 1990 as a part of Lanman Systems Group, one of the nation's leading systems integration and training firms. The company specialized in developing custom training materials for such clients as *L.L. Bean, The New England Journal of Medicine, Smithsonian,* the *National Education Association, Air & Space Magazine, Publishers Clearing House,* The *National Wildlife Society, Home Shopping Network,* and many others. The integration firm was among the most highly respected in the graphic arts industry.

To a great degree, the success of Systems Group can be attributed to the thousands of pages of course materials developed at the company's demanding client sites. Throughout the rapid growth of Systems Group, founder and General Manager Ellenn Behoriam developed the expertise necessary to manage technical experts, content providers, writers, editors, illustrators, designers, layout artists, proofreaders, and the rest of the chain of professionals required to develop structured and highly effective training materials.

Following the sale of the Lanman Companies to World Color, one of the nation's largest commercial printers, Ellenn embarked on a project to develop a library of training materials engineered specifically for the professional graphic artist. A large part of this effort is finding and working with talented professional artists, writers, and educators from around the country.

The result is the ATC training library.

Ellenn lives in Tampa, Florida with her husband Gary, and her dogs Boda and Chase.

About the Authors

Every one of the Against The Clock course books was developed by a group of people working as part of a design and production team. In the case of *QuarkXPress: Advanced Electronic Mechanicals*, there were two primary writers:

Rob McAllister has been speaking and writing about creating effective pages since before desktop publishing was invented. In the process of teaching others, he has written various "how to" guides and training manuals. Rob is a contributing editor for Hayden Books' FreeHand Graphics Studio Skills, and is the author of a series of eight books for Delmar Publishers on a variety of desktop publishing topics.

Rob is a technical editor for Electronic Publishing and contributing editor for Printing News in addition to Project Manager for Against The Clock.

David Broudy is an experienced prepress professional and works on many of the ATC projects. David lives in Rochester, New York, and is a graduate student in the College of Imaging Arts and Sciences at the Rochester Institute of Technology. He is currently writing a book on variable-data digital printing, and working on a thesis project in rotogravure cost reduction. David enjoys wine, and classical and alternative music.

Getting Started

Platform

The Against The Clock series is specifically designed to apply to both Macintosh and Windows systems — the courses will work for you no matter which environment you find yourself in. There are slight differences in the two, but when you're working in an actual application, these differences are limited to certain functions and actions.

Naming Conventions

In the old days of MS-DOS systems, file names on the PC were limited to something referred to as "8.3," which meant that you were limited in the number of characters you could use to an eight-character name (the "8") and a three-character suffix (the "3"). Text files, for example, might be called *myfile.txt*, while a document file from a word processor might be called *myfile.doc* (for document). On today's Windows systems, these limitations have been somewhat overcome. Although you can use longer file names, suffixes still exist. Whether you see them or not is another story.

When your system is first configured, the Views are normally set to a default that hides these extensions. This means that you might have a dozen different files named *myfile*, all of which may have been generated by different applications and completely different types of files.

On a Windows system you can change this view by clicking on *My Computer* (the icon is on your desktop) with the right button and choosing View>Options. From this dialog box you can choose whether or not to display these older, MS-DOS file extensions. In some cases it's easier to know what you're looking at if they're visible. This is a personal choice.

To ensure that the supplied student files are fully compatible with both operating systems, we've named all the files using the three-character suffix — even those on the Macintosh.

Key Commands

Key commands are fairly consistent between the Macintosh and the Windows versions of QuarkXPress. The major difference lies in the names of special function keys. The Macintosh has a key marked with an Apple and an icon that resembles a clover leaf. This is called the Command key. When you see this icon, hold this key down. The Command key is a *modifier* key; that is, it doesn't do anything by itself, but changes the function of a key pressed while being held down. A good example is holding Command while pressing the "S" key; this Saves your work. The same applies to the "P" key; hold down Command and press it to Print your work.

On Windows systems, the Control key is almost always the equivalent of the Command key on the Macintosh. (This is sometimes confusing to new users, since the Macintosh also has a Control key, although on the Macintosh it's hardly ever used in popular applications.)

Another special function key on the Macintosh is the Option key. It too is a modifier key, and you must hold it down along with whatever other key is required for a specific function. The equivalent modifier key on a Windows system is called the Alt key (for alternative). Besides these two nomenclature issues, there isn't really much difference between using a Windows system and a Macintosh system (particularly when you're within a particular application).

The CD-ROM and Initial Setup Considerations

Before you begin using your Against The Clock course book, you must set up your system to have access to the various files and tools needed to complete your lessons.

Student Files

This course comes complete with a collection of student files. These files are an integral part of the learning experience; they're used throughout the course to help you construct increasingly complex elements. Having these building blocks available to you for practice and study sessions will ensure that you will be able to experience the exercises and complete the project assignments smoothly using a minimum of time spent searching for the various required components.

In building the Student Files folders, we've created sets of data for both Macintosh and Windows users. Locate the the "SF-Adv QuarkXPress" folder for your platform of choice and simply drag the icon onto your hard disk drive. If you have limited disk space, you may want to copy only the files for one or two lessons at a time.

Creating a Project Folder

We strongly recommend that you work from your hard disk. However, in some cases you might not have enough room on your system for all of the files that we've supplied. If this is the case, you can work directly from the CD-ROM.

Throughout the exercises and projects, you'll be required to save your work. Since the CD-ROM is "read-only," you cannot write information to it. Create a Work in Progress folder on your hard disk and use it to store your work-in-progress. Create this folder while you're looking at your desktop so that it will be at the highest level of your system, where it will be easy to find. Name this folder "Work in Progress".

Fonts

Whatever platform you're working on — Macintosh or Windows — you will have to install the ATC font library to ensure that your lessons and exercises will work as described in the course book. These fonts are provided on the student CD-ROM. Separate versions for Windows and Macintosh are provided.

Instructions for installing fonts are provided in the documentation that came with your computer. If you're using a font utility such as Suitcase or Font Juggler, then be certain to refer to the instructions that came with the font management application for installing your ATC fonts onto your system.

Preferences

We recommend that you throw away your Preferences file before you begin the lessons in this course. The "XPress Preferences" file may be found inside your QuarkXPress folder.

Prerequisites

This book assumes that you have a basic understanding of how to use your system and have completed QuarkXPress 4: An Introduction to Electronic Mechanicals or have equivalent experience. Whether you're working on a Macintosh or a Windows workstation, the skill sets are basically the same.

You should know how to use your mouse to point and click, and how to drag items around the screen. You should know how to resize a window, and how to arrange windows on your desktop to maximize the space you have available. You should know how to access pull-down menus and how check boxes and radio buttons work. Last, you should know how to create, open, and save files.

If you're familiar with these fundamental skills, then you know all that's necessary to utilize the Against The Clock courseware library.

Notes:

CHAPTER 1

INTRODUCTION

CHAPTER OBJECTIVE:

To familiarize you with the structure of this book — *QuarkXPress 4: Advanced Electronic Mechanicals*. To get the most out of this course, we recommend that you first complete QuarkXPress 4, An Introduction to Electronic Mechanicals. In Chapter 1 you will:

- Review the chapters and their significance that will be taught to you, the designer, throughout this course.

- Be provided with an overview of what each chapter will cover in this course.

- Become familiar with the structure of the course book, broken down into chapters: Managing Workflow; Structuring Your Layouts; Working With Shapes; Complex Text Elements; Text and Graphics Living Together; Advanced Styles; Creating and Managing Multi-Page Documents; and Managing Output.

- Be introduced to a course that will provide you with the necessary knowledge, which when combined with your own practice and perseverance, will turn you into an advanced QuarkXPress operator. After completing this course you will be comfortable with implementing the features that will enable you to be a proficient and outstanding designer.

Introduction

This course is designed to improve your skills working with today's most popular page layout program — QuarkXPress. In this course we're going to provide plenty of opportunities for exploration of the more advanced functions, features, tools, and techniques available to you as a designer or professional artist.

Assumptions about Current Proficiency

Since this is an advanced course, and will explore some fairly complex issues, we assume that you're already familiar with most of QuarkXPress's basic tools and functions.

For example, you should already know how to create new QuarkXPress documents and create picture and text boxes; you should also be comfortable with using QuarkXPress to create, import, and arrange various components to create a document.

What We're Going to Learn

The course is divided into nine chapters, each specifically designed to teach you the advanced features of the newest version of QuarkXPress. Each chapter discusses specific functions, and, most importantly, shows you how to apply these concepts to the production of professional-quality designs, publications, and documents. Building on your existing knowledge of QuarkXPress, this course will introduce you to concepts and design techniques used by some of the nation's finest publication and advertising designers.

Managing Workflow: Knowing how to approach your projects, and how to control your working environment are important skills. We will learn to customize the QuarkXPress application to more precisely match your personal work styles and requirements.

Structuring Your Layouts: In this chapter we're going to explore advanced applications of grids and guides, teaching how proper structure can lead to dramatic, highly-professional results. We'll discuss and demonstrate how multiple versions of a design can be quickly and accurately produced from a single set of components and from only one template.

Working With Shapes: This chapter will explore the creation and management of complex shapes and custom objects. Besides the real-world use of Merge commands, *Working With Shapes* will provide extensive practice using the Bézier tool to create complex shapes. Image templates are provided to improve your speed and efficiency using anchor points and the Bézier tool for the creation of both picture and text boxes.

Complex Text Elements: In this chapter you will learn how to convert type elements into graphics and explore the use of merging and type conversion to create unique custom logos and graphics.

Text and Graphics Living Together: Although basic skills with QuarkXPress include the ability to place type and graphics together in a layout or publication, this chapter takes that skill to a new level by introducing a wide range of advanced techniques such as clipping paths, custom runarounds, and using imported graphics as text boxes.

Advanced Styles: In this chapter we'll introduce some of the more advanced applications of styles, both as they apply to paragraphs as well as to individual characters. The use of special styles to create graphic effects will be discussed, and you will learn how to create standard styles that reflect the way you work and the type of projects you work on. The concept of managing styles and templates specific to individual clients will also be introduced.

Working with Long Documents: This chapter will introduce critical skills to you that are relative to designing, creating, and managing long documents. Many job requirements call for long documents, even in the most design-intensive environment. This chapter introduces the advanced use of master pages and the creation and management of lists, such as tables of contents or tables of illustrations and figures.

Managing Output: The final chapter demonstrates and discusses many issues important to service providers and commercial printing companies when they accept your QuarkXPress files. How to control printer settings, the creation of custom print styles to improve efficiency, and color models and management will be introduced.

Chapter 2

Managing Workflow

Chapter Objective:

To learn how QuarkXPress can be customized to fit your production needs. To learn how to manage images and text; you will also discover the power of Templates and learn how to use them. In Chapter 2 you will:

- Learn the differences between Application and Document preferences, when to use them, and how to customize them to suit your design requirements.
- Explore the Display, Interactive, Save, and XTensions tabs of the Application dialog box, and understand their functions.
- Explore the General, Paragraph, Character, Tool, and Trapping tabs of the Document Preferences dialog box.
- Learn how to customize the Tool palette.
- Learn about the Color Management System (CMS) to maintain consistent color in images from scanner to monitor to press.
- Learn about Libraries; create and use a Library.
- Learn how to use Templates.
- Learn about managing images and image types.

Managing Workflow

Application and certain document preferences are saved into the "XPress Preferences" file, which is located in the same folder as the QuarkXPress program (the file has the same name on both Macintosh and Windows systems). Sometimes this file can become damaged and can cause QuarkXPress to crash when you try to launch it. If this happens, move the file out of the QuarkXPress folder and restart the program; if this works, get rid of the original Preferences file. This will reset all preferences to their default settings. If you make a lot of changes to your default settings, you should consider making a backup copy of your Preferences file in the event that it becomes corrupt.

In this section we'll discuss the many ways in which QuarkXPress can be customized to fit your production needs, how to manage images and text, and the use and power of templates.

QuarkXPress Preferences

Application vs. Document Preferences

QuarkXPress saves preferences in two ways: document-wide or application-wide. Any changes you make to the document preferences with a document open will be applied only to that document and saved with the document, and will revert back to their original state after you close the document. Changes you make to the document preferences with *no* document open will cause all new documents created afterward to use those settings. Application preferences are application-wide, and stay applied whether or not you have a document open. Application preferences are not saved with a document, so these settings won't affect anyone else who opens a file created with different application preferences.

Customizing Default Document Preferences

Customizing your document preferences with no document open before beginning a big project can save a lot of time. For example, the default setting for new text boxes is for runaround to be turned on. In many cases, this is unwanted and becomes annoying when you have to stop and turn off runaround for every new text box you create. Another example is that you might have a standard set of colors and styles that you use for all of a particular client's projects. Instead of tediously creating the colors and styles each time you begin a new project, you can add or delete your predefined preferences from the Colors and Style Sheets palettes. All new documents you create afterward will contain only the needed colors and styles. The same technique can be used for customizing the default behavior of object creation tools, H&Js, lists, runarounds, frame border thickness and color, fills, stroke colors, and other items.

Documents you open with differing document preferences may present the below dialog box.

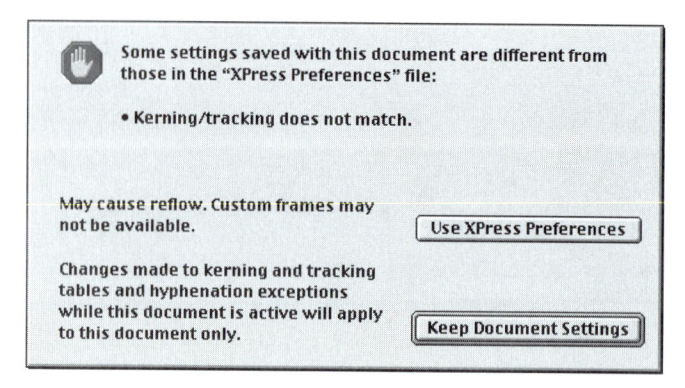

If you want to preserve the document's preferences, click Keep Document Settings. If you want to override the document settings with your own, click Use XPress Preferences.

Application Preferences

Application preferences control how QuarkXPress behaves in general and do not affect the contents or final appearance of a document. To access the Application preferences, choose Edit>Preferences>Application.

Changes in H&Js, tracking, kerning, and custom frames may cause text to reflow if you override the document preferences.

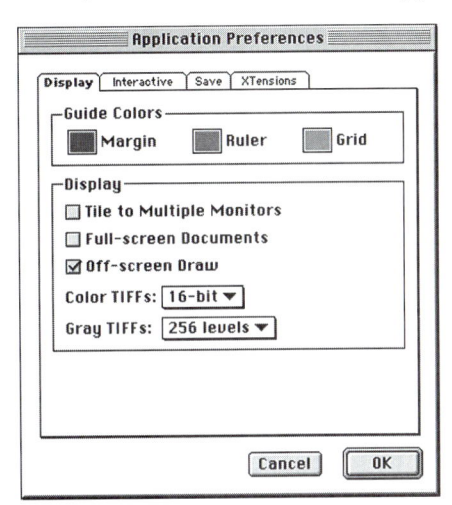

Preferences in this panel are divided into tabbed panels.

Display Tab

- You can change the colors of guides and grids to your own liking. Clicking on any of the three color swatches will display the Color Picker. You can edit the colors there and click OK to have them applied to the guide color you choose. The Margin color also previews the item boundary in the Runaround and Clipping Path dialog boxes; the Ruler color also represents a clipping path in an object; and the Grid color also represents the Runaround boundary of an object.

- If you have more than one monitor, you can spread multiple documents across all monitors when you choose View>Windows>Tile Documents. Check the Tile to Multiple Monitors check box to use this feature.

- Full-screen Documents (Macintosh only), when checked, will fit documents into the entire area of the screen when opened. The default is unchecked, which is why your documents will usually not fill the entire screen. Space is reserved for the Tool palette on the left and the Measurements palette on the bottom.

- Off-screen Draw causes all screen updates to appear at once instead of one object at a time. On a fast computer the screen will usually update quickly, depending on the complexity of the document. Having this option on or off makes no difference in the speed of the screen update.

Press Command-Option-Shift-Y (Macintosh) or Control-Alt-Shift-Y (Windows) to display the Application preferences.

CHAPTER 2/MANAGING WORKFLOW 11

Multiple monitors are automatically supported in Macintosh computers by adding a video card (or second video card) and another monitor. Windows computers may require careful configuration of multiple monitors for this feature to work properly. Multiple monitor support is a function of the operating system and not of QuarkXPress, so if the monitors are not properly configured, this feature won't work.

Changing the bit depth setting of Color TIFFs only affects images imported after the changes are made. Images already in the document display at the former bit depth. To force all images to the new bit depth, you must re-import them. Save and close the document, then choose File>Open to display the file name and click OK while holding down the Command/Control key.

- Color TIFFs lets you specify the color depth of color images placed into a document.

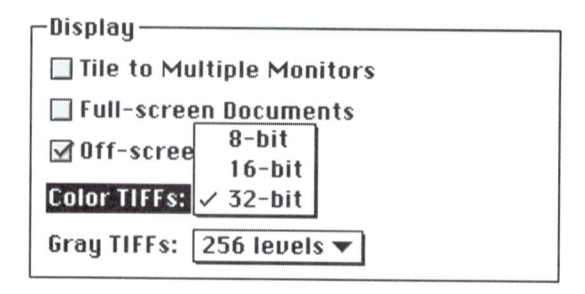

8-bit will allow the display of 256 colors. This speeds up screen updates and reduces the disk space required for the document, but it also degrades the image's on-screen preview (the actual image is unaltered).

16- and 32-bit allows the display of about 16,000 and several million colors respectively. These settings provide much truer color previews, but can significantly increase the file size of the document and can cause slow screen updates. Contrast settings (Style>Contrast) can only be applied to 8-bit previews.

See how much more detail is present in the right-hand image? It was imported at a 32-bit Color TIFF setting, while the left-hand image was imported at an 8-bit setting.

Gray TIFFs work similarly to Color TIFFs. Most grayscale images can be previewed at 16 levels without much degradation, but if you would like the most accurate previews, choose 256 levels.

Display DPI Value (Windows Only) allows you to set the number of pixels per inch (up to the maximum of your monitor). A rougher display will allow the monitor to refresh more quickly.

Straight quotation marks (primes and double primes) can make an otherwise outstanding project appear amateur and unprofessional. Look for examples in ads, signs, and billboards. It's amazing how many times this error appears.

Although the prime and double prime are often used for foot and inch symbols, there are special characters that should be used. These characters are found on the Symbol font, and in some math and other pi fonts such as Universal News. Using the Symbol font, press Option-4 or Alt-0162 to access the foot mark; Option-, or Alt-0178 to access the inch mark.

The Interactive Tab

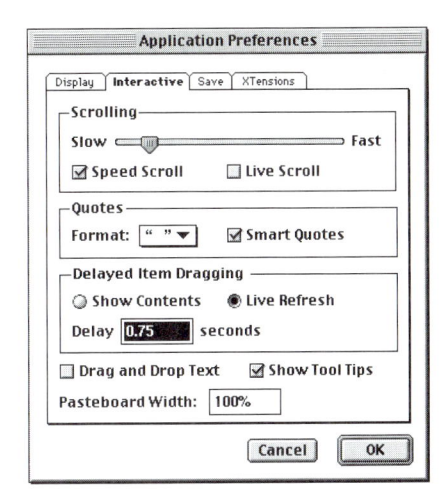

This panel lets you adjust display, scrolling, text editing, and quotation mark attributes.

- Scrolling (Slow to Fast) controls how quickly the document will scroll when you move the document's scroll bars or boxes.

- Speed Scroll causes images and blends to be *greeked* (displayed as gray items) while scrolling. Objects are redrawn after you stop scrolling.

- Live Scroll causes everything to be redrawn as you scroll. On a slow computer or with a complex document, this can become intolerably slow. Scrolling with the Grabber Hand (Item tool – Option/Alt) will always be a live scroll.

- Quotes — Choose a style for typographer's quotation marks under Format. Typographer's quotes for English and many other languages are "curly" or angled rather than straight, and their use is the hallmark of careful typography.

"Typographer's Quotes"   "Straight Quotes"

Some languages use a different standard quotation mark, so if you plan to do any foreign language typesetting be certain to choose the correct style of quotation marks.

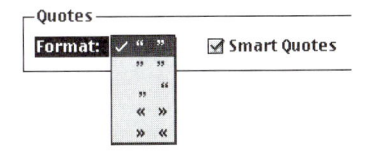

Use the accepted quotes standard for any international work and confirm that the style is correct for the country. Here are a few examples:

French: «Allons-y!»   **German:** „Schnell!"

Finnish: "Voi Luoja!"   **International English:** 'Let's go'

You pay a substantial price in performance when you use Live Refresh. Unless you have a good reason to use it, don't. The cursor in Show Contents mode is the familiar 4-headed arrow, which turns into a starburst when Live Refresh mode is active.

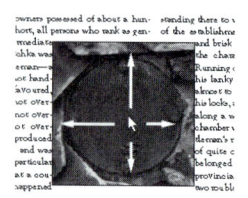

Option-Q will access one Symbol character. This works for all Macintosh characters and with all Windows characters that can be accessed directly from the keyboard, but not those accessed by typing Alt-XXXX.

The chosen style will automatically be applied to all quotation marks in any text imported into QuarkXPress and to any quotes that you type after you change the setting. Existing quotation marks will be unchanged. Apostrophes and single quotes will remain unchanged. Leave Smart Quotes checked unless you want to use the plain straight quote as symbols for inches and feet … and remember to turn it back on when you're done. It's usually best to leave Smart Quotes checked. You can access the prime (') or double prime (") by holding down the Control key (Macintosh) when typing the characters. In the Windows environment, hold down Control to access the prime and Control-Alt to access the double prime.

- Delayed Item Dragging — This controls what QuarkXPress displays as items are being moved with the mouse.

Click and hold the mouse on an image or text box. After a short delay, QuarkXPress will display the graphic or text as you drag it instead of a generic outline of the text or picture box. This is a helpful feature for fine-tuning layouts. To display the picture or text as it is being dragged, click Show Contents. Live Refresh takes Show Contents a step further, providing real-time text reflow and layering of graphic elements as the object is dragged. Delay Seconds allows you to set, in fractions of seconds, the amount of time you must click and hold a graphic or text element before you can drag it in Show Contents or Live Refresh mode.

Using Live Refresh for Accurate Runarounds

1. Open the file **Dsouls.QXD** from the **SF-Adv QuarkXPress** folder, then open the Application Preferences dialog box and click on the Interactive tab.

2. Draw a picture box that straddles the two columns and import the image **Sprocket.TIF** from the same folder.

3. Select the Item tool, then click and hold on the picture until the four-pointed Content cursor changes to a starburst.

4. Move the picture box around and watch the text rewrap around it.

Make certain that the settings match the ones above.

This is useful for finding an optimal position for an image with a runaround.

14 CHAPTER 2/MANAGING WORKFLOW

It's easy when dragging and dropping text to accidentally release the mouse button too soon. Be certain that the insertion point is placed exactly where you need it before letting go.

Some people use an XTension called Pasteboard XTension. Older versions of this utility modified documents in a way that prevented them from being opened unless you had the Pasteboard XTension installed. If you ever open a file and are informed that the Pasteboard XTension is required, track down the Pasteboard XTerminator from Markzware's web site (http://www.markzware.com /products/pasteboard.html (all one line, no spaces).

5. Close the file without saving.

- Drag and Drop Text — Using Cut and Paste isn't the only way to move a text selection. With Drag and Drop Text enabled, you can cut a selection of text and move it elsewhere by highlighting the section, dragging it to its new location and releasing the mouse. To copy text, highlight the selection, hold down the Shift key, drag it to its new location and release the mouse. The pointer will turn into an insertion point to help you place the text in the new location.

- Clicking Show Tool Tips will reveal pop-up descriptions of tools on the Tool palette if your mouse pointer pauses over them. If these become annoying once you master the tool set, you can turn them off in the Edit>Preferences> Application>Interactive dialog box.

- Pasteboard Width — The value in this field controls how much pasteboard appears around your document. Pasteboard space is useful for holding design elements that have been dragged from the document to be used elsewhere. The width of the pasteboard is expressed as a percentage of the width of the document. To have a pasteboard the same width as your document, leave it at 100%. To make it half the width of your document, type 50%. The pasteboard cannot be more than 48 inches wide or less than 1 inch wide.

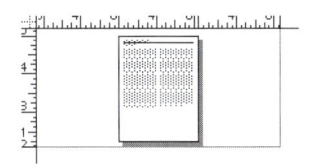

Pasteboard at 100% 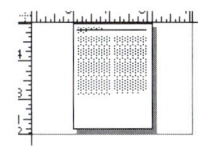   *Pasteboard at 50%*

CHAPTER 2/MANAGING WORKFLOW   15

Auto Save will not recover a document that has never been saved. As soon as you create a new document, you should name and save it.

Be careful with Auto Backup, especially with large documents. Auto Backup could possibly use all of your disk space if you specify too many revisions.

Save Tab

The options in the Save tab can help protect you from losing work caused by a system crash or power failure. You should specify a folder other than the folder in which the document resides.

- With Auto Save enabled, QuarkXPress saves your work in a temporary file at a time interval you specify (the default is every five minutes). If your system crashes or loses power, reopen the document and QuarkXPress will display an alert announcing that your last Auto Saved version will be restored. Your worst-case scenario — five minutes of lost work.

- Auto Backup creates a backup copy of the entire document each time you save the file. You can click the Document Folder button or specify another folder with the Other Folder button. Browse to choose the other folder. Backups are sequentially numbered <document name>-1, -2, and so on. You can specify up to 100 revisions, but try to keep this number at a reasonable level. Ideally, you will backup to a drive other than the one you're working on. Backups are for disaster recovery, not for versioning (use Save As with different file names to create multiple versions). When the document is complete, rid yourself of all those extra backups and save a copy of the complete document to the drive where archives are stored.

- Auto Library Save will save an open library each time you add an item.

- Save Document Position will preserve the placement, size, and proportions of your document window the next time you open it.

XTensions Tab

There are hundreds of XTensions available for QuarkXPress from Quark, Inc. and third party developers that add functionality to QuarkXPress. Some are free, but most have prices ranging from low to staggeringly high, depending upon the XTension's function. Some are highly-specialized products that can automate catalog and newspaper production, database publishing, or high-end prepress operations such as imposition. The XTensions Manager lets you create sets of XTensions, allowing you to have different XTensions available depending upon your needs.

If you have access to the Internet, start your web browser and go to http://www.quark.com/ftp004.htm (all one line, no spaces) to browse through a collection of free XTensions that you can download and install. There's also a detailed listing of many third-party XTensions, along with pricing and ordering information.

Press Command/Control-Y to display the Document Preferences panel.

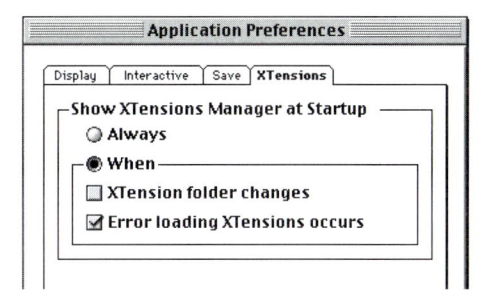

- Here's where you specify when you wish the XTensions Manager to automatically activate. You can make it appear every time you launch QuarkXPress, or only at certain times. You may wish to see the XTensions Manager only when the XTensions folder has changed or when there has been an error loading an XTension. If an XTension has caused an error, you can disable it until you determine the problem or reinstall it. XTensions Manager may be accessed at any time through the Utilities menu. XTensions opened with XTensions manager will be active the next time QuarkXPress is launched.

Document Preferences

Choose Edit>Preferences>Document. The Document Preferences dialog box includes comprehensive settings with tabs titled General, Paragraph, Character, Tool, and Trapping. Unlike application preferences, document preferences can be set for an open document, or set with no document open, which will apply the preferences to all subsequent new documents.

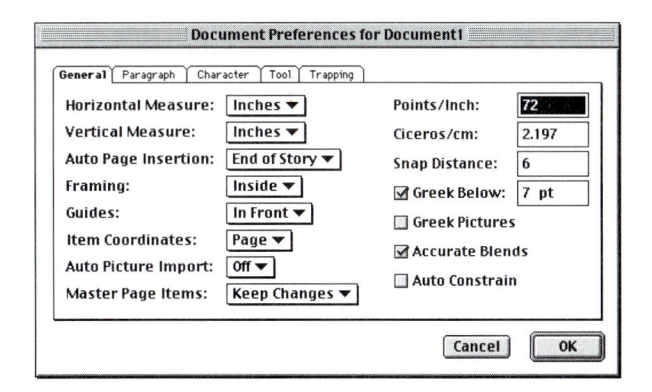

General

- Horizontal and Vertical Measure allow you to specify the measurement system with which you are most familiar.

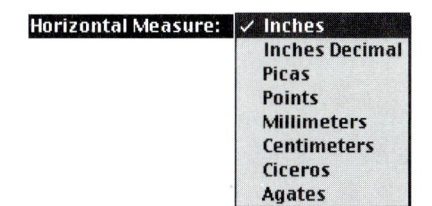

CHAPTER 2/MANAGING WORKFLOW 17

Auto Page Insertion only works when automatic text boxes are used. Ideally, you will create an automatic text box when you create a document, specifying it in the New Document dialog box. If you decide to create an automatic text box after the document has been started, go to the master page, draw a text box, and with the Linking tool active, click on the Link icon, then on the text box.

Inches is the default, though many designers prefer to work with picas, and some situations may call for different measurement units for horizontal and vertical axes.

Inches Decimal divides the inch measure displayed in the page rulers into decimal units (0.0625) rather than fractional (⅝). You can specify metric measure, ciceros (used in Europe), or agates, new to QuarkXPress 4 and the typical unit of measure for newspaper ads.

- Auto Page Insertion lets you specify where new pages will be placed when imported text overflows its text box.

Auto Page Insertion: Off / End of Story / End of Section / End of Document

This feature only works with automatic text boxes. When importing text into an automatic text box, QuarkXPress will automatically insert pages to contain any text overflow that occurs. Any new pages will be based on the current master page.

End of Story inserts new pages after the last page that contains the last text box containing story text. End of Section inserts new pages after the last page of the current section defined under Page>Section. End of Document inserts new pages after the last page of your document.

Setting Auto Page Insertion to Off keeps QuarkXPress from flowing overflow text; instead, a red checked box will appear at the end of the text box in which the overflow occurs. Choose Off to flow text manually.

- Framing lets you specify whether a frame stroke (line) is drawn on the inner or outer border of a picture or text box.

Framing: / Inside / Outside

Inside draws the stroke on the inside of the box; Outside draws the stroke on the outside of the box. Outside Framing applied to an existing box will change the dimensions and position of the box. Changing the Framing preferences only affects boxes created after you change the setting.

- Guides lets you have guides in front of all the items on the page or behind all the items on the page.

Guides: Behind / ✓ In Front

Choosing Inside Framing has its virtues — it can help mask edge imperfections in placed images but it isn't a magic bullet for images where the dimensions are short. Fix the problem in Photoshop for best results.

Having the guides in front can be very helpful in complex layouts where they might be obscured if they are behind everything.

- Item Coordinates lets you specify page rulers that measure only one page, or rulers that measure horizontally across page spreads.

- Auto Picture Import specifies how QuarkXPress handles imported images that have been changed.

If Auto Picture Import is set to On, and images are modified, then the next time the document is opened any modified images will automatically be updated. If you want to be alerted before any updating occurs, choose On (verify) and a dialog box will appear requesting confirmation of the image update. If you want to update everything manually, choose Off.

- Master Page Items — Master pages allow you to apply global changes to a document page with a single drag and drop. Master Page Items controls the behavior of master page items on document pages when a master page is applied to a document page.

Keep Changes will preserve alterations made to master page objects on a document page. When a master page is applied or reapplied to a document page, edited master items will be retained; unchanged master items will be deleted and new items from the master page will be added. Delete Changes deletes all master items on the document page, changed or not, and adds new items from the master page.

- Points/Inch — In traditional typography one inch is defined as 72.27 or 72.307 points, depending upon whom you ask. Now that computerized layout has become the norm, 72 points per inch is generally accepted as the standard. Similarly, the generally accepted standard for ciceros to centimeters is now 2.197.

- Snap Distance dictates the distance in pixels that an element can be from the page guide before it is snapped into place. Choose a higher number for a more

---

Be careful if you decide to turn Auto Picture Import off. A warning will appear when you try to print a document in which the images need to be updated, and you'll have to update every image manually. In a production environment, it's always a good idea to have Auto Picture Import turned on.

Be careful when applying a revised or different master page to a document page. It's easy to wipe out hours of work in about a second if your preferences are unintentionally set to Delete Changes.

aggressive snap or a lower number for more subtle snapping; the higher the number, the more often you may have something unexpectedly snap to a guide.

- Greek Below specifies the value below which text on-screen will be *greeked* (displayed as gray bars). This can speed up screen redraws, especially if there's a lot of small type in the document. This only affects text that displays on-screen below the specified point size in a particular magnification; it doesn't remain constant. If greeked text appears in a Fit in Window view, zooming up to 100 or 200% will display the text normally.

- Greek Pictures displays all imported TIFF images as gray boxes, which can dramatically speed up screen redraw. When you want to see an image, simply click on it. EPS artwork is always displayed without greeking.

- Accurate Blends displays color blends within a picture or text box more accurately and with less banding on 8-bit (256 color) displays. If your display supports 16- or 24-bit color, Accurate Blends is ignored, since these displays will show correct blends anyway.

- Auto Constrain — QuarkXPress allows for objects — picture boxes for example — to be constrained by one another. When a smaller picture box is drawn on top of a larger picture box so that the smaller box is contained within the larger one, the smaller one cannot be moved beyond the boundary of the larger one (until the constraint is turned off). Users of earlier versions of QuarkXPress will recognize this as the "parent" and "child" hierarchy of objects. There's really no need to enable this option.

Paragraph

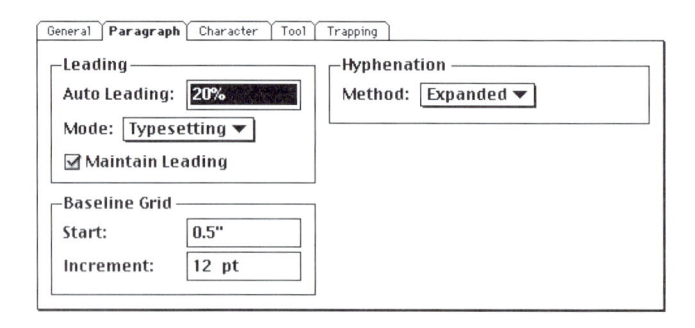

Changing the Auto Leading value changes it for all text in your document that uses automatic leading. Be careful! Massive reflow can result.

- Automatic Leading is defined as *percentage* or *points*. A percent value entered in this field determines how much larger the automatic leading value is in relation to the type's point size. If Auto Leading is set to 20% (the default), then 10 point type would be leaded at an amount 20% larger than the type, or 12 points. A point value (preceded by a + sign) specifies in points how much leading is added to the point size of the type. Setting Auto Leading to +2 would result in 10 point type with 12 point leading, or 18 point type with 20 point leading.

Many clients will supply a typographic specification to designers with a notation such as "Font: ITC Officina Sans, 10/12." This means that the point size is 10, and the leading is 12.

If you do a lot of foreign language or specialty typesetting you can purchase hyphenation rule files from Quark for many languages and for specialized terminology such as those used in medical and legal publishing. Contact Quark in Denver, Colorado or on the Web at http://www.quark.com.

- Mode determines how leading is measured.

  Typesetting Mode measures leading from baseline to baseline, and is the most commonly used and accepted leading measure. Word Processing measures leading from ascent to ascent and isn't as accurate.

- Maintain Leading — When a graphic or other element is moved into a column of text, the baseline of the first line of text forced down by the object is automatically snapped to the nearest leading increment, resulting in aligned baselines across columns.

- Baseline Grid — The baseline grid is an invisible grid that extends across a page. You can lock the baselines of type to the grid to achieve perfectly aligned type across all columns. Start specifies how far down from the top of the page the baseline grid begins. Increment defines, in points, the distance between grid lines, and should be set as the leading value, or a multiple thereof.

- Hyphenation Method determines which type of hyphenation will be used.

Earlier versions of QuarkXPress used different methods of hyphenation. If you convert an older document to QuarkXPress 4, hyphenation may change, which could affect runarounds and line endings. If you need to preserve the existing hyphenation, use Standard for QuarkXPress 2 documents and Enhanced for QuarkXPress 3 documents. The Expanded hyphenation in QuarkXPress 4 is more flexible and accurate, so it should be left selected for all new documents.

Character

Character preferences are more complicated than some of the other preferences we have examined; however, many of these settings are seldom changed after they have been set.

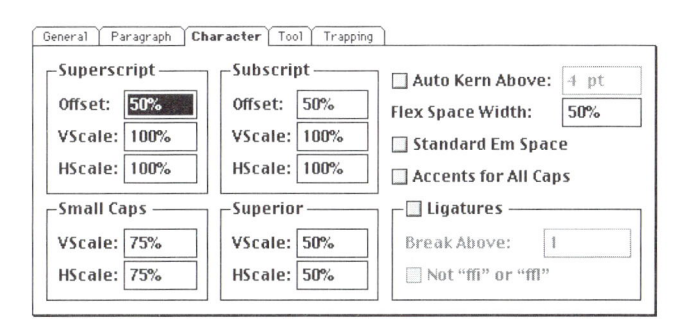

CHAPTER 2/MANAGING WORKFLOW   21

Small caps derived from regular caps look weak next to regular caps because they are reduced (the weight of the vertical stroke is disproportionately narrow). Cut caps from an Expert Set maintain type proportions that produce a more professional and readable effect.

PowerPC

Derived Small Caps

PowerPC

Cut Small Caps

Superiors are also available in Expert Sets, and are much more legible at small sizes than artificially-shrunken characters.

Press Option/Alt-Space bar for a breaking flex space; type Command/Control-Option/Alt-Shift-Space bar for a non-breaking flex space. Press Option/Alt-Space bar for an en space.

- Superscript has three settings for Offset, VScale, and HScale. The Offset setting specifies the amount of rise of superscript characters as a percentage of the point size measured from the baseline. VScale and HScale define the height and width of superscript characters as a percentage of the point size. The default V/HScale results in superscript characters that are the same size as regular characters.

- The same definitions of settings apply to Subscript. Because it is a definition of a percentage of the point size, this setting may need to be adjusted on a document-by-document basis. An offset appropriate for Minion (the typeface this book is set in) may be inappropriate for Cheltenham (a typeface with very tall ascenders).

- Small Caps and Superiors allow you to adjust the V(ertical) and H(orizontal) scale of the letters only. Small caps are normally the same height as the lower-case letters of a font, and should be adjusted to be pleasing. They are also somewhat expanded, as a rule. Expanding the small caps setting about 10% usually improves their appearance.

$e = mc_2$ — subscript

$e = mc^2$ — superscript

$e = mc^2$ — superior

- The default Small Caps value can be a somewhat weak or ineffectual with some typefaces. Try other settings to obtain a pleasing balance, or better yet, use an *expert set* of the typeface that contains "cut" small caps, which retain the weight of the standard caps.

- Auto Kern Above sets a size above which all type will be automatically kerned according to the *kerning pairs*, such as WA, Wa, Yo, and so forth, which are built into most professional-quality fonts. The effects of automatic kerning may not be very noticeable, especially at sizes under 12 points, but kerned text produces type of good color and readability. The default value of 4 points is usually acceptable.

- Flex Space is a special type of space character that is specified in terms of percentage of an en space, half an em space, as it is defined (see below). The default value of 50% creates a traditional thin space, but you may set it to a higher or lower value to suit your needs. Setting it to 200% will give you an em space.

- A Standard Em Space is defined as a square the width and height of the nominal point size. Therefore an em space in 12 point type is 12 points wide. However, QuarkXPress has typically measured an em space as the width of two zeroes. That is great for aligning columns of numbers, but since it is variable according to the typeface being used, it is not measurable. Check the box by Standard Em Space if you want to use the traditional em space instead of the width of two zeroes. Uncheck the box by Standard Em Space if you want to use QuarkXPress's version of an em space.

Special ligatures are available for the typesetting of historical documents or decorative effects.

ct ff st

- Accents for All Caps is fairly self-explanatory. In foreign language typesetting it is usually a matter of linguistic custom whether or not uppercase letters are accented, so this can be set as needed.

  This feature only affects CAPS created by styling characters (Style>Type Style> All Caps or click on the K in the Measurements palette) and does not affect capital letters that are "naturally" generated. A caution surrounding this feature is that QuarkXPress considers all accents equal — and they are not. A tilde (˜) and an umlaut (¨) are necessary to pronunciation and should always be used, as opposed to the diacritical marks.

- Ligatures (Macintosh only) are special pairs of characters joined together to prevent the appearance of overlap. Typically these character pairs are fi, fl, ff, ffi, and ffl. Most professional-quality typefaces include the fi and fl ligature; you'll usually need to purchase an Expert Set of the typeface to get the other ligatures. QuarkXPress will automatically substitute the special ligature characters for fi and fl if Ligatures is checked and will treat them as separate characters for hyphenation and spelling. The ffi and ffl ligatures are simulated with a regular f and fi or fl ligatures. You may specify that ffi and ffl combinations do not use ligatures, even though ligatures are turned on, if you wish.

  fi fi fl fl ff ff ffi ffi ffl ffl

  Examples of ligatures: The first pair is not a ligature; the second pair is. Ligatures from the Expert Set are shown for ff, ffi, and ffl.

  Because ligatures are not included in Windows font sets, if there is even a remote possibility that the document will be moved cross-platform, it is recommended that ligatures be turned off to prevent the possibility of lines reflowing.

- Break Above, specified in units of tracking or kerning, defines the threshold when QuarkXPress will break a ligature. (A tracking or kerning unit is 1/200 of an em space). Checking Not "ffi" or "ffl" will prevent QuarkXPress from forming ligatures of these combinations.

Tool

Tool preferences are among the most powerful of all QuarkXPress's preferences. You can easily predefine a tool's default behavior; for example, if you want all picture boxes to have no runaround, a fill of 25% Cyan, and a 2 point border of 100% Magenta, you can specify this by altering the picture box tool's preferences. You can set preferences for every tool that creates an object based on any available options in the Modify dialog box for that tool. Tool settings that you can change include background color for picture and text boxes, frame width, text inset, line width, and runaround type. You can also alter the settings for the Magnify tool.

You can restore all preferences to their original defaults by deleting the XPress Preferences file in the QuarkXPress application folder.

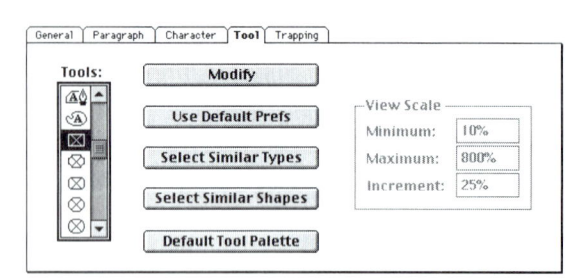

To edit Tool preferences, select the icon of the tool or tools you wish to edit. Click Modify. The Modify box will appear, allowing you to customize your tools to work exactly as you desire. Note that some settings may be grayed out when you select multiple tools, since not all settings apply to all tools.

==To edit all similar tools in one step, click a tool (a picture box tool, for example), then click Similar. Changes will apply to all picture box tools.==

Customizing Tools

1. Create a new document.

2. Press Command-Y (Macintosh) or Control-Y (Windows) to display the Preferences dialog box. Click on the Tool tab.

3. Select the Rectangular Picture Box tool.

4. Click Modify.

5. The Modify dialog box appears.

6. The Box tab usually appears first. If not, click the Box tab.

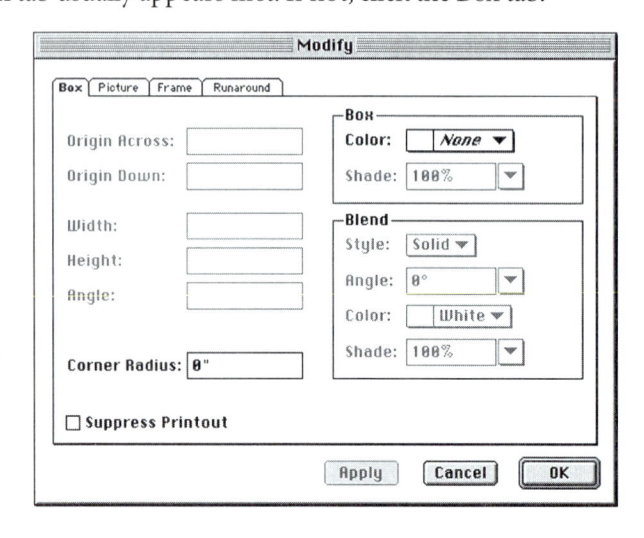

QuarkXPress outputs unpredictably when TIFF images are placed in picture boxes set to a fill of None. To avoid any potential for error, you should change all the picture box tools to have a default fill of either White or 0% Black.

24 CHAPTER 2/MANAGING WORKFLOW

Remember to set the Frame to Inside or Outside. Inside is used most often, because Outside will cause the picture box to grow in size and to change position, which can mess up a layout.

Use 0.25 pt. in place of a "hairline." A hairline is defined as one tenth of a point wide. On a high-resolution imagesetter a hairline will usually vanish because the emulsion of the media cannot reproduce a dot of that size. If your design calls for very thin lines, set the preferences of all the line-drawing tools to 0.25 pt. to avoid the disappearing hairline.

7. Set the Box color to White.

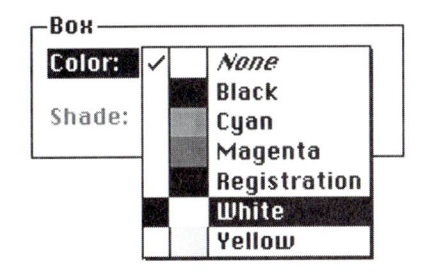

8. Click the Frame tab.

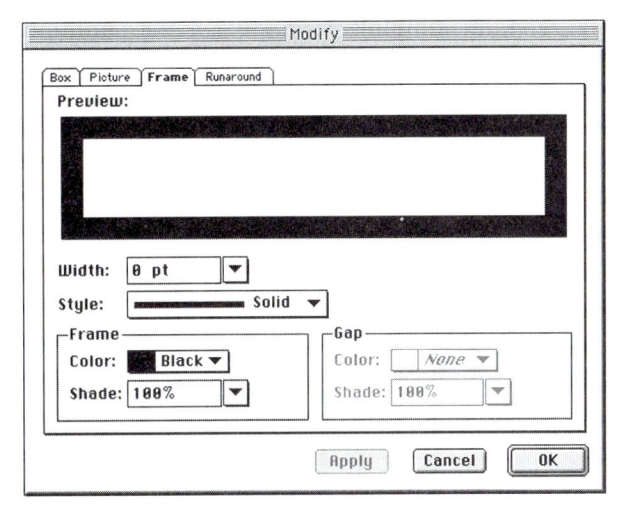

9. Specify a Width of 0.25 pt. This setting isn't on the pop-up menu, so type it into the Width box.

   You can also set a frame color, style, and shade, but we're just going to alter the width. Fanciful default picture boxes with 8 pt. dashed magenta and yellow lines probably aren't much good for production work, but again, you have the ability to specify just that if you must.

10. Click the Runaround tab.

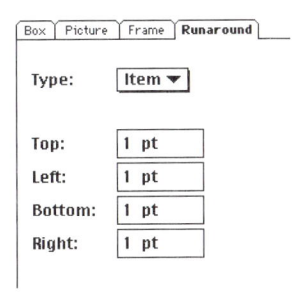

    Set the Runaround Type to None.

CHAPTER 2/MANAGING WORKFLOW

One of the first things you should do is to set the default behavior of text boxes to a fill color of White or 0% Black with a runaround of None. The default text box drives many people up the wall when they try to place text boxes near each other, or over each other, and things start to disappear.

11. Click OK.

12. Draw a rectangular picture box and verify that it has fill of White, a 0.25 pt. frame, and no runaround.

13. Close the file without saving.

You can set the preferences of multiple tools all at once. Select a tool, then click Select Similar Type or Select Similar Shape. To edit the settings of *all* types of picture boxes, click any picture box tool in the list and click Select Similar Type. Click Modify to change the settings. Note that the Runaround tab is not available for multiple types. Clicking Similar Shape will select all rectangular tools, for example, or all Bézier boxes.

Zoom pertains only to the Magnification tool. You can specify the minimum and maximum magnification, and the amount of zoom for each mouse click.

Customizing the Tool Palette

You can set up the Tool palette to use the tool types you prefer. For instance, if you click and hold the Text Box tool, the available types of text boxes appear.

The tool selection remains in the Tool palette, even if you quit and restart QuarkXPress or open another document. To reset the Tool palette to the default tools, open the Document Preferences dialog box, click the Tool tab, and click the Default Tool Palette button.

Trapping

See the Color Output section of this book for more information about Trapping. Trapping can be a very complex and time-consuming process and is best left to printing professionals, so it's a good idea to leave the Trapping preferences alone.

Communicate clearly with your service provider or printer about trapping. A quick phone call can save hundreds or thousands of dollars in added charges for rework, or in the worst-case scenario, a reprint at your expense. In most cases, your service provider or printer should be the only one to adjust QuarkXPress's trapping preferences to suit the prepress equipment, paper stock, inks, and the type of printing press to be used for your job.

Color Management

A Color Management System (CMS) is a software-based system for maintaining consistent color in images (scans, typically) from scanner to monitor to press. High-end scanners and prepress equipment operate in CMYK color, and computer monitors work in RGB color. Differences are bound to occur between what you see on your screen and what emerges at the end of a printing press. A CMS helps map the RGB screen display to an approximation of the final CMYK image. If the screen display is outside the range of what can be printed as CMYK, the display is adjusted to within the range of CMYK. Note that it is only the *display* that is adjusted; the actual image is not adjusted, so this is not a replacement for traditional color correction, but it does make color viewing more accurate.

A CMS requires *profiles* for each input, display, and output device you will use. Typically these profiles are small files supplied with a scanner, monitor, or printer; but in practice the use of a CMS requires extensive and time-consuming calibration of each device in the production loop. In most cases, end users and designers need not worry about a CMS; this is something that your printer or service provider may use.

To turn on Color Management, choose Edit>Preferences>Color Management and click the check box next to Color Management Active. You must quit and restart QuarkXPress for changes to take affect. In general, leave Color Management off unless you are certain that all devices in your workflow are properly calibrated.

Libraries

Libraries are a special type of QuarkXPress file that you can use to store and organize objects (boxes of any kind, with or without contents, lines, text on paths, or grouped objects). You can create as many libraries as you like, and the contents of any open library will appear on a palette. Libraries are very useful for projects that require a large number of repeating elements; you can simply drag an object out of the palette onto a document page.

Creating and using a Library

1. Create a new letter-size document. Name it "Wine.QXD".
2. Draw a picture box 5 inches × 3 inches with a color of White and a frame of 0 pt.
3. Duplicate the picture box twice.

A library doesn't actually store imported images; it creates a proxy of the item, which is what you see. If you drag an image to a page, the links to that image are maintained and you will still need to supply the original image with the document when you send it to a printer.

If you store library items that use named colors, those colors will be added to the Colors palette if the entry is dragged to another document.

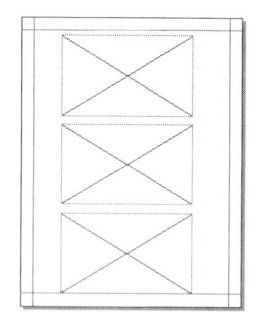

4. Import **Cab.EPS** from the **SF-Adv QuarkXPress** folder into the top box.

5. Import the pictures **Sb.EPS** and **PS.EPS** into the other picture boxes.

6. Create a library by choosing File>New>Library. Name the new library "Wine.QXL" and save it to your **Work in Progress** folder.

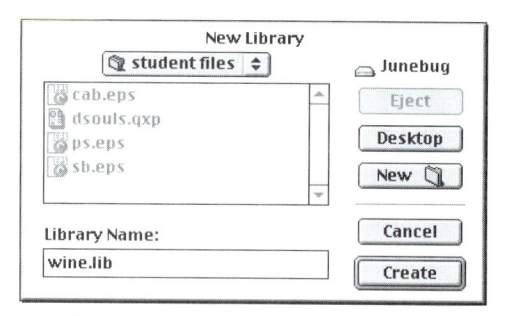

The new empty library appears.

7. Select the Item tool, then click and drag the top image and its box to the Library palette.

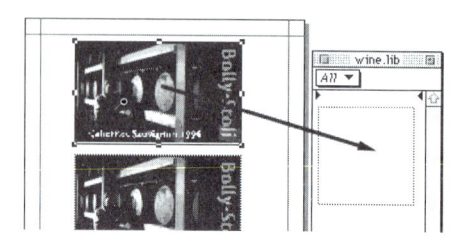

8. Repeat this procedure for the other two picture boxes.

It's possible to become carried away with libraries. If you have a very large number of images to work with, such as a collection of digital stock photos, a library may not be suitable for your needs. You should look into a Digital Asset Management system that allows you to create a database of all your images and lets you search for an image by keywords that you can create for each image. Many newspapers and magazines use such a system, and have digitized and referenced most of their photo archives. As you can imagine, this results in thousands of images that one could never hope to just flip through in a reasonable amount of time; sophisticated search routines are built-in to these management systems.

9. Name the top library entry by double-clicking on it in the Library palette.

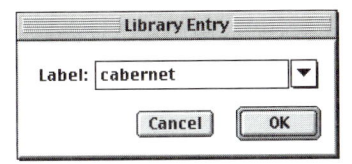

   Type "cabernet" and click OK.

10. Repeat with the other two entries, naming them "sauv blanc" and "petite sirah".

11. Click on the pop-up menu at the top of the Library palette.

    Select **Sauv Blanc**. The other library items disappear. This is useful for finding named items in large libraries.

    Select All to show all of the entries.

12. Close the document **Wine.QXD**; save it if you like.

13. Create a new letter-size document.

14. Drag the Cabernet thumbnail to the page.

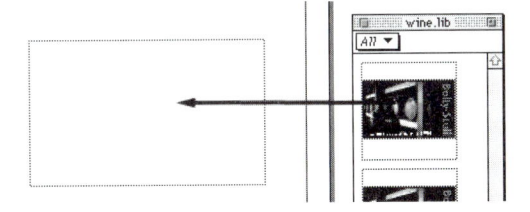

15. Close the file without saving.

16. Close the library by clicking in the box in the upper left (Macintosh) or the box with an X in the upper right (Windows).

It's easy to imagine the power of libraries. In the exercise above you could have created a series of Cabernet library items, each a different size, and stored them in a library for use in laying out bottle labels, a wine catalog, brochure, or other items that might require a specific size of the image. Libraries are a terrific means of storing frequently used objects.

CHAPTER 2/MANAGING WORKFLOW   29

Templates

A template is a read-only document that serves as a starting point for new documents. You build a template just like any other document, but *save* it as a template. When you open the template, QuarkXPress makes a copy of it and opens the template as a new, untitled document.

You already know that a few minutes invested in creating custom settings can return hours in dividends. The wise use of templates is perhaps the most important time-saving discipline a QuarkXPress user can cultivate. Templates allow you to design your commonly used documents once and for all, instantly retrieving all of the vital elements needed for each subsequent job. Typical templates include a myriad of custom elements — master pages, colors, style sheets, H&Js, grids, text boxes, and many other timesaving presets.

Creating a Template

One of the most common uses for templates is for designing business cards. Business cards are almost always the same size, and most print shops will expect them to be set up in multiples on a page. Here, we'll set up a business card template. The printer has asked you to supply a "6-up" *imposition*; that is, six business cards on a page, all lined up and positioned so that when the page is printed and cut, the cards won't need any further trimming. The client has supplied a set of specifications regarding colors and typefaces, and has supplied a logo on disk. Your job is to design cards for everyone in the company and supply them to the printer ready to print. The client specifies that the logo is to bleed on three sides.

1. Determine the dimensions of a page that will hold six business cards. North American cards are typically 3.5 inches wide and 2 inches tall, so the live area of the page is 7 inches wide and 6 inches tall. Since we are building an imposition, we have to allow room for crop and registration marks. An inch all around is plenty. Create a new document 9 inches wide by 8 inches tall with no automatic text box, margins all set to zero, facing pages off.

2. Drag the zero point over and down 1 inch.

An imposition is a special type of document that is made up of multiple pages arranged on one large page in the manner that is required for efficient printing. Templates are a powerful method for creating impositions and for creating exacting items such as music CD inserts, video tape boxes, printed cartons, and other types of packaging.

30 CHAPTER 2/MANAGING WORKFLOW

3. On the master page, draw guides to create six areas that are the same size as a single card. Place vertical guides at 0, 3.5, and 7 inches, and horizontal guides at 0, 2, 4, and 6 inches.

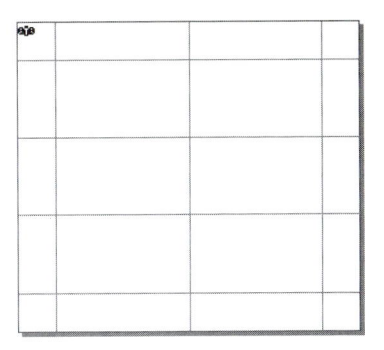

Press Command/Control-Y to open the Document Preferences dialog box.

crop marks
step + repeat
horizontal + vertical

4. Save the file into your **Work in Progress** folder as "Buscards.QXD".

5. Open the Document Preferences dialog box (Edit>Preferences>Document) and click the Tool tab.

6. Select the rectangular Text Box tool and click Modify.

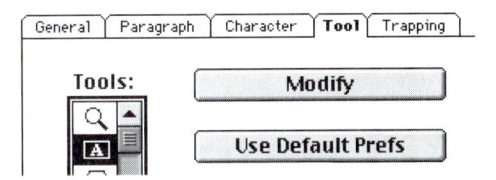

7. In the Box tab, change the default text box color to None.

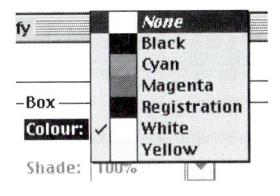

Press Shift-F12 to display the Edit Colors dialog box.

8. In the Runaround tab, change the default runaround to None.

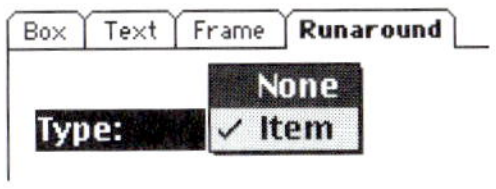

9. Click OK to save the changes.

10. Modify the rectangular Picture Box preferences to have a Box color of White and a runaround of None.

11. Click OK, then click OK in the Document Preferences window to save the changes.

Press Shift-F11 to display the Edit Styles dialog box.

CHAPTER 2/MANAGING WORKFLOW 31

12. Choose Edit>Colors. Select two new colors from the Pantone Solid to Process library: 492 and 3308. Uncheck the Spot Color check box because the logo is a four-color process image and the client does not want to pay for extra inks. Click Save.

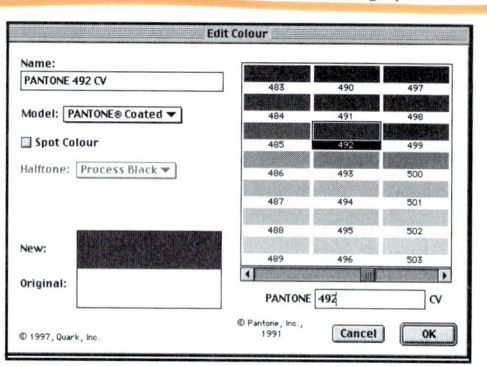

13. Choose Edit>Style Sheets. The client has specified two Paragraph styles of ATC Flamingo for all the copy on the cards. Create two new styles: "company", using ATC Flamingo Bold, 14 pt., Pantone 492, track amount 30, alignment right; and "name", using ATC Flamingo Regular, 9 pt., Black, track amount 10, leading 11, space before 11 pt., alignment right.

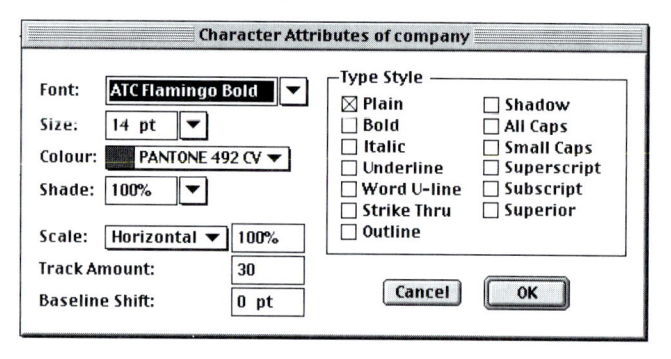

14. On the master page, draw a picture box 0.5 inches wide and 2 inches tall. Place it in the left upper corner of the first card at X and Y coordinates of zero. Import the image **Cardpic.EPS** from the **SF-Adv QuarkXPress** folder into the picture box and adjust it so that the "B" in Bolly and the "i" in Stoli center within the box.

The New Line, or soft return is accessed by pressing Shift-Return/Enter.

15. Draw a text box 2.5 inches wide and 1 inch high. Position it at X: 0.75 inch and Y: 0.25 inch. Type "Bolly-Stoli Winery, Inc." into the box. Apply the Company style. Select the hyphen and color it Black; select "Stoli" and color it Pantone 3308.

Press Command/Control-G to group selected items.

Press Command/Control-0 (zero) to fit the page in the document window

Press Command/Control-Option/Alt-D to open the Step & Repeat dialog box.

With the Item tool selected, press Command/Control-A to select all items on the page.

Click an insertion point after the period in Inc. Press Return once and enter the following: "7 Lacroix Road <new line> Holland Park, CA 94765 <new line> tel: 888.555.0000 <new line> fax: 888.555.0000". Apply the Name style to this text.

16. Draw another text box 2.5 inches wide and 0.5 inches tall. Position it at X: 0.75 inch and Y: 1.375 inch. Type the following as placeholder text: "Name <new line> Title <new line> E-mail". Apply the Name style.

17. With the Item tool, select all the objects and choose Item>Group.

18. Choose View>Fit in Window. Choose Item>Step and Repeat.

19. We're going to duplicate the group twice, stepping and repeating it with numbers to get absolute precision. Type the values shown into the Step and Repeat dialog box and click OK.

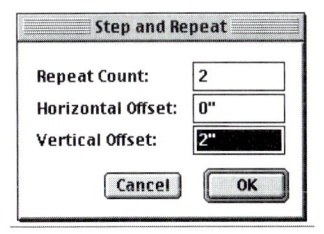

This creates all the cards for the left side of the page.

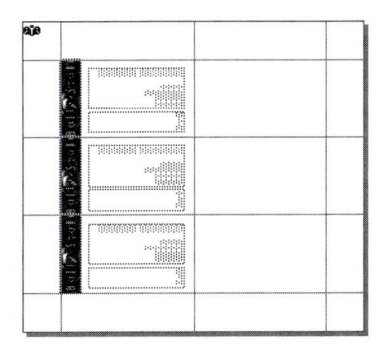

CHAPTER 2/MANAGING WORKFLOW   33

What about the right-hand cards? The client wants the logo to bleed. We can't have the logo bleed on the right without rotating those cards 180 degrees, so we'll do the right side next.

20. With the Item tool, select all three groups. Group them again into one object. Step and Repeat the group as Repeat Count: 1, Horizontal/Vertical offset: 0. This places a copy exactly on top of the original. Navigate to the Measurements palette, enter 180 in the Rotation field, and press Return/Enter.

The group rotates 180 degrees.

21. Look carefully at the X and Y values for the rotated group.

When you rotate an object, the reference point for its X and Y coordinates changed along with it. The Measurements palette is now measuring these from the lower right-hand corner.

22. We want the rotated copy to be in exact relation to the original. It is already at the correct Y coordinate, but we need to move it over. Notice where the far-right guide is: 7 inches. The X coordinate should be set to the same value. Click the rotated group and type 7 into the X coordinate and press Return/Enter.

23. The last step is to set the bleed. Each card needs separate bleeds; corner cards need bleed on two sides, while middle cards just need it on the left edge.

With the Content tool, select the upper-left corner point of the top left picture box. Drag the point up and to the left 0.125 inch to create the bleed.

34 CHAPTER 2/MANAGING WORKFLOW

Here's the bleed:

A bleed of 0.125 inch is standard in most printing applications.

24. Repeat the same procedure with all the images, pulling the corners 0.125 inch out on corner cards and the one edge out 0.125 inch on the middle cards.

25. Because this is a press form, we can't use QuarkXPress's crop marks option in the Print dialog box. We have to create crop marks and registration marks. Zoom in on the upper left-hand card.

The point at which the guides intersect the outer perimeter of the form is where crop marks will be needed.

26. Double-click on the Line tool and change its preferences to 0.25 pt. and a color of Registration.

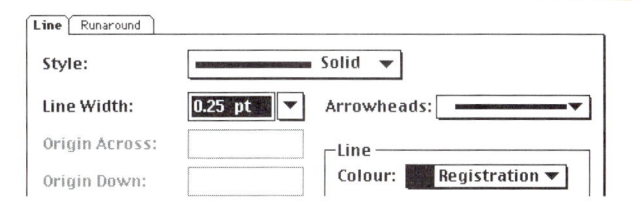

Draw a short line on the two intersecting guides, making certain that the line does not enter the live area (we've used 1 pt. lines here for clarity; 0.25 pt. lines are the norm for crop marks).

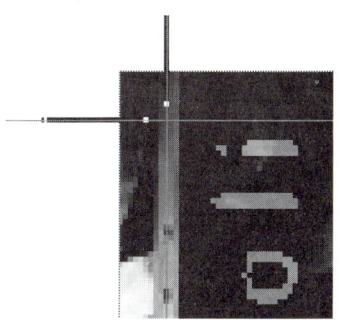

Double-click on any object-creation tool or the Magnify tool to show the Preferences dialog box.

0.25 pt. crop marks may be difficult to see if your guides are set to In Front. Choose Edit>Preferences> Application to set guides Behind, and you should be able to see the crop marks.

Alternately, you can toggle the guides on and off by pressing F7.

CHAPTER 2/MANAGING WORKFLOW 35

"Registration" is a special color. While it appears to be Black, it is only useful in cases where you need to create crop and registration marks by hand instead of using QuarkXPress's built-in crop and registration marks. Coloring an object Registration will result in that object printing on all pages of a color separation, whether it is spot or process. This provides a point of reference for each ink. A press usually requires adjustment in the initial stage of printing, called make-ready, and a press operator will fine-tune the press's controls until the registration marks on the printed sheets line up precisely. A registered press will print marks that are solid black. A misregistered press will print marks that have a bit of color showing on the edges.

27. Step and Repeat the horizontal crop mark three times with a horizontal offset of 0 inch and a vertical offset of 2 inches.

28. Step and repeat the vertical crop mark twice with a horizontal offset of 3.5 inches and a vertical offset of 0 inch.

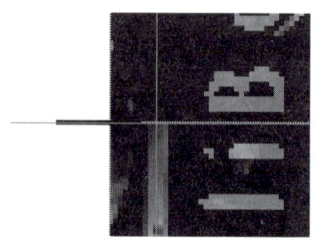

29. Draw crop marks for the right side and bottom. The result should look like this:

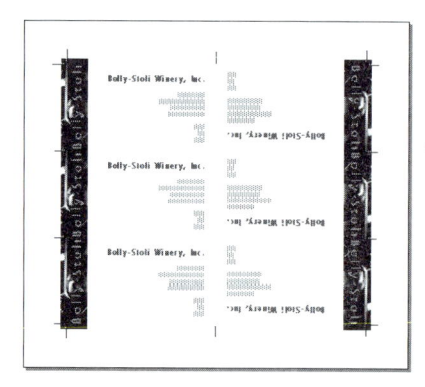

30. Now we need registration marks. These are used when the job is printed to make certain that the color separations on the press are "in register" and are not misaligned.

Typical registration mark

Draw a 0.5 inch square picture box and place the file **Regmark.EPS** from the **SF-Adv QuarkXPress** folder. Scale the contents equally to 25%. Place the picture box near the bottom, in the middle of the page, under the center crop mark.

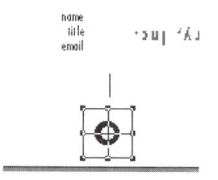

31. Duplicate the registration mark three times and place the copies on the top, left, and right sides of the page.

36 CHAPTER 2/MANAGING WORKFLOW

32. Because this document will be printed with automatic crop marks off, we need to add separation names to the imposition, so that when the final films are used to make printing plates, the plating technician will know which separation is to be used for the correct process color.

   Create a 3 inch × 0.5 inch text box at the bottom of the imposition in the area used for crops and registration marks. Type "Cyan Magenta Yellow Black" (the default font of Helvetica/Arial 12 pt. is fine). Select each word and color it accordingly.

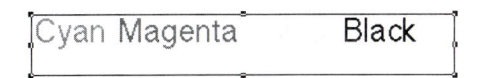

   Each word will print only on the corresponding color separation.

33. Save the file, then choose File>Save As. Rename the file "Bustempl.QXT" and select Template from the Type pop-up menu.

   The final template:

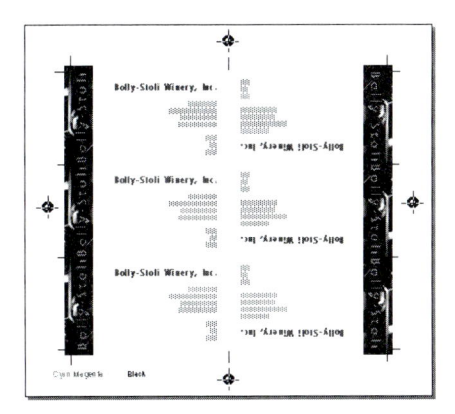

You now have a template that can be used repeatedly. This is helpful in cases such as business cards for a medium-sized company where the only things that change are a few lines of text. Each time you get an order for more cards, all you need to do is open the template, select the Content tool, and replace the placeholder text from the master page with the name, title, and e-mail information for each employee (and even though the cards on the right are upside down, you can still edit them) on the document page, adding pages as needed.

This can also be used as a standard business card template that you can edit for other clients, now that you have all the measurements and crop marks set up. Templates are ideal for odd-sized items such as artwork for the discs, inserts, and tray liners that are used in packaging for a compact disc. Many companies that produce CDs, video cassettes, packaging, books, and other products where correct measures are critical often provide templates to their customers upon which to base their artwork.

The EPS file format is one of two definitive standards for the exchange of graphics in the graphic arts industry. The other is TIFF, which is used for color and black-and-white photos. Other formats that are becoming popular are Adobe's Acrobat (PDF), and TIFF/IT, which is an extension of TIFF that allows very high-resolution of type and line art to avoid the inherent "jaggies" in this type of art in the plain TIFF format.

Managing Images

Getting images into QuarkXPress is easy, but once there you might have a few issues to deal with before your job is ready to be printed.

Image Types

Images can be loosely divided into two types: bitmap (or raster) images or vector images. Bitmaps can be saved as TIFF or EPS files; vector images are always saved as EPS files. EPS files can contain either type of image or a combination of both. Other formats can be used if necessary, though converting these to either TIFF or EPS will decrease the likelihood of problems when the document is printed. QuarkXPress can only color-separate EPS and TIFF images.

QuarkXPress can import the following types of images:

Vector	Bitmap	
EPS	TIFF**	JPEG*
DCS EPS	EPS	Scitex CT
	DCS EPS	PICT
	PAINT	PCX*
	OS/2 BMP	Windows BMP
	Kodak Photo CD*	

* Requires a QuarkXPress import filter.
**LZW-compressed TIFFs require a QuarkXPress import filter.

QuarkXPress's installation utility will automatically install import filters for these formats. If you don't use these formats you can turn off the filters with the XTensions Manager (Utilities>XTensions Manager).

Vector EPS files usually come from illustration programs such as Illustrator, FreeHand, and CorelDraw! TIFF and bitmapped EPS files usually come from image-editing programs such as Photoshop. Scitex CT files are produced by high-end Scitex imaging workstations. DCS EPS files are similar to regular EPS files except that DCS (Desktop Color Separation) files are pre-separated when they are exported from the originating application. Ask your printer if they prefer DCS files, which usually process faster than EPS files.

Deciding whether to save a bitmapped image as TIFF or EPS depends on a few factors. If you have created a clipping path in Photoshop you can use either format because QuarkXPress 4 now supports TIFF images with embedded clipping paths. QuarkXPress 3 only supports clipping paths in EPS files, and many people still use QuarkXPress 3, so for maximum compatibility, save images with clipping paths as EPS. Duotones *must* be saved as EPS. CMYK images can be saved in either format with no difference in the final quality of the image. You can sometimes get a better preview of an image in QuarkXPress if you save it from Photoshop as EPS with a TIFF preview. If your printer wants you to supply DCS files, these must be saved as EPS. A DCS EPS is pre-separated into the four process colors, plus any used spot

Macintosh users who plan to share material with Windows users should get into the habit of using the old MS-DOS file naming conventions. Even though Windows 95, 98, and NT allow long file names, these may not survive a Windows-to-Mac conversion, and older machines running Windows 3.1 will chop off long file names, replacing "a nice photo.tif" with "ANICEPHO.TOT." To maintain compatibility, use an eight-letter file name, a period, and then a three-letter extension. Windows depends heavily (and dangerously at times) upon file extensions to determine the file type.

Common file extensions:

TIFF	.TIF
EPS	.EPS
QuarkXPress	.QXD
JPEG	.JPG

colors, and can be a single file, or a preview file with four or more files, one for each separation.

PICT, PAINT, PCX, GIF, OS/2 BMP, and Windows BMP aren't well suited for quality printing. Typically they are low-resolution bitmap files that will print poorly. If you want to use them in a layout that will be printed, it is better to open them in Photoshop and convert them to TIFF (line art, grayscale, or CMYK) images before using them in a QuarkXPress layout.

WMF (Windows Meta File) is a vector graphic format, but the Macintosh version of QuarkXPress will convert these to a low-resolution bitmap PICT file. Always convert WMF files to EPS before transferring them to a Macintosh. Freehand 8 for Macintosh can open and convert WMF to EPS.

Photo CD and JPEG images can be used, but it is better to open them in Photoshop and convert them to CMYK TIFF images.

JPEG is a highly-compressed image format that achieves its sometimes spectacular compression levels by discarding portions of the image that the compression routine considers expendable. This is called *lossy* compression. *Lossless* compression, such as an LZW-compressed TIFF, preserves all of the image data. People who use JPEG images for printed material are unpleasantly surprised when *compression artifacts* (unacceptable mottling and patterning that appear especially across areas of flat color and around edges) appear in the printed piece. The higher the level of compression, the more data is discarded from the image, and the artifacts will become more and more pronounced. JPEG images can also cause problems at the print shop because not all prepress imaging systems can successfully color separate them. The shop may have to convert all JPEGs into TIFF or EPS files, and you'll have to pay for their time. Converting a JPEG image to another format does *not* eliminate compression artifacts; it merely makes the file print more easily. Avoid using JPEG images for printing. Uncompressed TIFFs will take up a lot more storage space, but the image quality will remain uncompromised. JPEG is better suited for projects meant to be displayed on a computer screen, such as a web page or a presentation, because artifacts won't be nearly as apparent on a monitor.

Color Issues

A lot of time and money is wasted when a job arrives at a printer and the prepress operator discovers that the job is essentially unprintable because the images and colors are not set up properly. Expensive rework is required to get the job on press. Here's a few pointers on preparing your files before sending them to the printer:

- If your job is printed with just Black (or any single ink), use grayscale or line art TIFFs, and create vector art with only Black and tints of Black.

- If your job is printed with spot colors (including Black) be certain that the spot color names in all programs used to create the project are identical. If not,

CHAPTER 2/MANAGING WORKFLOW

QuarkXPress will treat misnamed colors as separate spot colors. Your two-color job may suddenly become a four-color job because QuarkXPress treats "Pantone 116 CVC" and "Pantone 116 CVU" as two separate colors. It's a good idea to avoid using "Pantone Process Black" for Black in an illustration program; to QuarkXPress it is just another spot color.

While it is possible to remove and convert colors through the Colors palette, that is one more opportunity for an error to occur.

TIFF images in spot color jobs should be saved as grayscale or line art and then colored in QuarkXPress, or you can create duotones of Black and/or spot color inks in Photoshop. You can use from one to four inks with Photoshop duotones. Watch the color names! Photoshop 5 allows the use of spot color in images without having to create duotones or separate color channels.

- If your job is to be printed in four-color process, spot colors must be converted to process colors before printing; otherwise you'll end up with extra separations and a whopping bill. If you plan to use both spot and process colors in a job, convert all named colors to process except for the ones that will print as spot separations.

- QuarkXPress imports any named spot colors in EPS files (including Photoshop duotone files). If you import EPS files to a 4-color process job and any new colors appear in the Colors palette, convert the colors to process in the original application (or convert a Photoshop duotone to a CMYK TIFF or EPS) and re-export it. After you update the image in QuarkXPress you can delete the spot colors from the Colors palette. QuarkXPress can be set to convert all imported or QuarkXPress spot and RGB colors to CMYK, but the results may not match what you expected.

- Be wary of enlarging bitmapped images (TIFF or EPS) in QuarkXPress. The image quality degrades and it will become pixelated at enlargements that are much over 110%. Always try to scan or create bitmapped images at the actual size you plan to use. Alternately, if you don't know what the final size will be, you can *oversample* an image when scanning or creating it by using a higher resolution. Typically, images are scanned at twice the value of the lines per inch (lpi) screen ruling that will be used in the printed piece. If your job will be printed at 150 lpi you should use a 300 ppi resolution. If you aren't certain of the final size or screen ruling you can scan it at a higher resolution, and when you decide on the size you can reduce or enlarge the image in Photoshop and then *downsample* it to the optimum resolution.

Always try to use the optimum resolution. If you reduce a 300 ppi image to 50% it becomes a 600 ppi image and will take much longer to print than it would at 300 ppi without any increase in quality. Conversely, a 300 ppi image enlarged 200% becomes a 150 ppi image, and will look terrible when printed.

Pantone spot colors are named according to the swatch book type. Colors picked from the Pantone Coated color library end with CVC; colors picked from the Pantone Uncoated library end with CVU; colors from the Pantone Solid to Process library end with CVP (the "CV" stands for "Computer Video" simulation). QuarkXPress recognizes each as a discrete color. It's good to get in the habit of removing the CV extension from colors created in QuarkXPress and illustration programs.

An exception to the ppi = 2 × lpi rule is scanned line art, which is always black-and-white. Because this type of artwork is usually sharp and detailed, it should be scanned at the actual resolution of the final output device. If your printer's imagesetter is run at 2400 ppi, then scan line art at 2400 ppi. The same warnings about enlargement and reduction apply to high-resolution line art.

- QuarkXPress can convert RGB images to CMYK when you print separations, but this will almost always result in a final image that may look quite different than the original RGB image. Always convert RGB images to CMYK (or grayscale or duotone, depending upon your print process) before you import them. This will allow you to see how much the image's colors might change, and you can make any needed adjustments in the image's original application. The same applies to named RGB colors in illustration programs and in QuarkXPress. Always define colors according to the printing process used: spot or four-color process. A printer will charge you extra to make these conversions and you may have little control over any necessary color correction.

Text Issues

Text in QuarkXPress arrives in one of two ways: from imported files or from typing it directly into a document. Most types of text import issues are covered in Chapter 7, "Advanced Styles." One issue you might face is importing a plain text (ASCII, raw text, unformatted text, and so forth) file into QuarkXPress. Often these files have hard returns at the end of each line instead of at the end of a paragraph, and the text will never flow or justify properly. You can use QuarkXPress's Find and Replace feature to correct this problem, rather than deleting them manually.

You might encounter plain text files if you receive copy by e-mail, download a text file from a web site, or from someone using a different computer platform who has saved the file as plain text to ensure the broadest compatibility.

Cleaning up a Plain Text File

1. Create a new document, US Letter-size, 0.5 inch margins, Automatic Text Box On, 2 Columns, Gutter Width 1p, Facing Pages Off.

2. Click the Content tool in the automatic text box and import the file **Dsouls.TXT** from the **SF-Adv QuarkXPress** folder. About five pages will be added to the document.

3. What a mess. The text has hard returns after every line and doesn't fit in the columns.

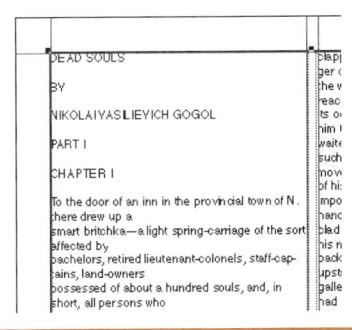

Click an insertion point at the very beginning to the left of the first line that reads "Dead Souls". Choose Edit>Find/Change… to display the Find/Replace palette.

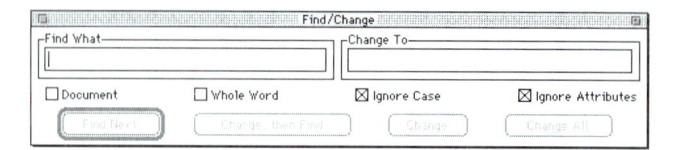

4. To specify returns in the Find What field, type Command/Control and then press the Return or Enter key twice. The Find What field will show these somewhat cryptic codes: \p\p. QuarkXPress uses this type of code to search for non-printing characters such as returns and tabs.

    In the Change To field, type: "@@".

    The code \p represents a single return in the Find/Change palette. We want to remove all hard returns at the ends of the lines, but just deleting *all* the returns would turn the entire story into a large blob of text. Double returns are used in the file to denote a new paragraph. We'll replace those double returns with the symbols @@, which we will return to shortly.

    Check the Document check box and click Find Next. If QuarkXPress beeps at you, check to make certain that the insertion point is at the beginning of the text: The first instance is found.

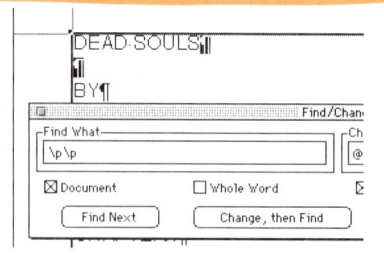

    Now click Change All. The search is performed and a message appears stating how many instances were changed.

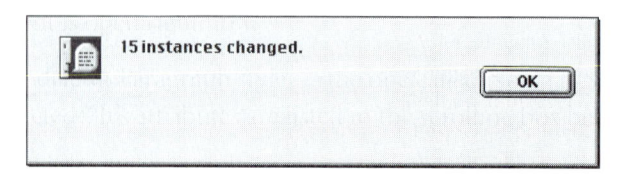

    Click OK. All double returns have been replaced with @@.

5. In the Find/Change palette, delete \p\p in the Find What field. Press the Command or Control and the Return key once. In the Change To field, delete @@

Holding down the Option/Alt key will change the Find Next button to a Find First button, so you can go from the end of the document back to the top without having to manually reposition the cursor.

and press the Space bar one time. Make certain that the insertion point is at the very beginning. (After a multi-page search and replace, QuarkXPress will often display the last page of the document.)

Click Find Next, then Change All. Click OK in the Instances Changed message.

6. Now there are *no* returns in the file. We need to resurrect the double returns that signify a new paragraph. Replace \p in the Find What field with @@ and press Command/Control-Return in the Change To field (be certain to replace the space character) and perform the replacement.

7. We now have a plain but usable text file that can be styled to fit your needs.

8. You can also export the text into a file to be used elsewhere. Click the insertion point in the story and press Command/Control-A to select the entire story. Choose File>Save Text… and name the file "DsoulsASCII.TXT". Select ASCII Text for the Format and click on Selected Text. Alternately, you could place the cursor anywhere in the document and select the Entire Story button for export.

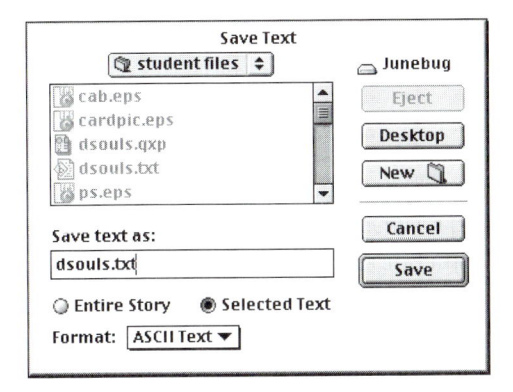

9. Close the document without saving.

CHAPTER 2/MANAGING WORKFLOW 43

You can export text in many types of word processing formats such as Microsoft Word, Word Perfect, and others, or in more universal formats such as RTF-Rich Text Format (Windows only) or XPress Tags. See Chapter 7, "Advanced Styles" for more information.

Chapter 3

Structuring Your Layout

Chapter Objective:

To learn how to approach a job through proper planning and construction, the most important skill a designer can learn. In Chapter 3 you will:

- Understand the use of non-printing grids.
- Learn how to build grids.
- Learn how to use text boxes to create custom grids.
- Perform an exercise creating column grids.
- Understand managing Styles and Baseline Grids.
- Learn how to apply Baseline Grids to Styles.
- Review copy and layout fitting; and kerning and tracking.
- Understand the "color" of type.
- Learn more about H&Js.

Projects to be Completed:

- **Gym Ad**
- Recipe Book
- Tropical Suites Brochure
- Staying Alive Newsletter
- Automation Booklet
- GASP Newsletter

A solid design is pleasing to the eye; it makes intelligent use of white space, balances the text and images, and provides the reader with the information that it's meant to convey quickly and efficiently.

This chapter will show you some of the tricks and methods used by the pros to develop and maintain a professional style with all their projects.

Structuring Your Layouts

If someone asked us the single most important skill to look for in an experienced operator, we would say it was how they approached a job. Did they immediately sit down at QuarkXPress and start clicking and dragging stuff around, or did they begin by planning the job and properly constructing the mechanical *before* they put anything on the page. Another word for this approach is how designers or artists *structure* their own jobs.

That's what we're going to study in Chapter 3 — Structure: how you use grids and guides, how you approach the fit and look of your work, and how to use QuarkXPress to create truly structured and professional-looking documents.

Grids

The most important consideration when you're creating structured documents is the use of non-printing grids. There are many different types of grids and guides available in QuarkXPress, and we're going to cover most of them in this chapter.

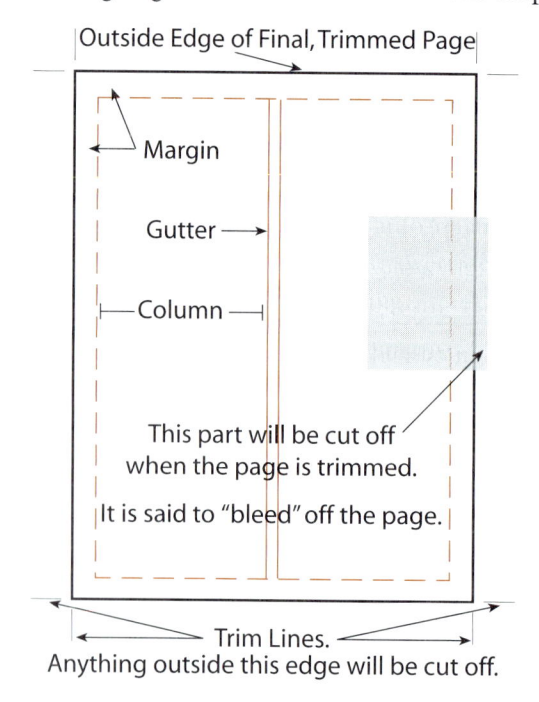

Outside Edge of Final, Trimmed Page

Margin

Gutter

Column

This part will be cut off when the page is trimmed. It is said to "bleed" off the page.

Trim Lines. Anything outside this edge will be cut off.

In its simplest definition, page margins and trim guides can be thought of as a grid. They provide the artist or designer the boundaries within which design elements — pictures, illustrations, shapes, type, rules and so on — must fit. This simple "inside the margins" grid is called the *live area* of the page. The clean area around the outside edge is called the *margin,* and any elements that hang off the page (and will be cut off when the job is cut or trimmed) are *bleed* elements.

Studying grids and templates provides you with the opportunity to examine the work of others to understand how they're using structure in their documents. Pick up a magazine and examine the way it's laid out, how the designers achieve consistency from department to department and from article to article, even though they might look different at first glance.

Beyond that simple definition, grids become very powerful tools that you can use to gain consistency, establish and maintain a "look and feel" for your documents, and ensure that every object on the page is exactly where it is supposed to be.

Using Custom Grids and Template Files

Most of the print work you see today is executed on workstations such as the one you're working on right now. If you were able to see the actual files that were used to create these ads, magazines, books, and publications, you would invariably find that they were built using custom grids and template files. For example, the course book that you're reading right now is built on a grid. There are several different type of master pages; and guides are predefined in the document before we start laying in text and graphics.

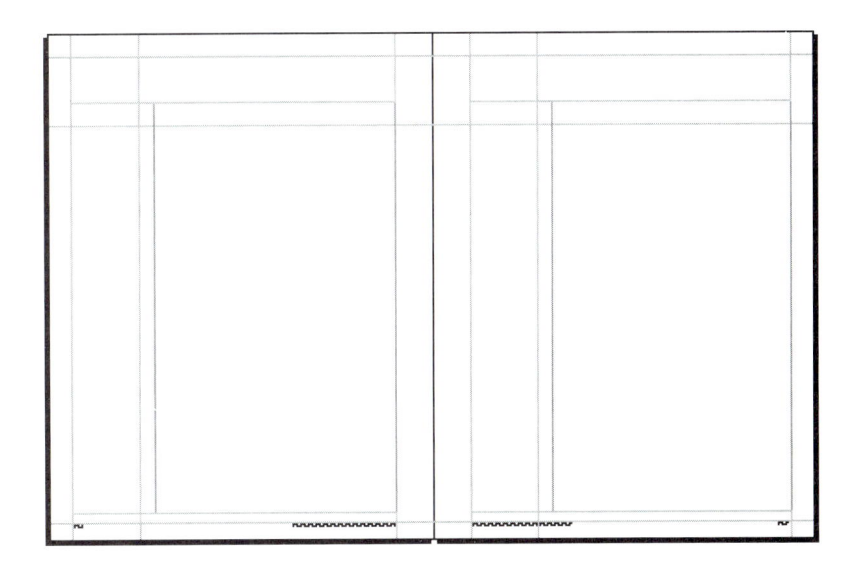

Dividing Pages

The first thing to understand about grids is that they are used to divide the page into logical regions. Within these regions, the designer places specific elements such as type, graphics, color, blends, rules, and so on. As we stated before, the page's margins are the first component in the grid; the second component is guides that split the page into vertical areas.

The best way to split the page into vertical and horizontal regions is by using text boxes, specifically, rectangular text boxes. This is a trick that very few designers use, yet it's extremely simple and elegant; it eliminates the need to use a calculator to figure out where you should place the guides.

Building Grids

1. Create a new document, letter-size, single page, 0.25 inch margins.

2. If you can't see the margin guides, select the View menu, then select Show Guides or press F7.

3. Make certain that your rulers are turned on by pressing Control-R (Windows) or Command-R (Macintosh). If the rulers aren't showing in inches, choose Edit>Preferences>Document and select the General tab. This is where you can change the measurement units from that dialog box.

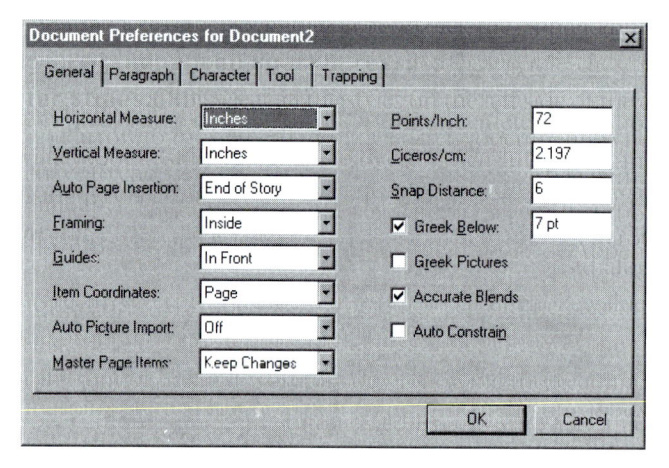

4. Select the Rectangular Text Box tool. Draw a rectangle that stretches from margin to margin.

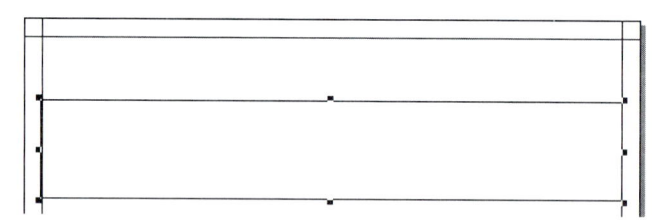

5. The simplest division of a page is to split it in half horizontally and vertically. Since all square or rectangular boxes have anchor points on their corners and midway between each line, you can use these markers to split the page. Zoom in to the center point and drag a vertical ruler to the middle of the handle.

An excellent exercise for the new artist or designer (and not bad for the experienced designer, either) is to take a piece of tracing paper, place it over a series of display ads or publication pages, and draw the grid that was used to build the mechanical. It will not only give you the ability to just "see" the grid as soon as you look at a design, but will expand your own creative repertoire.

You can turn guides on and off (called "toggling") by pressing the F7 key.

48 CHAPTER 3/STRUCTURING YOUR LAYOUTS

The closer you are to the page when you place your rulers, the smaller the increments are and the more accurately you will be able to place your guides. Don't drive yourself crazy, but always try to place your guides as accurately as possible.

6. Resize the box until it fills the margins. Split the page horizontally in the middle.

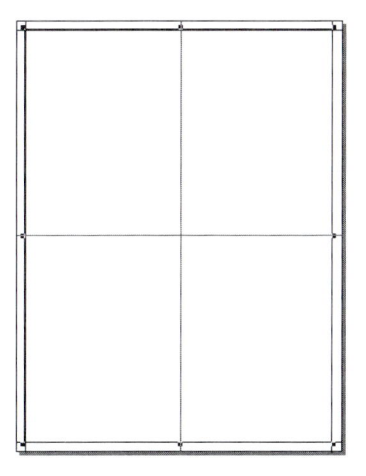

Once you've built this grid, visualize how you might use it to build a dramatic, interesting page. Something to think about when you look at a grid like this is that you could build it into any corner simply by resizing the box we're using as a measurement aid into the upper-left corner or one of the lower corners. This type of grid gives a page "direction"; it tends to weigh the look of the page toward one or another corner and is a very popular grid used by many professional designers.

7. Resize the text box to occupy the upper-right quadrant of the page. Drag horizontal and vertical rulers over the midpoint anchors. Resize the box one more time into the upper-right region. Split the area again with horizontal and vertical rulers.

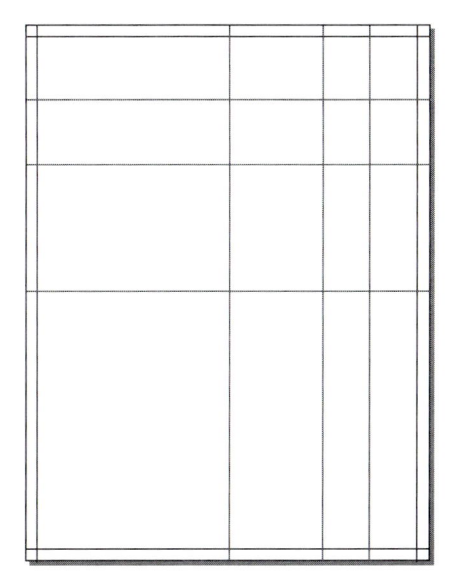

8. Name the page "Grid Practice.QXD" and save it into your **Work in Progress** folder.

CHAPTER 3/STRUCTURING YOUR LAYOUTS 49

There are books available that contain dozens of ideas for grids and page structuring. Just check out your local art bookstore or log onto www.amazon.com and look through their selections. They have an excellent find function to help you search. You will never find an award-winning professional designer that doesn't have an extensive library of graphic arts books, magazines, and publications. Source material is extremely important in the development of your own personal creative style.

Gutter width is the space between the columns.

Using Text Boxes to Create Column Grids

Earlier, we mentioned that a text box is the best type of box to use as a measurement aid when building your grids; this is because of their unique ability to split page regions into uneven regions. In the last exercise, we used a box simply to split regions in half, and in half again. Any box could be used for this purpose. To split regions into odd areas, though, the text box proves unique.

Many documents are built on three, four, and five column grids. Using column grids is different than simply using a text box set to several columns, as you'll see from this next exercise.

Creating Column Grids

1. Navigate to your **Work in Progress** folder and open the **Grid Practice.QXD** file that you created in the last exercise.

2. If you're using a Macintosh, hold down the Option key and click the horizontal ruler at the top of the window (for Windows users, use Alt-click). The horizontal rulers disappear. Do the same to the vertical rulers by Option- or Alt-clicking the ruler on the left side of the window. This is an easy way to remove all the guides on a page with a few clicks.

3. Choose File>Revert to Saved and click OK to restore the page to its previous condition (with the guides from the last exercise still in place).

4. Add another page to the document by selecting Page>Insert and clicking OK to add a single page after page 1.

5. Turn to the new page by pressing the Page Down key. Draw a text box that fills the page within the margins. Using the Item tool, double-click the box. Select the Text tab. Enter 3 for the number of columns (it defaults to 1 unless you change the defaults) and 0.25 inch for the gutter width. Click OK.

50 CHAPTER 3/STRUCTURING YOUR LAYOUTS

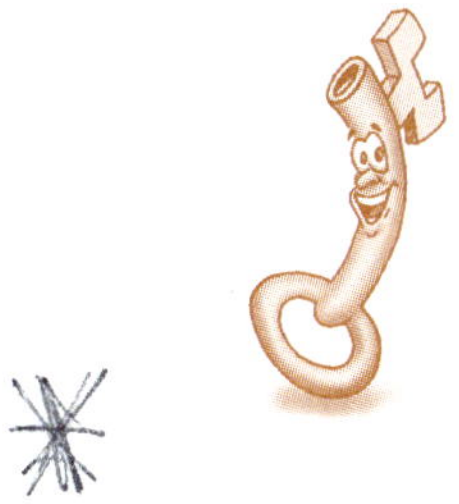

For those using a Windows system to run QuarkXPress, you can right-click on any item and choose several options from the pop-up menu that appears.

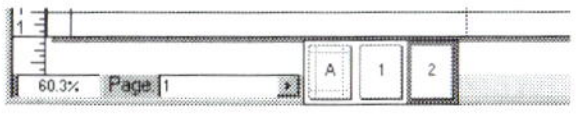

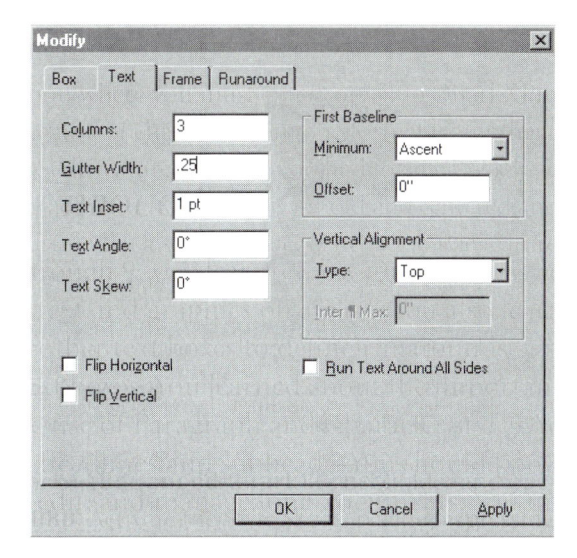

6. Zoom in to the top of the page. Carefully drag vertical guides to mark the edges of each column guide, as well as the centers. You will have six vertical guides on the page when you're done.

7. Drag the top of the text box to the 1.5 inch mark. You just made room for the headline on the page. Put another text box in the space at the top of the page. It should only have one column.

8. Add another page (page 3) and go to that page. Drag a horizontal guide to the 1.5 inch mark. Create a text box the width of the page. Double-click with the Item tool and set the columns to 5 and the gutter to 0.125. Save the document.

9. Drag vertical guides to the center of each of the column breaks. When you're done, delete the text box.

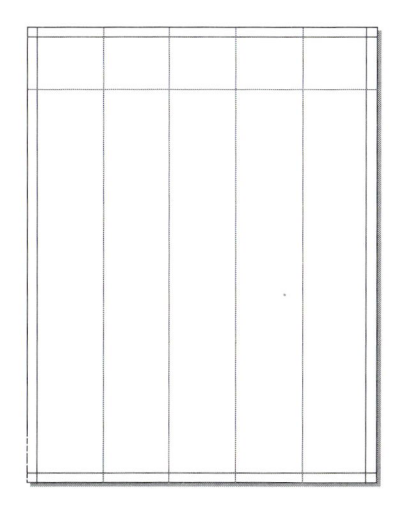

You can immediately go to any page in a document (including the master pages) by clicking the Page pop-up menu in the lower left side of the window.

CHAPTER 3/STRUCTURING YOUR LAYOUTS 51

Another way to jump to a specific page is with the Jump command — Command/Control-J.

To jump to the first page of a document, press Command/Control-Home.

When you design a grid that you think you might want to use again, or develop a format that you like, try using the Template function. Choose Save as, and select Template from the pop-up menu. Name the file XXXX.QXT instead of XXXX.QXD. A QXT file is a QuarkXPress Template file. When you open the file, QuarkXPress will open a copy named Untitled. You will be prompted to give the file a name. The template will remain intact.

10. Return to the first page. Draw a picture box that fills the live area of the page — side to side and top to bottom. Get the picture from the **SF-Adv QuarkXPress** folder named **Thinking Man.TIF**.

11. Notice how the grid could be used to position copy to the man's right side in the direction he's facing. The headline could be positioned at the first or second horizontal guide, and so on. In many cases, you can look at an image and see what kind of grid you'll need — weighed to one corner, weighed to the top or bottom, and so on.

12. Save and close the document. We'll be using this file again throughout the balance of this chapter.

Using Grids as Design Aids

Be aware that even this simple grid provides the designer or artist with almost unlimited options for dramatic layouts. For example, we could use the grid to determine the location and even the direction of an image.

When you place type on the page, the grid helps even more. In this simple layout you can begin to see the power of using grids to develop structured and effective designs. Not only do they keep the design fresh, but they also make it easier to try out different ideas.

Not all professional documents are built on very tight specifications and well-defined grids. A good exercise is to spend some time at the newsstand finding examples of very structured publications and some that are not-so-structured. There are plenty that come to mind. New York Magazine, Esquire, and others are extremely well structured, yet very elegant and effective. Wired is an excellent example of a magazine that pushes design boundaries while maintaining a superb publication. One style isn't any better than another; just different. The more versatile you are, though, the more effective you'll be.

The Baseline Grid

There's another grid system built into QuarkXPress — one that's designed to give rigid structure over the vertical placement of body text. It's called a *Baseline Grid*. It's particularly useful when your assignment calls for a great deal of accuracy and control over how body type is positioned.

Most documents have more than one Character and Paragraph style. Headlines are usually one style, selected to catch the attention of the potential viewer. If there are more than a few paragraphs of body text, then the document might also contain style definitions for subheadings, bulleted or numbered lists, captions, credits, and more.

In the case of Paragraph formats and styles, their type size, leading, space before or after, and rules above or below can all affect the horizontal position of type. So, too, can the Baseline Shift command, which can move type up or down in extremely small increments.

Managing Styles and Baseline Grids

1. Open the **Grids Practice.QXD** file that you created earlier; this should be in your **Work in Progress** folder.

2. Page two of this document has a three-column grid in the body with space for a headline. Select that page.

3. Select the Content tool and click on the large, three-column text box. Press Command-E (Macintosh) or Control-E (Windows) to import a story. Navigate to the **SF-Adv QuarkXPress** folder and select the story named **Meeting.TXT**. It will flow into the three-column format that you previously created. Zoom in to the upper-left corner of the page.

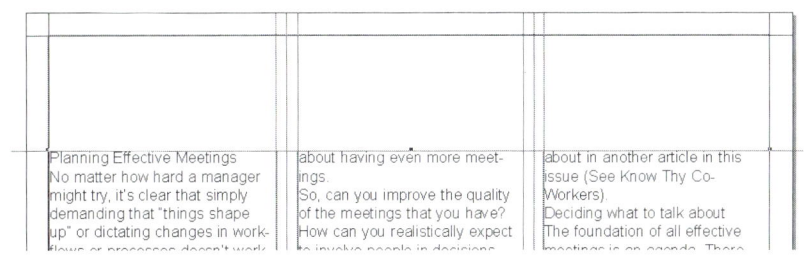

4. Highlight the first line (Having Effective Meetings). Cut it from the page by pressing Command-X (Macintosh) or Control-X (Windows). Put the text cursor in the box at the top of the page and press Command-V (Macintosh) or Control-V (Windows) to paste it into place. Just leave it there for now; we'll return to it a little later.

5. There is probably an empty line in the first column before the first paragraph. Delete it.

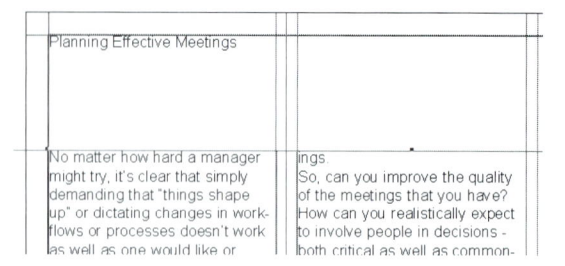

6. Quadruple-click (four times) inside the first paragraph; it will become highlighted. First, set the type attributes to ATC Colada, 9 pt. on 13 pt. of leading.

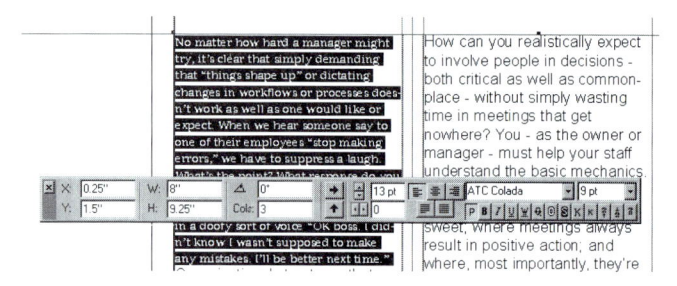

7. Press Shift-F11 to access the Style Sheets dialog box. Click the New button and select Paragraph from the pop-up menu.

If you're building long documents and you're not using style sheets, shame on you! Set the attributes you want on a single paragraph or character, highlight it, and press Shift-F11. Click the New button, name the style, give it a keyboard equivalent, and go to work. Whenever you need that formatting applied, press the keystrokes that you assigned and the attributes will automatically be applied to the selection.

The Edit menu has many keyboard equivalents. This is the Windows menu, so if you're working on a Macintosh you need to substitute the Command key for the Control key (shown as Ctrl on this menu).

8. The highlighted copy automatically provides the attributes for the new style. Name the new style "First Paragraph".

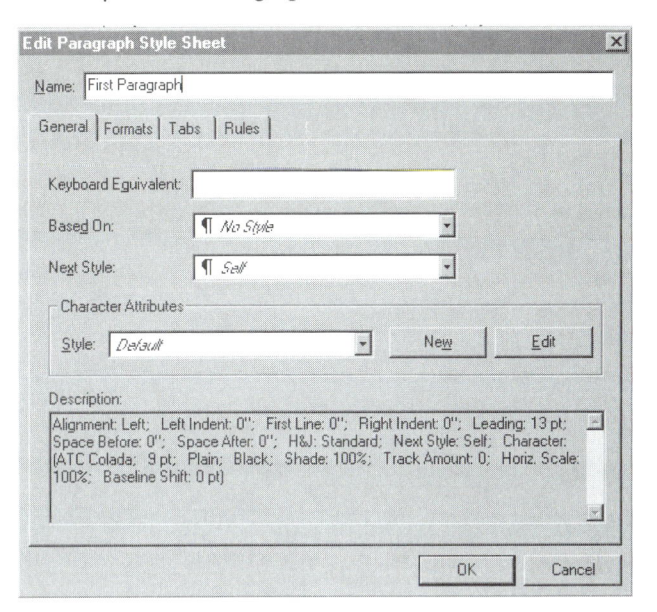

9. Click OK. When the Style Sheets dialog box appears, make certain that the First Paragraph style is highlighted, and click the Duplicate button. This creates a copy of the style that you just created. Click the Formats tab and set the first line indent to 0.15 inch. Name the style "Body Text". Click OK to exit the Paragraph Style Sheet dialog box, and Save when you're done.

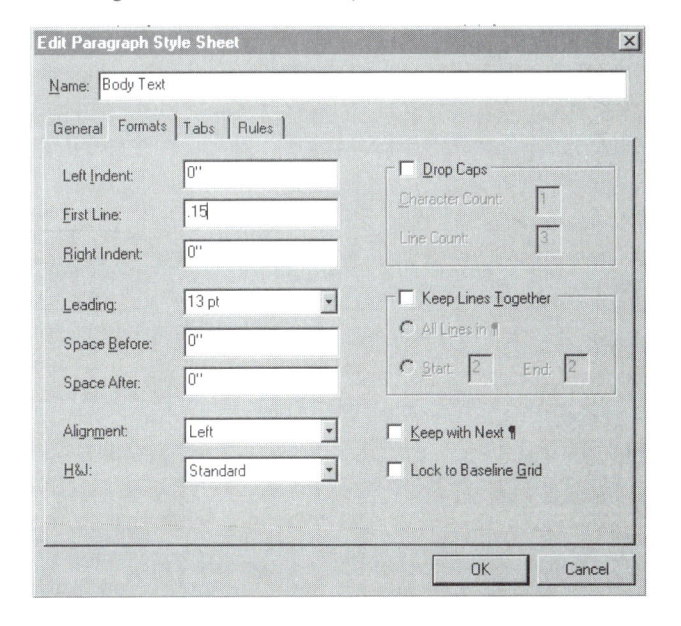

CHAPTER 3/STRUCTURING YOUR LAYOUTS 55

Using style sheets is an extremely effective technique, and one that we feel is tremendously underutilized by many of the professional designers and artists that we meet. What many designers do is learn only as much of the software as they need to know to get their page components properly positioned. They feel that learning more about the software is a waste of time. That's all well and good, but what they fail to recognize is that the better they are, the faster they are; the faster they are, the more time they have to try out ideas, which makes them better designers. Style sheets are a perfect example of something that can save major time (you can edit them later to try out different looks). Take the time to learn more about them and how to use them.

10. Assign the styles. The first paragraph should be assigned, appropriately, the *First Paragraph* style. The second and third paragraphs should be assigned to *Body Text*. When you get to the fourth paragraph, stop. It's not text; it's a subheading.

11. Highlight the headline (triple-clicking will ensure that you grab the entire line of text). Set the type attributes to ATC Tradewinds Ultra, 12 pt. on 14 pt. of lead.

12. Set the Paragraph specifications. Since it's a subhead, let's make certain that there is always a small amount of extra space before the style. Select Style>Formats or press Shift-Command-F (Macintosh) or Shift-Control-F (Windows). Put 0.25 inch space before and 0.15 inch space below the paragraph. Click the Keep with Next ¶ box.

13. Select the Rules tab. Place rules above and below the paragraph. Here are the attributes:

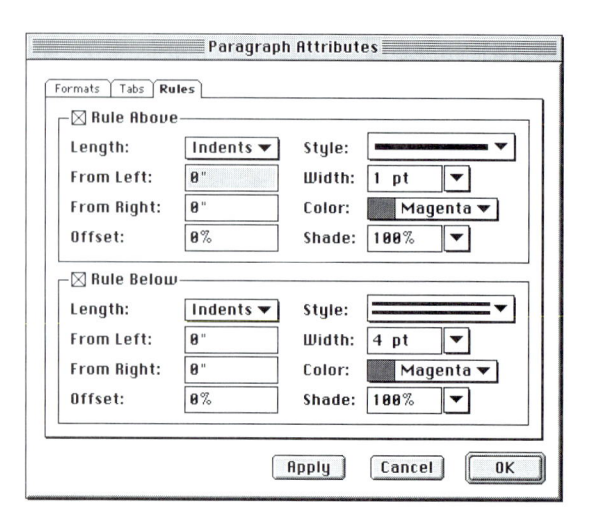

56 CHAPTER 3/STRUCTURING YOUR LAYOUTS

The reason we have two different types of body copy (one called "First Paragraph" and one called "Body Text") is because the first line after a subhead shouldn't have an indent. The same rule applies to the first paragraph in an article or story. It looks better because indents are meant to separate paragraphs, and the first paragraph doesn't need to be separated from the one above.

You might consider using the Next Style attribute when you create Subhead styles and make the next style "First Paragraph". This way you will be assured that first lines don't indent. This feature only works, however, when text is typed directly into QuarkXPress.

14. Click OK to apply the changes. The subhead formatting we're going to use is now established.

15. Select the text, create a new style called "Subheads" and save the file. You should now have three paragraph styles showing in the Style Sheets palette.

16. Put your cursor in the next paragraph. Assign the First Paragraph style. Move down through the page, assigning Body Text to the copy, Subheads to the word Agenda, First Paragraph to the paragraph immediately underneath that subhead, and Body Text to the rest of the copy. When you're done, you'll see that the bottoms of your columns no longer line up.

CHAPTER 3/STRUCTURING YOUR LAYOUTS   57

When you highlight a range of type or a paragraph and then use it to define a new style, that the new style isn't automatically applied to the selected text; you have to apply it yourself or the selected text will simply show as Normal+ (or whatever style it was when you redefined its attributes). The + sign lets you know that the original style assigned to that text has been directly modified.

17. It could be even worse. Select the Subhead style and change the space before to 0.15 (it's now set at 0.25). While you're at it, edit the Character Attributes of the style and change the point size to 14 pt. Look at what happens now:

18. Save the file. If you want to, you can close it and put it away for a while; we're going to use it again.

Ranging Defined

Clearly, if we have all these uneven sizes within one of the styles (the Subheads style in this case), we can never make the bottoms of the columns line up. There's more space before and after, and a different amount of leading in that one style. If you have three, four, five, or more styles in your document (which isn't unusual in many projects), then the problem would be even greater. The more styles you have, and the more inconsistent they are in vertical measurements, the more ranging will become a problem. Ranging is when column bottoms don't line up, or more accurately, when the baselines of the primary copy (in this case the First Paragraph and Body Text styles don't line up). Body copy should always align in a long document. It makes the document easier to read and to look at. It's a sign of well-detailed, professional typography and document design.

Applying Baseline Grids to Styles

1. If it's not already on-screen, open the file named **Grids Practice.QXD**.

2. Select Edit>Preferences>Document>Paragraph. Change the start location to 0.25 in. (the top of the document's live area) and the baseline grid increment to 13 (the default setting is 12 pt.). Click OK.

3. Edit the two primary copy styles (First Paragraph and Body Text). Under the Format tab for each, check the Lock to Baseline Grid option. Click Save. Look at the page; it's perfect. Each line of those two styles are now locked to the baseline grid, which you've now set to reflect the leading for the primary copy (13 pt.). Note, however, how QuarkXPress achieves this: Additional space is added below the subheads to force the first lines of the paragraphs to the grid. The result is overall "neatness," but with a resultant difference in spacing below the subheads. If some of the subheads went to two lines, the space below would be erratic.

We refer to a document as having a "well detailed" look. Think about this for a moment. You might spend ten hours designing and completing a design, and yet not have detailed the work. Detailing refers to the little things such as ranging (discussed here), consistency in the amount of space above and below graphics, even highly-esoteric typesetting issues such as ligatures. Ligatures are special type characters contained in some fonts that group together certain characters, such as "ff" or "fl." Font in the "Expert" series and fonts with old style figures often have ligatures built into the face.

The default Auto Kerning setting of 4 pt. is awfully small. Such tiny type will probably benefit from a slight positive tracking value, which will retain the Auto Kerning.

4. Save and close the file. We'll return to this file later in the course. You're not done yet.

Copy and Layout Fitting

You will often be called upon to fit a specific amount of copy into a predefined region of the page. There are several methods that you can use to squeeze or stretch your copy to fill the space provided in your design.

In a perfect world, the writer or editor would sit beside the designer editing the copy on the fly and making certain that it fits. In large-scale editorial environments there is actually a specialized application available from Quark that automatically links the editors' workstations with the designs put forth from the art department. As the writers and editors work on the text, they can see if it fits or not, but they don't have the ability to change the layout. The designers are happy, the editors are happy, and copyfitting is efficient. The software is called *CopyDesk*, part of QPS, QuarkXPress Publishing System. Most of you, though, won't have this luxury; you'll have to figure it out for yourself.

Kerning and Tracking

Kerning and *tracking* are the adjustment of spacing between letters expressed as a value in QuarkXPress from 500 to –500. Each kerning or tracking unit (both use the same measurements) represents 1/200 of the width of an em space, which traditionally is the width of the nominal point size (an em space in 10 point type is 10 points wide). Kerning is the adjustment of spacing between two letters; tracking is the adjustment of space in a range of characters. Positive values increase space between letters; negative values decrease space. All characters can be kerned or tracked, including punctuation.

Most professional-quality typefaces have built-in *kerning pairs* that specify how much space to add or subtract from pairs of specific letters; and you can create custom kerning pairs with QuarkXPress's Kerning Table Edit command. Pairs such as WA, Wo, Va, Ye, and others benefit greatly from kerning, and many other letter pairs also

CHAPTER 3/STRUCTURING YOUR LAYOUTS   59

Although we're simulating the creation of a magazine or newsletter page, these concepts work with all types of documents — anything that would benefit from structure and consistency of design, layout, and component placement. Other examples of this type of project include brochures, annual reports, technical bulletins, and many others.

Don't forget that styles can contain colors — not only for text or paragraph elements, but for rules above and below. Always make certain that the colors you use are suitable for the output you want.

benefit to an extent from a small amount of kerning; in most cases, space is removed between pairs. You can specify that QuarkXPress automatically kern all text above a certain point size in the Document Preferences>Character tab. Kerned text is more pleasing to the eye and helps improve readability.

Tracking can be used to make text tighter or looser. Tracking applies a tracking value to a range of text. You can specify a tracking amount in a style sheet for all text of that style, or you can use tracking to tighten or loosen specific copy to fit a layout.

Unkerned letter pairs:
Va Ve Vo

Kerned letter pairs:
VaVeVo

Tight tracking:
Château

Loose tracking:
C h â t e a u

As you can see, too much negative kerning or tracking can impair legibility, but subtle negative tracking or kerning can help fit copy into a layout without affecting legibility. Positive values can be used to create many typographic effects.

Kerning and Tracking for Copyfitting Headlines

1. Open the document you created previously: `Grids Practice.QXD`.

2. Go to page 2. Click the Item tool in the text box and press Command-A (Macintosh) or Control-A (Windows) to select all the text. Set the headline as follows: ATC Coconuts Extra Bold, 32 pt., auto leading.

3. Resize the headline text box so that the right edge is between the last two columns.

4. We want the text to spread across the width of the box, but it's somewhat short. You could force-justify the headline to fill the box, but we'll use tracking as an alternative. With all the text selected, click once on the negative (left) tracking arrow in the Measurements palette.

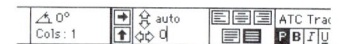

5. Oops! One click on the tracking arrow enters a value of −10 in the tracking value box. This is a little too much.

60 CHAPTER 3/STRUCTURING YOUR LAYOUTS

QuarkXPress uses the width of two zeros to determine the em space. You can use the traditional em space by selecting "Standard Em Space" in Edit>Document Preferences>Character.

The headline has been tracked –5, and adding kerning of –5 between "M" and "e" gives it a total kern/track value of –10; but if you click in the line and move the insertion point left or right with the arrow keys, the kerning value displayed for all the other pairs will be zero. Removing tracking still preserves the –5 kerning of the "Me" pair.

Do not figure in additional tracking for the kern value. QuarkXPress will take any added kerning into account when a selection of text is tracked.

Having Effective Meetings

6. Let's see what clicking the right arrow will do. Click the right arrow twice and see what happens.

7. Double-click in the tracking value box, type –5, and press Return. The line seems to fit, but let's see if it can be opened up any further. Enter –4 and press Return. Too much. Set the tracking to –5.

Having Effective Meetings

8. Zoom in on the headline and look carefully for any extra white space between the letters or for letters that seem scrunched together. Compared to the rest of the letters, the letter pair "Me" in Meetings seems to have a little more space between the letters.

Meetings

9. Click an insertion point between these two letters, then click once on the left kerning arrow. –10 appears, and it is too much.

Meetings

10. Set the kerning value to –5 and check the results.

Meetings

11. Manually kerning letters, especially in headlines, can greatly improve the overall balance of the word. A reader's eye is likely to notice the extra space between "M" and "e", so fine-tuning letter pairs with kerning is usually worth the effort, although in small body copy it is usually unnecessary.

CHAPTER 3/STRUCTURING YOUR LAYOUTS   **61**

Kern/Track shortcuts:

*decrease 10/200 em:
Cmd/Ctrl-Shift-{*

*increase 10/200 em:
Cmd/Ctrl-Shift-}*

*increase 1/200 em:
Cmd/Ctrl-Opt/Alt-shift-{*

*decrease 1/200 em:
Cmd/Ctrl-Opt/Alt-Shift-}*

12. Add the kerning value for this letter pair to the font's kern pairs for future use. Since the pair doesn't seem to have a kern pair setting in the font, auto kerning won't work. Open the Kerning Table Edit dialog box by choosing Utilities>Kerning Table Edit…. It may take a moment for the Kerning Table Edit dialog box to appear if you have a lot of fonts active.

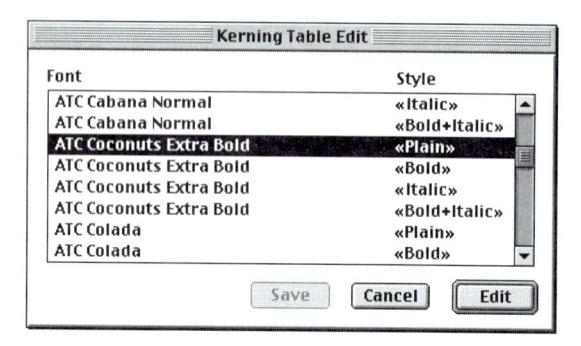

13. Select ATC Coconuts Extra Bold in the font list, then click Edit.

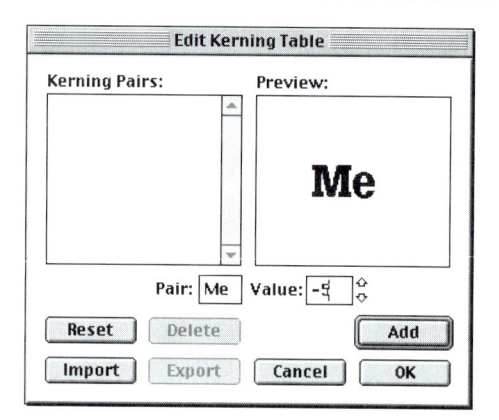

14. Type "Me" into the Pair box. Enter –5 in the Value box.

15. Click Add, then click Save. The new kerning value is applied to the "Me" pair. You can override values from a kerning table at any time by changing the kern value in the Measurements palette.

16. Leave the file open.

Generally, you won't need to edit kerning pairs very often, but some fonts do not contain any kerning pairs, or contain only a few. Kerning pairs added to a font only affect that font's kerning in QuarkXPress and not in any other program.

To copyfit long text, use tracking. You can add tracking values to a style sheet to apply overall tracking, or you can track parts of a story to fine-tune a layout. It's recommended that any partial-story tracking be minimal so that it doesn't look obvious or clash with untracked copy.

Most typeface manufacturers will give you a free specimen book of all their typefaces. You can also find type specimen books at the Library, usually in the graphic design or graphic arts sections.

Tracking for Copyfitting Body Text

1. Open the Style Sheets dialog box by pressing Shift-F11. Double-click on the Body Text style.

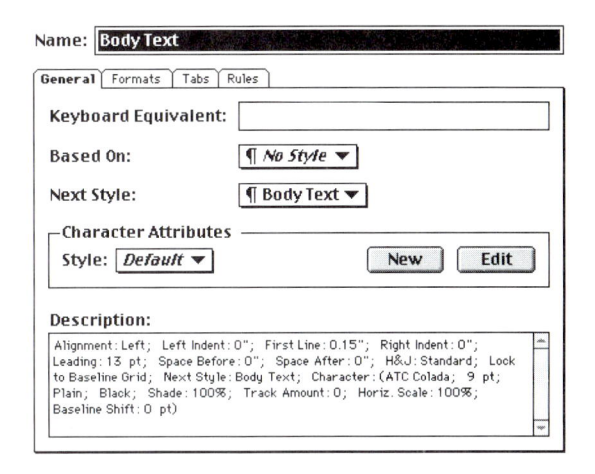

2. Click the Character Attributes>Edit button.

3. Enter –3 in the Track Amount field.

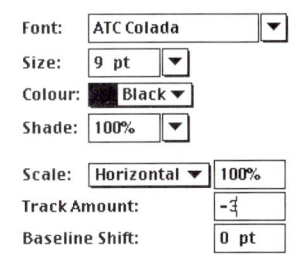

4. Click OK, then click OK in the Edit dialog box. Repeat the kerning value change for the First Paragraph style. When finished, click Save.

5. The entire story reflows. You can use this technique to get more copy on a page or in a text box, but use this feature with caution. Too much tracking can significantly impair legibility.

6. Leave the file open.

The Color of Type

A block of type has color. Not in the sense of colors such as red or yellow, but in the overall look of the text. Type color depends on the typeface used, the size, leading, tracking values, and the column width. Narrow columns call for a lighter type color than wide ones. The choice of a typeface can have an enormous impact upon the readability of long passages of body text; this may not be the case with headlines, which should be readable at a glance in most any typeface. Compare the examples on the next page.

Foreign language and specialty (medical, legal) typesetting creates a few problems with hyphenation and spelling. If you don't know the language or the technical terms used, you can't be certain that any hyphenation QuarkXPress applies is accurate. Quark sells a product called QuarkXPress Passport, which is a version of QuarkXPress that supports add-in hyphenation and spelling dictionaries for many foreign languages. You can also get some foreign language and specialty dictionaries through vendors of Quark XTensions that work with the standard version of QuarkXPress.

See www.quark.com for more information about available XTensions.

His arrival produced no stir in the town, and was accompanied by no particular incident, beyond that a couple of peasants who happened to be standing at the door of a dramshop exchanged a few comments with reference to the equipage rather

His arrival produced no stir in the town, and was accompanied by no particular incident, beyond that a couple of peasants who happened to be standing at the door of a dramshop exchanged a few comments with reference to the equipage rather than to the individual who was seated in it. "Look at that carriage," one of them said to the other. "Think you it

His arrival produced no stir in the town, and was accompanied by no particular incident, beyond that a couple of peasants who happened to be standing at the door of a dramshop exchanged a few comments with reference to the equipage rather than to the individual who was seated in it. "Look at that carriage," one of them said to the other. "Think you it will be going as far as Moscow?" "I think it will," replied his companion. "But

Each column is the same text, set in 10 point type with 12 point leading (the image is reduced to fit this page), but the typeface used in each example gives a different flavor. The left column is set in ITC Bookman Light, which despite its name is a fairly heavy typeface and is too heavy for use in a narrow column. The middle is set to ITC Garamond Condensed Book, which is slim but not too light and is suitable at small point sizes in narrow columns. The right column is set in Futura Condensed Light, which is very thin and quite unsuited for use in nearly any type of body copy. The ideal color of type is achieved by the careful balance of typeface, column size, point size, leading, and tracking.

In general, avoid slim, condensed type in wide columns and use generous leading so that wide columns of text don't become too dense. You have more tracking options with a wide column, and sometimes the default tracking value of most commercial typefaces is actually too much. Narrow columns require typefaces that are economical of space and benefit from tighter tracking and leading. The typeface of this book's body copy, Adobe Minion, is well-suited to this column width at 11 pt., leading of 14 pt., and –3 tracking. You should always adjust typefaces, sizes, leading, and tracking to achieve a good type color in body text.

Hyphenation and Justification (H&Js)

Most body copy benefits greatly from hyphenation, which helps prevent gaps between words and *rivers* (excessive white areas) in justified copy.

His arrival produced no stir in the town, and was accompanied by no particular incident, beyond that a couple of peasants who happened to be standing at the door of a dramshop exchanged a few comments with reference to the equipage rather than to the individual who

Acceptable H&Js

His arrival produced no stir in the town, and was accompanied by no particular incident, beyond that a couple of peasants who happened to be standing at the door of a dramshop exchanged a few comments with reference to the equipage rather than to

Poor H&Js

QuarkXPress will automatically hyphenate words as needed based upon its built-in hyphenation dictionary. You can add custom hyphenation examples, specify that certain words never be hyphenated, and turn hyphenation off completely, which is recommended for headlines and subheads.

Justification refers to the spacing of words and letters in justified paragraphs such as the two examples above. You can adjust word and letterspacing in combination with hyphenation to produce clear, legible, justified columns of text. You can adjust letterspacing and hyphenation in unjustified text to help create a less ragged margin. Sets of hyphenation and justification settings are called H&Js in QuarkXPress, and you can apply them with Style>Formats to selected paragraphs, or you can incorporate them into a paragraph style sheet.

The H&Js Dialog Settings

To edit H&Js, choose Edit>H&Js .

Changing Justification settings may seem similar to using tracking to adjust word and letterspacing, but tracking only affects letterspacing, not word spacing.

Clicking the Edit button lets you edit the Standard H&J settings. Here's where you can add new ones. The settings for the Standard H&J are shown below.

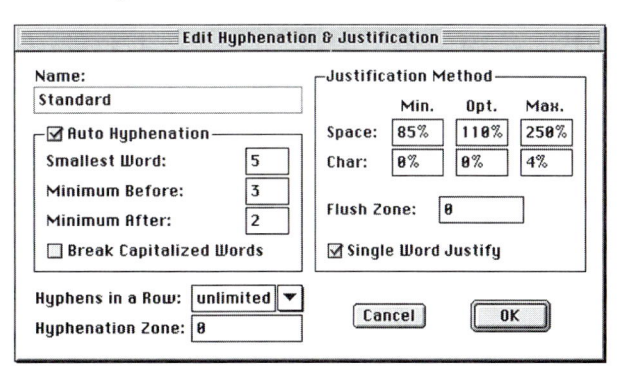

- Unchecking Auto Hyphenation turns off hyphenation completely.

- The Smallest Word value sets the number of letters in a word below which QuarkXPress will not hyphenate the word.

- Minimum Before sets the smallest number of letters that must precede a hyphen.

CHAPTER 3/STRUCTURING YOUR LAYOUTS 65

- Minimum After sets the smallest number of letters that can follow a hyphen. The default value of 2 produces some odd hyphenations, so a setting of 3 is recommended.

- Unchecking Break Capitalized Words prevents hyphenation of proper names, corporate names, trademarks, and other words. These, and the first word of a sentence, should not be hyphenated, although it may be necessary if there are narrow line lengths to contend with.

- Hyphens in a Row controls how many consecutive lines can have hyphens at the end. Usually it's best to set this to a value of 2 or 3, because more than three lines in a row with hyphens impairs readability.

- Hyphenation Zone is measured from the right margin of unjustified paragraphs. The default of zero inches means there is no hyphenation zone; QuarkXPress will either hyphenate the word according to another of its rules or will wrap the entire word to the next line. A word within the hyphenation zone will be hyphenated only if the preceding word is outside the hyphenation zone and an acceptable hyphenation point within the word falls within the zone.

- Justification Method controls how QuarkXPress will handle paragraph justification. The Min, Opt (Optimum), and Max values for Space determine the size of spaces between letters used to fully justify a paragraph based on the size of the space designed into the font. The Min, Opt, and Max values for Char control the percentage of an en space that can be added between letters to justify a paragraph. The Opt values for Space and Char determine spacing in unjustified paragraphs. To change the spacing attributes, enter higher or lower values in the fields. Lower values give tighter spacing; higher values, looser spacing.

- The last line of a paragraph is not justified unless its last character falls within the Flush Zone. To justify last lines, you can set a value for the Flush Zone, which is measured from the right indent of the paragraph.

- Single Word Justify controls whether a long word that occupies an entire line will be justified within the paragraph indents.

Creating Custom H&Js

1. Open the file you just worked on, `Grids practice.QXD`.

2. Go to page 2 and draw a rectangular text box 2 inches × 2 inches with a text inset of 3 points, vertical alignment Centered, frame of 2 pt. Black, runaround type Item with 5 pt. offset on all sides between the second and third columns. Position the box to straddle the columns and set the X and Y coordinates to 4.7 inches and 2.9 inches respectively. This will be used to hold a pull quote.

3. Type the following into the box: "Making sure that the discussion is kept clear and structured is [an] important requirement." Set this text to ATC Coconuts Extra Bold, 16 pt., with leading set to auto, Centered. Select this text and create a Paragraph style based upon it and call it "Pull Quote".

4. The copy to the left is very ragged and on the right has poor hyphenation. Justify all body copy to exaggerate the effect. Command/Control-click on the Body Text style and set its alignment to Justified.

Repeat for the First Paragraph style, and click Save. All the body copy is now justified, and the page looks even worse:

5. Choose Edit>H&Js… to display the H&J dialog box and click New.

6. Name the new H&J "Tighter Copy". Set the specifications as shown below.

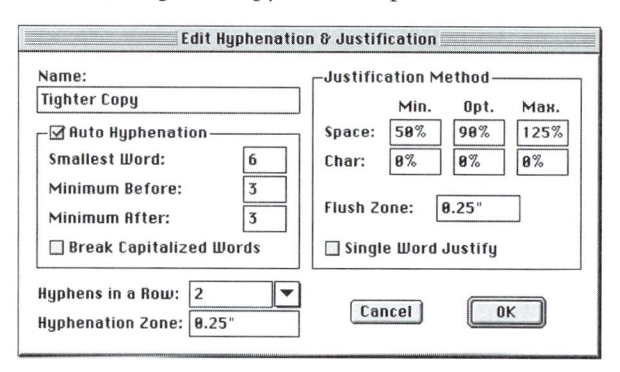

   Click OK.

7. Create another new H&J called "Looser Copy", with the below specifications.

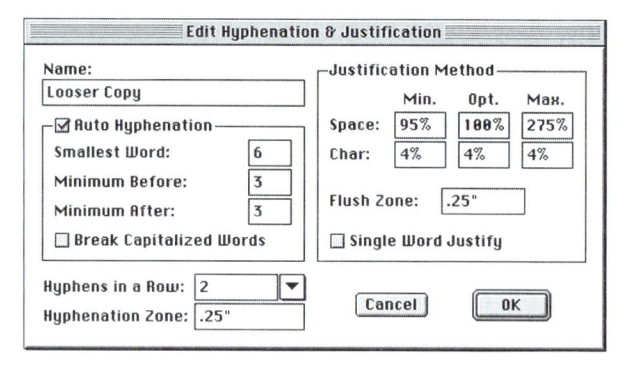

8. Create one more new H&J called "No Hyphens". Uncheck the Auto Hyphenation box and leave the rest of the settings alone. Click OK, then click Save.

9. Apply the new H&Js to the Text styles. Press Shift+F11 to open the Styles dialog box. Click on Body Text, then Edit. Click the Formats tab and set the H&Js to Looser Copy.

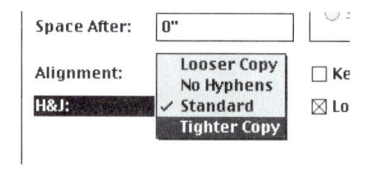

   Repeat this for the First Paragraph style.

Working with writers and editors can be frustrating for a designer. You have to balance the client's need for a clean design against his or her inevitable urge to provide you with more copy than will fit in the layout. Be reasonable but firm about copy length, and never criticize the content of the copy.

10. Set the H&J of the Pull Quote and Subheads to No Hyphens. Click Save to apply the new H&Js to the styles.

11. The Looser Copy H&J increases word and letterspacing too much. Change the H&J of Body Text and First Paragraph to Tighter Copy.

12. The copy is tighter, but there are now a few large gaps in the copy around the pull quote. Open the H&Js dialog, reset the Tighter Copy H&J to these values, then save the H&J.

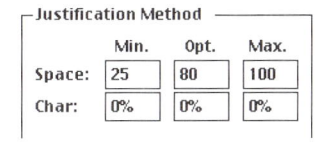

Justification Method	Min.	Opt.	Max.
Space:	25	80	100
Char:	0%	0%	0%

We're taking away far too much space, and words are starting to run together. We need to go in the other direction. Open the H&Js dialog box again, and edit the Tighter Copy H&J as shown below.

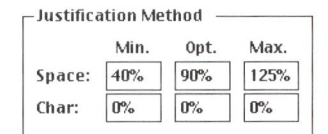

Justification Method	Min.	Opt.	Max.
Space:	40%	90%	125%
Char:	0%	0%	0%

This produces a nice overall spacing of letters but there are probably a few big gaps still remaining. Look to the right and the word "progress" is probably not hyphenated at all, even though the hyphenation specifications should include this word, creating a huge, ugly gap in the copy. (The actual hyphenation in your document may vary if you are working on a Windows computer.)

13. You can force a word to hyphenate by using a discretionary hyphen. This special hyphen can be used to break a word manually, but if the text reflows and a hyphen is no longer needed, the hyphen will disappear. Click an insertion point between "prog" and "ress", and type Command/Control- (Hyphen key) to break the word appropriately.

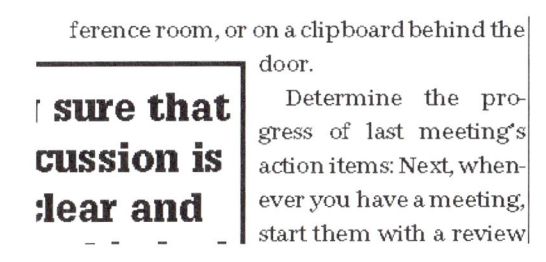

If you're uncertain about hyphenating a word that's not in the hyphenation dictionary, look it up in a real dictionary. Most dictionaries show a word's correct hyphenation breaks.

If there's a specific word that you never want hyphenated, type it into the Hyphenation Exceptions box exactly as written.

14. A better way to hyphenate a word that is not in QuarkXPress's hyphenation dictionary is to add it. You can tell if a word isn't in this database by clicking the insertion point in the word and choosing Utilities>Suggest Hyphenation. The word will appear whole if it is not in the dictionary.

    Add the word "progress" to the hyphenation dictionary by choosing Utilities>Hyphenation Exceptions.... Type "prog-ress" into the lower field, click Add, then click Save.

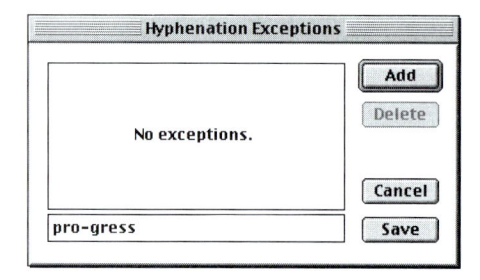

    The word is now and forever hyphenated correctly. Or is it? There are two different hyphenations for the word "progress." The word we used, the noun, is hyphenated "prog-ress" but the verb is hyphenated "pro-gress." Let's reopen the hyphenation dictionary and delete our hyphenation exception. It's better to hyphenate manually than to run the risk of hyphenating incorrectly.

15. Save and close the file.

As you now know, fitting copy into tight columns can be a difficult task. Adjusting tracking, H&Js, type size, and leading are suitable workarounds for fitting copy. Ideally, copy should arrive to you already edited for content and written to fit the style and size of the document. This is how newspapers always seem to fit copy perfectly no matter how long the story is. That's because newswriters know beforehand how much space is available for a story and use the newspaper's standard text formats to determine how much copy will fit into the space *before* the pages are laid out. Changing typefaces is a drastic step and one that should be avoided at all costs. Your client or employer will probably not react favorably to a typeface change, but probably will react positively if you send copy back to be edited for length because it will not fit within an agreed-upon design. *Never edit a client's copy without permission.*

It can be very difficult to arrange images within narrow columns of justified text simply because no matter how much you fiddle with tracking and H&Js, there's only a finite amount of space available. In situations such as our exercise, it's sometimes impossible to fit copy around an image without it looking terrible. When such occasions arise, you must question the validity of the design. Stop working on it for a while and come up with alternatives that work better before spending hours trying to force copy into places where it just won't fit.

Complete Project A: Gym Ad

Notes:

Chapter 4

Working With Shapes

Chapter Objective:

To learn how to work with the QuarkXPress drawing tools to create custom shapes that can be used for holding imported text or graphic components. In Chapter 4 you will.

- Learn about Complex Merging, which brings to you the ability to merge different types of shapes together for your desired designs.
- Exercise applying the Merge commands.
- Learn how to apply Blends to Merged objects.
- Study advanced Bézier tool techniques.
- Review the different Bézier tools, and understand their features.

Projects to be Completed:

- Gym Ad
- Recipe Book
- Tropical Suites Brochure
- Staying Alive Newsletter
- Automation Booklet
- GASP Newsletter

While you can definitely save time by using QuarkXPress's powerful drawing tools, you shouldn't think that you can live without a solid illustration program. If you're at all like the artists and designers we know, you will use the QuarkXPress tools for common tasks such as flowing text into a shape or shaping a picture box, but fall back on stand-alone illustration software for the tough and complex jobs.

Working with Shapes

The ability to create custom shapes into which text or graphic components can be imported is a designer's dream. In the past, this was an extremely difficult and complex process. In many cases you had to use another program such as Adobe Illustrator or Macromedia FreeHand. You had to use their drawing tools to develop a shape and then use it to define the boundaries of copy or an imported graphic element. Once you had it working there, you imported it into your QuarkXPress page, and if you had to edit it you went back to the original software used to create it.

With your ability to develop complex custom boxes in the QuarkXPress layout environment you can often avoid having to go back and forth between programs while developing extremely complex designs. You can now easily create complex text containers.

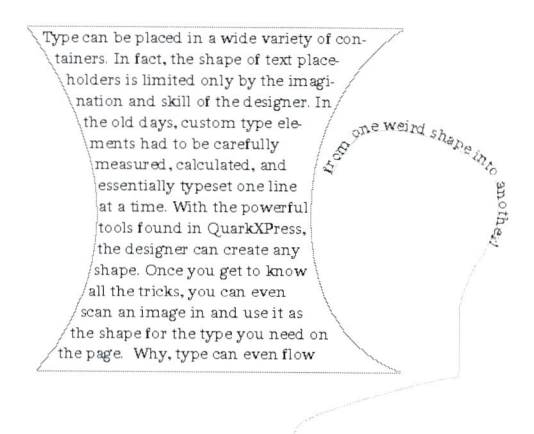

Or, using one of the many available options, you can create innovative custom shapes to hold the graphics on your page.

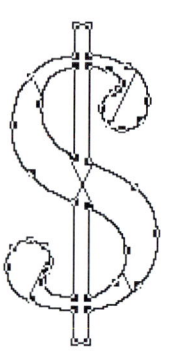

74 CHAPTER 4/WORKING WITH SHAPES

Complex Merging

One powerful set of techniques that should be in your design arsenal is the ability to merge different types of shapes together to create designs that you either cannot draw by hand, or would prove very tedious and time-consuming to develop. While you may have some experience using the Merge command (particularly if you went through the ATC course *QuarkXPress 4.0: Introduction to Electronic Mechanicals*), there are many creative possibilities offered to you by this set of commands that you may not have tried yet.

The best way to review the Merge commands, or to familiarize yourself with them (in case you've never used them), is to work through a series of exercises.

Applying the Merge Commands

1. Create a new document, letter-sized, landscape, with a 0.25 inch border.

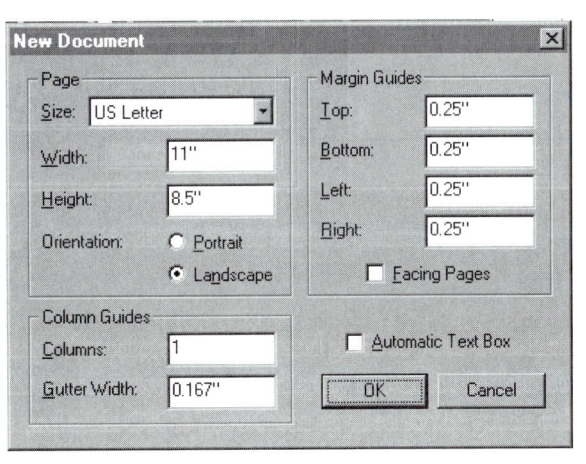

2. Once the document appears, create a circular picture box. Draw it about 2 inches around. When it is close, double-click on it with the Item tool and enter the numbers to make it perfect.

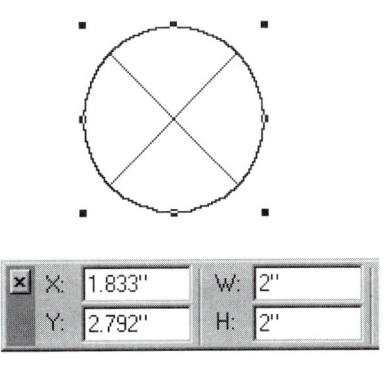

You should always try to reduce the number of steps necessary to achieve a given effect. That's why it's always better to spend a little time thinking about what you're trying to accomplish before you start clicking away with the mouse.

CHAPTER 4/WORKING WITH SHAPES 75

It is our belief that the more an artist or designer takes advantage of keyboard commands, the more efficient he or she is. If you watch really efficient operators, they are using menus, keyboard commands, and the mouse in a sort of rhythm. Try mousing around to music sometimes — it's very cool.

3. Step and Repeat the circle by pressing Command-Option/Control-Alt-D. Make the horizontal offset 0.5 inch and the vertical offset –0.5 inch. Using the Measurements palette, enlarge the new circle to a 3 inch diameter.

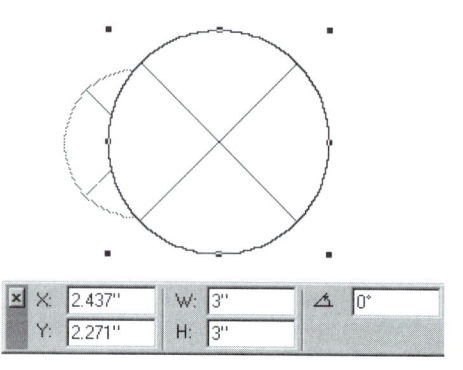

4. Select both circles with the Item tool. Choose Item>Merge>Difference.

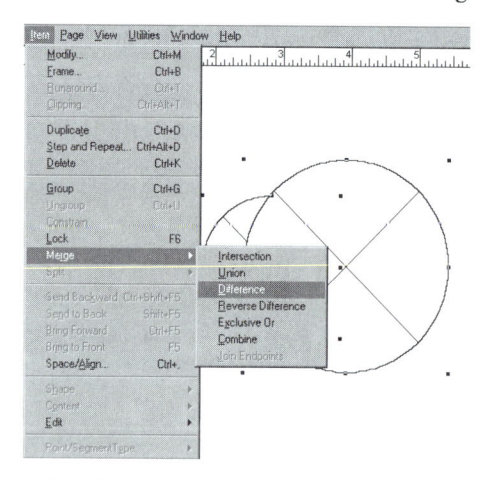

5. Now select the Freehand Line tool and draw a nose for the moon man (of course, he's a moon man).

6. While the nose (we never said we were artists, just teachers and writers) is still selected, choose Item>Shape and select the Freehand shape (it looks like an artist's palette).

76 CHAPTER 4/WORKING WITH SHAPES

Whenever you use the Freehand Line tool to create a shape, you should convert it to a closed shape using the Item>Shape menu. The two ends do not automatically join with this tool, unlike the Freehand Picture Box tool.

7. When you do this, QuarkXPress warns you that you're about to convert a rule into a thin (extremely narrow, as they put it) box, which isn't normally what you're trying to do when merging shapes. Click OK, then press Undo (Command or Control-Z).

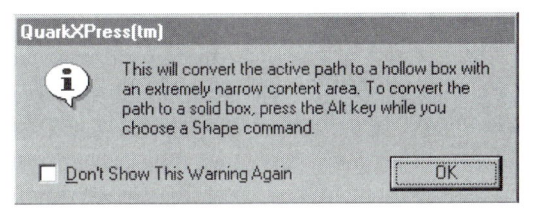

8. Hold down the Option key (Macintosh) or the Alt key (Windows). The nose will turn into a solid shape. Select the two shapes (the moon and the nose) and use the Item>Merge>Union command to turn them into one piece.

9. Make a smile for the moon man. Repeat the same series of steps. First draw the mouth with the Freehand Picture Box tool, then select it and the moon man and cut it from the moon man shape using the Item>Merge>Difference command. The result will be a smiling moon man. If he only had eyes.

CHAPTER 4/WORKING WITH SHAPES　77

There are times when you might want to convert simple rules into a picture box. One example might be a sort of "ribbon" effect, where a group of rules were drawn, merged, and then changed into a single, big picture box containing an image. You would draw a bunch of thick lines and then convert them into picture boxes by first changing them into a closed path (Item>Shape and select the little artist's Palette icon) and then converting their content type to Picture using Item>Content>Picture.

10. Make the eye socket you see in the picture above using the Oval Picture Box tool and the Merge Difference command.

11. Inside your **SF-Advanced QuarkXPress** folder there's a file named **Moon Texture.TIF**. Press Command-E (Macintosh) or Control-E (Windows) to import the texture into the moon man. Use the Content tool to move the texture around inside of the shape. Notice that the eye, which was "cut" from the shape, remains transparent.

12. Position the texture to fill the moon man picture box.

13. Draw a rectangular picture box. Convert the Content to None (Item>Content>None) and choose View>Colors to display the Colors palette. Drag the Magenta color chip onto the rectangle.

78 CHAPTER 4/WORKING WITH SHAPES

Whenever you're scanning an image to use in an unusually shaped picture box, be certain to take into consideration that the picture has to be large enough to completely fill the shape — you don't want any white areas showing through. You can always size the image up in QuarkXPress, but this effectively reduces the resolution of the original scan. You need twice as many dpi in the scan as you have halftone dots on press. If you're running a job with a 150 line screen, you need 300 dpi resolution. If you enlarge a 300 dpi image to 200%, you're now working with a 150 dpi image (resolution divided by the enlargement).

The opposite also holds true if you reduce a 300 dpi image to 50%; you now have a 600 dpi image. That's more than you need and might result in slow output or unexpected darkness in the image.

14. Move the rectangle beneath the eye (you'll have to use Item>Send Backward to get the "stacking order" correct). When you've got it right you should be able to see the rectangle underneath the eye socket.

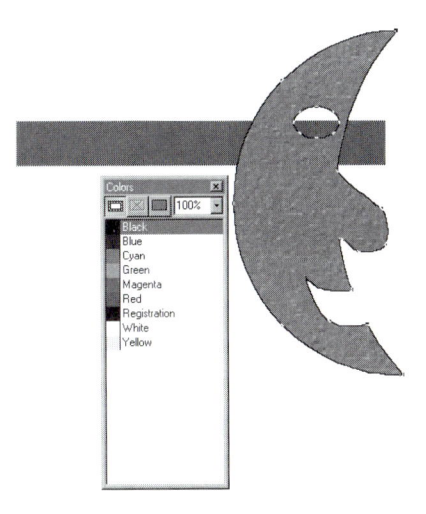

15. When you're done, you can choose to save the file in your **Work in Progress** folder, or discard it by choosing not to save the changes.

CHAPTER 4/WORKING WITH SHAPES   79

Applying Blends to Merged Objects

Objects don't have to be touching to be merged; this function allows the designer or artist to use merged objects and blends to achieve some interesting effects.

Practicing with Blends and Merged Objects

1. Create a new document, letter-sized with 0.25 inch borders and a landscape orientation.

2. Draw a rectangle with the Picture Box tool to fill the entire margins of the document.

3. Zoom in to the upper-left corner of the page. Drag a vertical ruler to the 0.5 inch point inside the margin. Do the same with the horizontal ruler.

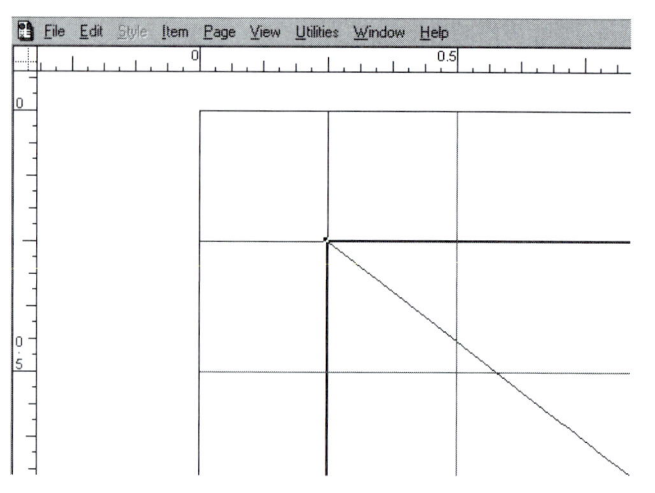

4. With the Content or Item tool active, use the Option key (Macintosh) or Alt key (Windows) to activate the Grabber Hand and move down to the lower right of the page. Repeat the same procedure. Put rulers 0.5 inch inside the margins at the 8 inch and 10.5 inch marks.

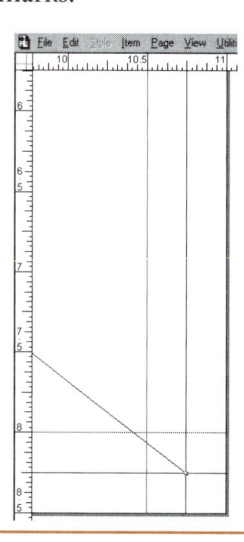

A method of navigation that is popular among many artists is to use a combination of the "Fit in Window" command (which is either Command-0 if you're using a Macintosh or Control-0 if you're using a Windows system) and the Magnifying Glass tool. Press Command/Control-0 (that's a zero, in case you can't tell), select the Magnifying Glass tool, and draw a square around the area you want to fill the monitor with. Zoom out and Zoom in as needed until you have your guides in the correct location.

80 CHAPTER 4/WORKING WITH SHAPES

This technique of zooming in and out of the corners of a page to place rulers in specific spots is a useful method of quickly adding grids and guides to a page. For more information, check out the chapter that focuses on the advanced use of grids and object placement.

5. Draw another picture box inside these new margins. You will now have two rectangles on top of each other.

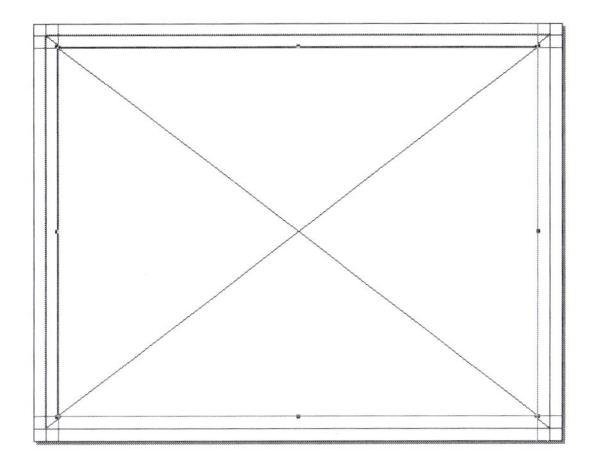

6. Select both items by pressing Command-A (Macintosh) or Control-A (Windows). Note that you have to have the Item tool active when using this command.

7. Select Item>Merge>Difference.

8. Select Item>Content>None.

9. Double-click the object with the Item tool. Click on the Frame tab and set the frame around the object to a 1 pt. black rule.

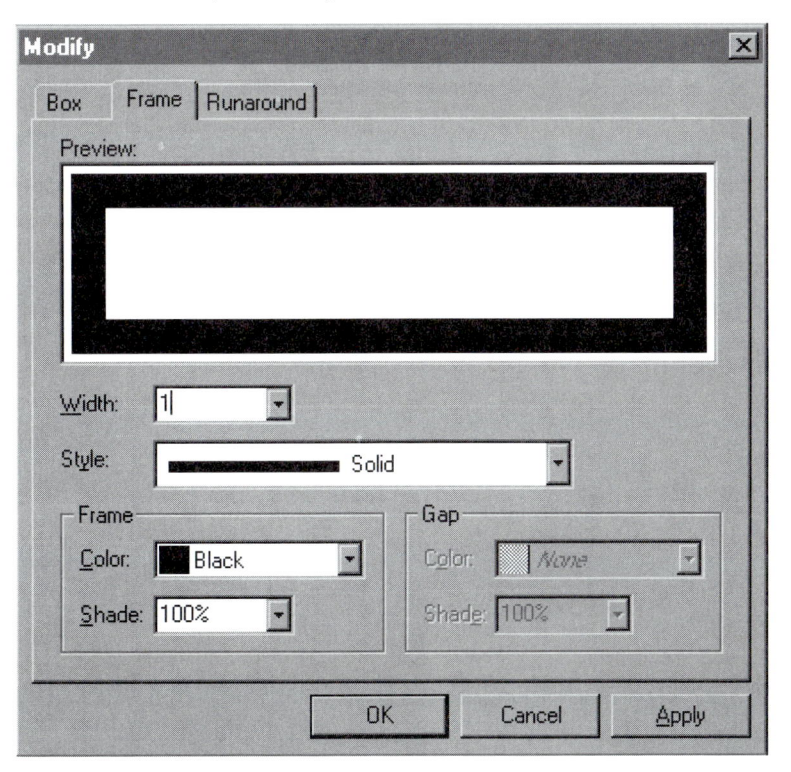

CHAPTER 4/WORKING WITH SHAPES 81

We're going to use the alignment functions of QuarkXPress in these next few steps to avoid having to measure the boxes and figure out the correct Step and Repeat numbers. We're going to draw a second box, place it at the upper right side of the page, and then simply duplicate five more boxes from that one. We'll drag them into place and then align and distribute them — once again an example of minimizing steps.

10. After you've done this, choose View>Hide Guides (F7) and examine what you've created.

11. When you're done, save the file in your **Work in Progress** folder. Name it "Framed.QXD". If you want to, you can close it and return to this lesson later.

At this point we can simply add a blend to the frame and we will have created a pretty cool effect that would be difficult to achieve under other circumstances. In the old days of page layout programs you couldn't even apply a blend to an object created within the application. To achieve this effect you would have had to use a drawing program to create the frame; that frame would have been imported into a large picture text box with a fill of None. But by creating the effect that you just performed in the last exercise, you have the object completely isolated (independent of other objects), and you have accomplished it in very few steps. Counting mouse clicks is always important, and your goal should always be to try to use the least amount of steps to execute a given thought.

Blends in Multiple Merged Objects

1. Open the **Framed.QXD** file from your **Work in Progress** folder. Drag horizontal and vertical rulers to the 1 inch mark in the upper left corner of the page. In the juncture of the two rules, draw a 0.5 inch picture box.

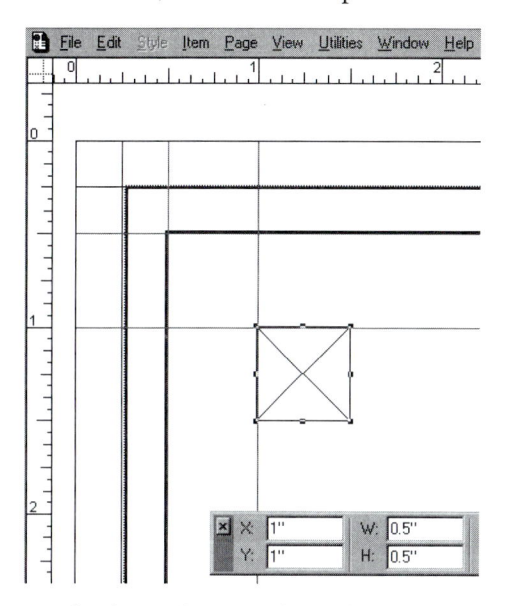

2. Drag another vertical ruler to the 10 inch mark.

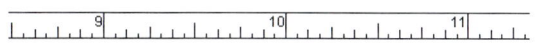

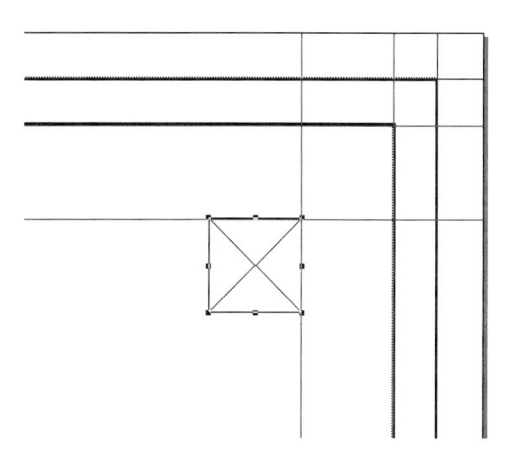

3. Step and Repeat the original box eight times with a horizontal offset of 1 inch and a vertical offset of 0. Drag the last box (the one that's still selected) to the juncture of the upper-right rulers.

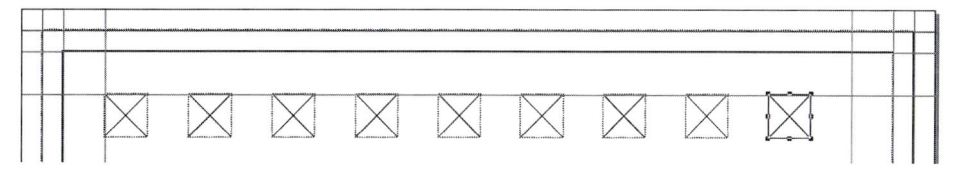

There is just no way to gain true efficiency with any page layout program without liberal use of non-printing guides. We continue to stress this throughout the course because we are aware of so many designers and artists — really talented ones — who would have so much more time to think and actually design if they became truly proficient with their tools. Instead, they sit at their computers and waste a lot of precious time. We know that many artists don't like to measure and don't like the math, but without it, constructing documents will simply take a lot longer.

CHAPTER 4/WORKING WITH SHAPES 83

This idea of disconnected picture boxes that can be filled with blends or contain a single image offers dramatic and almost unlimited creative possibilities. This example is a simple exercise designed to familiarize you with the technique. You should try some other ideas and see if you can come up with ways to use this powerful feature in your own designs.

4. Using the Item tool, select all the boxes by drawing a marquee around them. Choose Item>Space/Align. Check the Horizontal box, Distribute Evenly, and choose Items from the pop-up menu. Click the Apply button to make certain that it does what you want it to, then click OK.

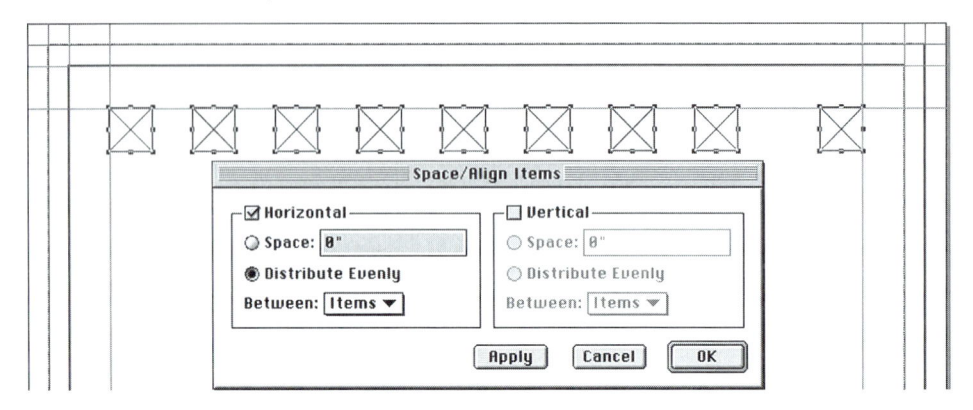

5. While all the boxes are still selected, press Command-D (Macintosh) or Control-D (Windows) to duplicate the entire set of boxes. Immediately go to the Item menu and select Merge>Union. All nine boxes will become one item — similar to a series of windows through which you could see parts of a large image.

6. We're going to fill some of these objects with blends. First, move the long, sectioned picture box beneath the individual boxes for a moment. Select the first, third, fifth, seventh, and ninth individual boxes. Double-click one of them with the Item tool and choose the Group tab. Create a blend with the following attributes:

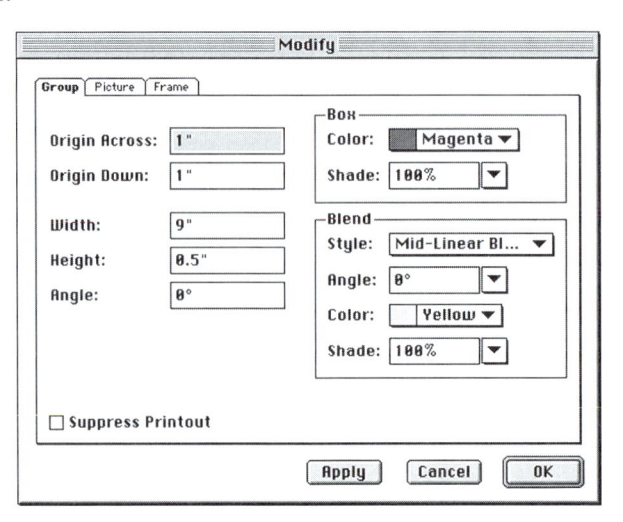

84 CHAPTER 4/WORKING WITH SHAPES

Now you can see that if you merge a selected group of objects — even if they're not touching each other — that any colors, images, blends, or graphics imported into them will show through the entire set. Individual elements still require that you apply attributes or import images individually.

7. See what happens? Each of the individual boxes fills with the mid-linear blend, with the blend compressed to fit the 0.5 inch squares.

8. Now apply the blend to the merged boxes. The blend fits that shape, filling all the boxes in the merged unit as if they were one long, thin series of openings over the top of the blend.

9. Put a blend into the first frame that you built on this page in the beginning of the chapter. Here are the settings to use:

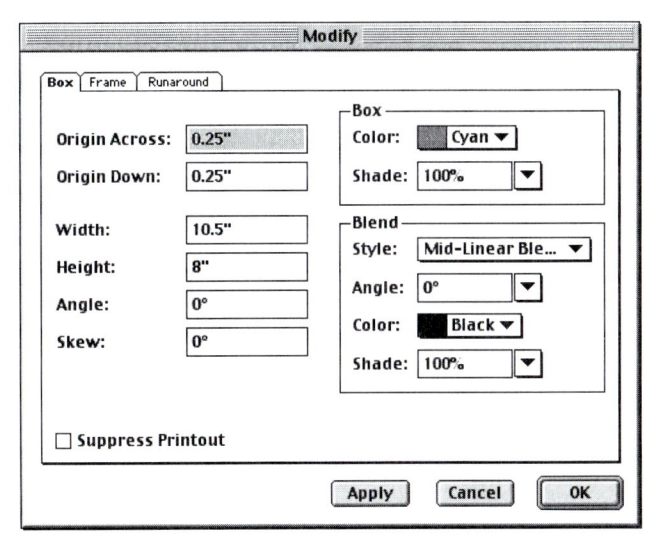

10. Now let's put a picture on the page to take advantage of all these cool graphics. Draw a picture box that fills the margins and covers everything. Draw a picture box 10.25″ × 7.75″, with X and Y coordinates of 0.375″. With the Content tool selected, navigate to the **SF-Adv QuarkXPress** folder and select the image named **Bare Bottoms.TIF**. Position the sign in the lower center of the frame.

11. Choose Item>Send to Back and take a look. Notice how you can slide the image around in its frame with the Content tool.

12. Turn off guides (F7) and view your framed image.

CHAPTER 4/WORKING WITH SHAPES 85

Bringing items to the front of a stack or sending them to the back of the stack can be easily accomplished with keyboard commands. So can moving an item one layer at a time in either direction. Draw a few objects partially on top of each other and select one of them somewhere in the center of the stack. Now examine the Item menu; it shows all the keyboard equivalents. For Macintosh users, simply substitute the Command key for the Control key shown here, and the Option key for the Alt key. The Shift key is the same on both machines. You should always carefully study menus, since they almost always show the keyboard equivalents for the commands that they contain.

13. Save the file and close. We're going to use similar techniques in a project assignment at the end of this chapter.

Advanced Bézier Tool Techniques

Proper use of the Bézier tools within QuarkXPress opens yet more creative possibilities to the designer or layout artist. If you've ever used an illustration program such as Adobe Illustrator or Macromedia FreeHand you may already be familiar with how curves work. If not, then let us assure you that spending the time it takes to fully familiarize yourself with the operations of QuarkXPress's Bézier tools is well worth the effort.

One thing to remember about using a Bézier tool (and there are quite a few offered in the QuarkXPress environment) is that all curves and anchor points work the same way. There are several reasons you might choose to use one of the Bézier tools:

- To draw curved or shaped lines that will contain text.

- To draw curved or shaped lines for use as simple graphic elements.

- To draw closed shapes to act as containers for text or graphic elements.

- To draw closed shapes for use solely as graphic elements to hold a single color or blends between colors.

- To create shapes that will be used with one of the Merge commands to develop a complex shape that can't easily be drawn using only one tool. An example of this might be an object that has a shape "punched" out of its surface to allow objects behind the shape to be seen through the hole.

Tracing as a Drawing Method

In this section of the course we want to improve your ability to use the Bézier tools for complex and difficult tasks. The best way to learn the intricacies of these tools is through tracing. There are very few professional artists working on computers that don't first sketch out an idea for the finished piece and then work from there. That's exactly how you should think about the Bézier tools. For all but the most elemental graphics, you will benefit by using a sketch as a "template" for the drawing. This short series of exercises will give you a good feel for what we're talking about.

Working from a Sketch

1. Create a new document, letter-sized, portrait orientation, 0.25 inch margins, no facing pages or automatic text boxes.

2. Using the Rectangle Picture Box tool, draw a box beginning at X and Y coordinates 0.25 in. to about the 3.75 in. mark, spanning the width of the page between the margins.

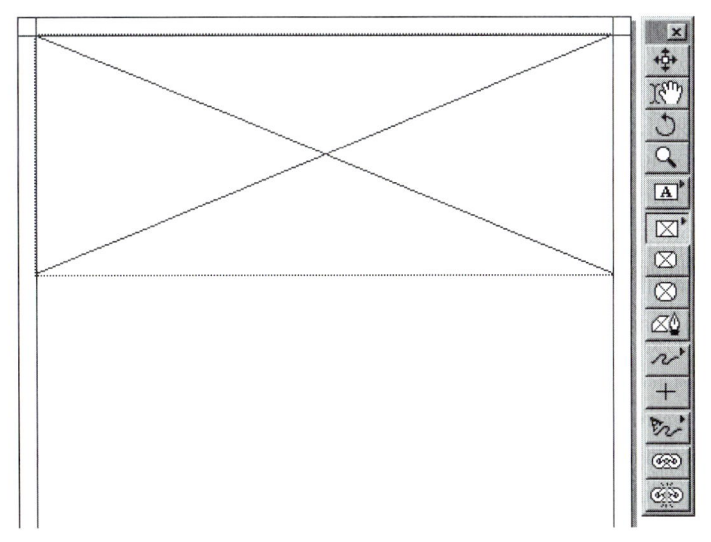

3. Press Command-E (Macintosh) or Control-E (Windows) to import a picture into the box. Navigate to the **SF-Adv QuarkXPress** folder and import the image called **Curve Practice.TIF**.

4. Press F6 to lock the picture box down to the page. We don't want it moving around as we're working with the Bézier tools.

5. Click on the Text-Path tool and hold down the mouse button. Slide over and select the Bézier Text-Path tool. It's the one with the little pen nib icon.

6. Zoom in to the top of the page. This image was a simple curve that was drawn on a piece of paper and scanned into the system as a TIFF file.

Many artists still choose to have a full-featured, dedicated drawing program in their design arsenal. They feel, justifiably in our opinion, that knowing how to use these powerful applications will ultimately benefit them in their design careers. While it's more expensive to own several programs, and more of a challenge to learn them, there are things that you can do with a dedicated drawing program that you simply can't achieve with the Bézier tools found in QuarkXPress.

If you speak to a professional designer or artist, they will be quick to say that their computers (and most people in the industry now work on computers) are only a tool to aid in the design or illustration process.

You should always keep this in mind — that's why we continuously urge you to plan your designs before you implement them. It's certainly true that the computer can let you attempt a number of design ideas in the time it would take to complete only one by hand, but you should begin by knowing where you want to arrive in the end.

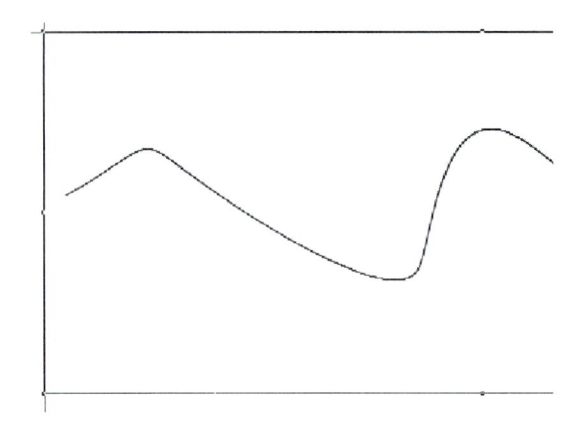

7. Click the Bézier tool (and hold down the mouse button) at the beginning of the line. Pull the mouse slightly up to the right, along the line. The idea is to get the line going in the same direction as the template.

8. The second point is going to be at the very top of the first curve. Click there, then hold down the Shift key, and pull slightly to the right. Holding the shift key constrains the handles to 45° increments. You will see the line start to fit the curves.

9. The third point is going to be placed at the very bottom of the next curve. Once again, hold down the Shift key; this helps you shape the curve. You can hold the key down and let it go while you're building the shape.

10. If you simply click up on the right side of the curve now, the shape won't fit properly because the length of a curve's handle determines how round (or flat) it is. You need to shorten the right handle. Hold down the Command key (Macintosh) or Control key (Windows) and move the cursor over the right

Something else to consider that we strongly recommend is to look at the work of the real professionals; the people creating ads and publication design for the big national magazines are a good place to start. Look at their creative, and imagine yourself being assigned the mechanical work required to put the job together. It's OK to practice with other peoples' designs as long as you don't steal them.

handle. Click on it and move it slightly to the left. You want it to be about one third the length of the handle on the left. The curve on the left is much flatter than the curve on the right; this is reflected in how long the handles happen to be.

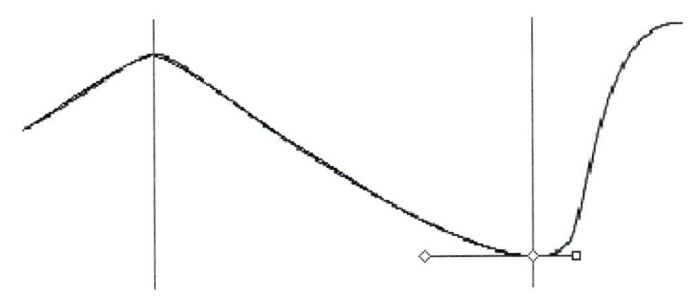

We're beginning to put guides on the page. This is to give you an idea of where the points actually are on the curve.

11. Now you're going to place the fourth point slightly up the side of the curve. It should be just above the end of the right handle.

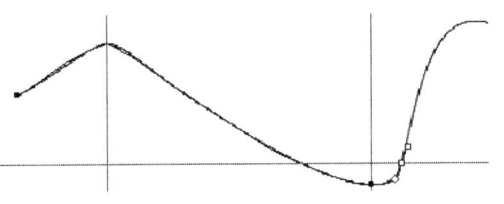

12. The next point is up on the top of the next curve. Sometimes you have to put the points on either side of the curve, and at other times you have to position a point on top of a curve; it just depends on the shape. Again, you can see that holding down the Shift key, which constrains the direction of the handle to increments of 45 degrees, helps us shape the curve.

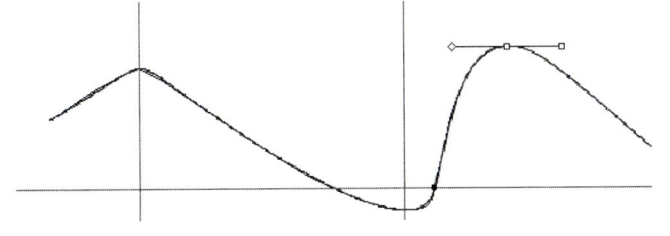

13. The next point is going to be at the bottom of the slope to the right. Once again we used the Shift key to hold the handles flat to the bottom of the curve.

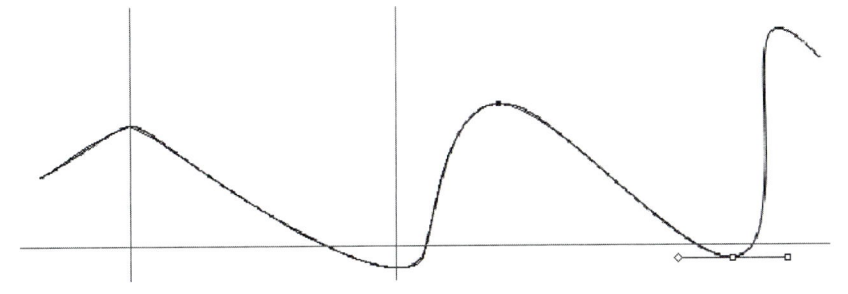

CHAPTER 4/WORKING WITH SHAPES 89

If you stop drawing a curve using QuarkXPress's Bézier tools, the line is ended; you cannot select another tool, do something, select the line again, and continue drawing. This is a serious weakness in the Bézier tools offered by QuarkXPress when compared to dedicated illustration programs, in which you can simply click the end of a line with the Bézier tool and keep drawing. You should try to get through this exercise in one continuous motion. If one of your curves doesn't fit you can always come back and edit it later.

14. The handle on the right side of this curve is going to have to be shortened in the same way that we shortened the handle of the fourth point. Hold down the Command key (if your on a Macintosh) or the Control key (for Windows users) and shorten the handle slightly.

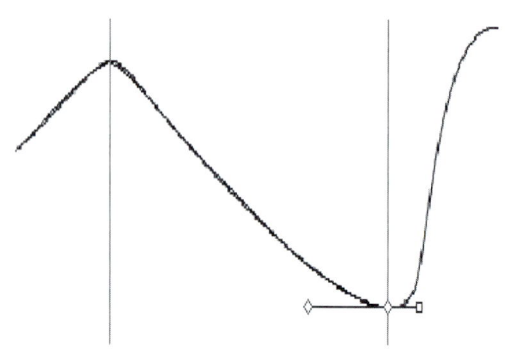

15. Make the seventh click, just up the side a little at the start of the long, vertical curve.

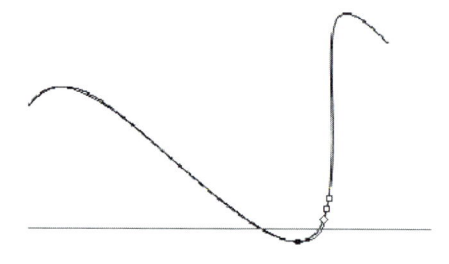

16. The eighth curve shows an instance where the anchor point needs to be on the side — not the top — of the curve. You'll see what we mean when you place the ninth and final point in Step 17. Pull the handle slightly up to about the level of the top of the curve.

17. Click on the very end of the line and pull the handle down and to the right a little, carefully fitting the Bézier path onto the tracing template.

90 CHAPTER 4/WORKING WITH SHAPES

If you do something that causes the path to be deselected, simply select it with the Item tool and press Delete. Start again; the practice won't hurt you.

18. Unlock the template and delete the picture box. Click the Content tool and enter some text onto the line.

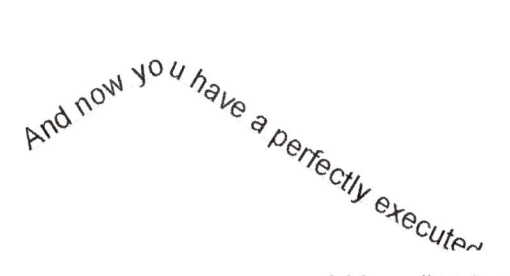

And now you have a perfectly executed

19. Save the file into your **Work in Progress** folder as "Bézier Practice.QXD".

Turning Corners

In the last exercise, we used the Bézier Text Path tool to create a series of smooth curves that matched the hand-drawn template that we imported into the picture box at the top of the page. Learning where to position the anchor point to get a perfect fit on your curves is an important skill and one you should work to master.

Unfortunately, not all shapes are built only of curves. Most are a combination of curves and corners, round edges, and straight lines. That's why you have to learn how to combine different types of points to fit any shape you may have to create or trace.

Creating Corner Points

1. Create a new document, letter-sized, single page, 1/4 inch margins, with Facing Pages and Automatic Text Box unchecked.

2. Create a picture box at the top of the page. Import the image named **Shape Practice.TIF** from the **SF-Adv QuarkXPress** folder.

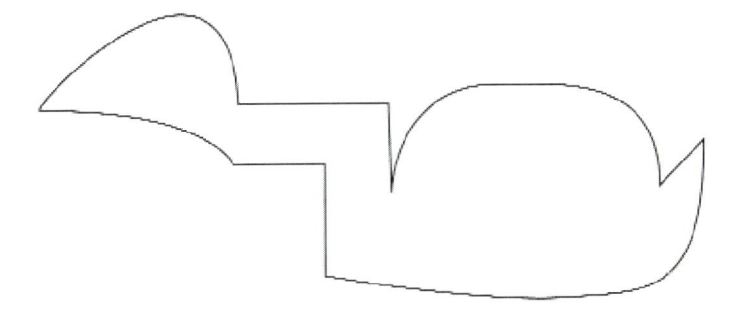

In this section you're going to learn how to make corner points, where a line abruptly changes direction — not with a smooth curve but with a sharp point.

3. Clearly we're not going to walk you through each and every point. You're going to execute this one largely on your own. We will, however, "point out" how to make a curve into a point. Select the Bézier Picture Box tool (the one with the pen nib icon). Click on top of the curve on what appears to be a head of some weird bird. Pull the curve handles out to the left.

CHAPTER 4/WORKING WITH SHAPES **91**

If you notice, we're starting this shape by moving from right to left, yet in the last exercise we started on the left and worked to the right. The end result is no different whether you start right to left or left to right; it's more a matter of personal preference. We did it both ways to show you that it makes no difference to the shape. We decide on the direction when we look at the shape. Once we pick a point, we keep on moving until the shape is done or we have to take a break.

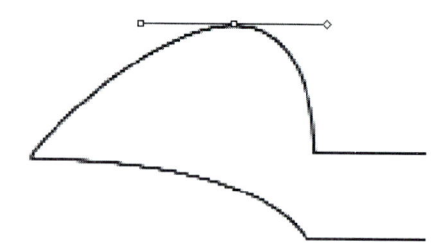

4. The next point is going to be at the "beak." Click there and pull the handles down and slightly to the left.

5. The next point is to the right, at the bottom of the curve where it meets the straight line. If you just click there, the beak of the bird will have a long curve — not the sharp point that we need. Try it and then immediately undo the anchor point by pressing Command-Z (Macintosh) or Control-Z (Windows).

6. Hold down the Command and Option keys (Macintosh) or the Control and Alt keys (Windows). Position the cursor over the lower handle and click it; it will disappear. The point now shows up as a small triangle, which indicates that it's now a Corner point.

Tracing is absolutely the best way to get a feel for using Bézier curves. It's the same way we teach students how to use Adobe Illustrator or MacroMedia FreeHand, providing feedback on the shape of curves and where to place anchor points that no other teaching method achieves.

7. Now click on the next point. Pull the curve until it fits and watch what happens.

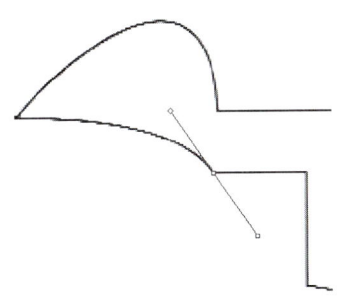

8. Press Command-Option/Control-Alt and click on the lower handle to retract it, as you did in step 6.

9. The next two points are simply a matter of clicking.

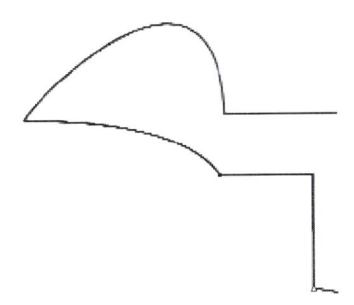

10. Finish the shape. Don't forget that if you need to, you can use the Content tool to move points or pull on the curves to make them fit better.

11. When you're done, save the file in your **Work in Progress** folder and name it "Making Shapes.QXD", then close it before you move on to the next section.

Joining Complex Paths

Sometimes the best way to create a complex shape is to do it in pieces. Other times, you might accidentally select another tool while you're trying to develop a complicated shape and the line stops, forcing you to develop the shape in several pieces.

This raises the argument that no matter what type of closed shape you're trying to create, you should start out with the simple Bézier Line tool, develop the shape in pieces, and join the anchor points together at the end. Once you do that, you can use the Item>Content selection to change the shape into a picture or text box.

Remember that joining and merging and content-type conversion are all techniques that are designed to be used together in combinations so that you're never really limited to what you can create. These are tools that require a good amount of thought — it's not a push-button process. We stress the importance of looking at how professional artists and designers put their images together. Looking at commercial work and then figuring out how to accomplish the method using QuarkXPress is a mental and physical exercise that will, over time, dramatically improve the look of your own work and the skills with which you execute your designs.

In this example, we draw one curve using the Bézier line tool, then draw a second curve, continuing until we have all the parts for the weird bird shape. We've pulled one of the sections away from the shape to show you how it's been constructed from individual pieces.

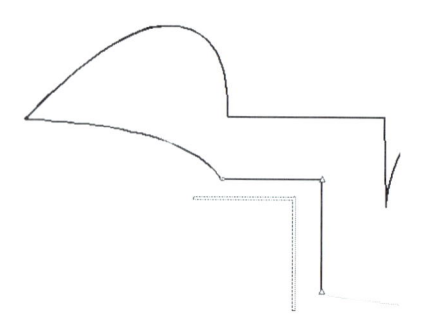

To join the paths together, we use the Content tool and draw a marquee to select the end points of two paths.

Then we choose Item>Merge>Join Endpoints.

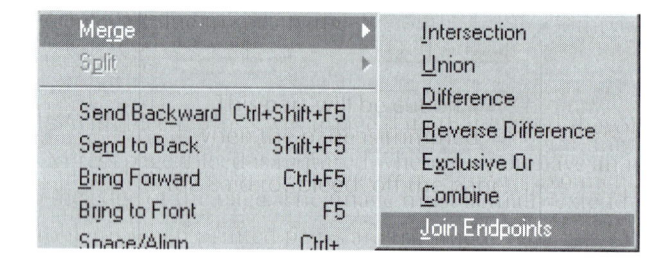

The two line segments become one, and the curves or points can be pulled and edited to conform to the shape being traced.

94 CHAPTER 4/WORKING WITH SHAPES

Once we're done connecting all the points, we can then change the content type into whatever we need it to be.

Which Tool to Use

As we've already mentioned, since you can easily and quickly change the content type of any shape from, for example, a picture box to a text box and back again, you might decide to use only the Bézier Line tool and simply join, merge, and convert the shape to the type of text box you will eventually need.

As you become more proficient with the Bézier tools, however, you may decide to use the correct tool type from the start, and simply join or merge if you need to. Here's a breakdown of the tools and how they work:

The Bézier Picture Box tool is used by clicking and dragging around the outside of the shape that you want to draw.

The Freehand Picture Box tool is used by dragging only.

The Bézier Text Box tool is used by clicking and dragging.

The Freehand Text Box tool is used by dragging.

The Bézier Text Path tool is ussed by clicking and dragging.

The Freehand Text Path tool is used by dragging.

The Text Path tool is used by clicking and dragging.

CHAPTER 4/WORKING WITH SHAPES 95

Notes:

CHAPTER 5

COMPLEX TEXT ELEMENTS

CHAPTER OBJECTIVE:

To learn the advanced text element handling features of QuarkXPress 4 — its typographic controls, style features, and type management functions, which are the most powerful text management tools in any page layout program today. In Chapter 5 you will:

- Learn how to turn text elements into graphic objects.
- Learn how to convert text to paths.
- Learn how to create logotypes.
- Learn how to put type inside of character-based graphics.
- Learn how to combine text and picture box characteristics.
- Learn how to put text on paths, curved paths, circles, and ovals.

PROJECTS TO BE COMPLETED:

- Gym Ad
- **Recipe Book**
- Tropical Suites Brochure
- Staying Alive Newsletter
- Automation Booklet
- GASP Newsletter

Complex Text Elements

If you've been working with professional illustration programs such as Adobe Illustrator or MacroMedia FreeHand to create special text effects, you should consider using the built-in text tools provided by QuarkXPress. In some cases they're as powerful as those found in stand-alone programs. This doesn't mean that you won't find yourself occasionally using drawing programs for text treatments; some are still outside the capability of a page layout program. Many effects, however, can be created right on your page without leaving the program; this is often more productive than switching back and forth between applications.

Even in its earliest versions, QuarkXPress has been famous for its ability to manage text elements. Its typographic controls, style features, and type management functions have always been considered the best in any page layout program. With the latest version of the program, this feature set has become even more effective and powerful.

With power comes responsibility. We don't mean that to be flippant, but to get the most out of QuarkXPress's text features, you have to study and practice, and use its more advanced features in the real-world, where experience will round out your abilities.

In this chapter we're going to explore some of the more advanced features QuarkXPress offers the designer and artist.

Converting Text to Paths

A perfect example to begin with is the ability to turn text elements into graphic objects. Illustrator, FreeHand, and CorelDraw! all offer this ability; it's a very powerful function, providing you with tremendous flexibility in designing elements such as logotypes, type that contains images, or type that contains blends, textures, or other graphic treatments. It also lets you actually modify a specific character or group of characters to meet your specific design requirements.

Your creative options are almost unlimited, from simple effects such as applying a blend to a type selection.

Or complex masks that contain photographic images.

Using Modified Type Elements for Special Graphic Treatments

A powerful technique that's been employed by professional graphic artists for many years — even before the advent of computers — is the use of modified, altered, or composite type characters. There are dozens of examples around you at any time. Probably one of the most popular is the creation of "logotypes." Logotypes are the use of modified type characters to create a corporate or organizational logo.

There are so many variations on this theme that it's virtually impossible to explore them all. Let's examine a few so that you can get a feel for converting type characters to graphic elements, and then use those graphic elements to build complex logo and design elements.

Creating Graphics from Type Characters

1. Create a new document, letter-sized, no automatic text box, with 0.25 inch margins.

2. Create a fairly large text box. Using the Content tool, click inside the box and enter the letter "T". Highlight it and change it to ATC Monsoon, 196 pt.

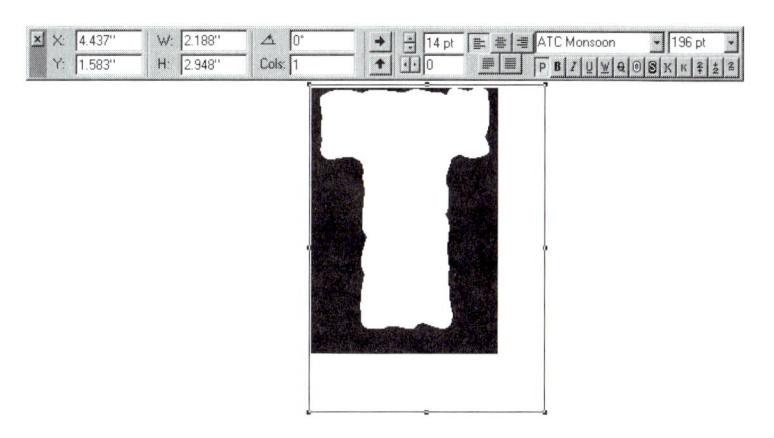

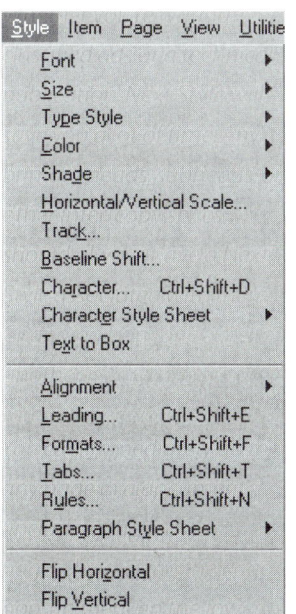

3. Create another text box and enter the letters "ropical". Make the type ATC Monsoon 60 pt.

4. Create another text box, and this time enter the letter "I" at 134 pt. Using the Measurements palette, rotate the letter 90 degrees.

5. You now have three different type components on the page: the first "T", the sideways "I", and the letters "ropical".

The Style menu provides you with the option of converting any type character to a picture box — complete with anchor points.

CHAPTER 5/COMPLEX TEXT ELEMENTS **99**

6. Highlight the letter "T". From the Style menu choose "Text to Box." You now have another copy of the letter "T"; this one isn't text, though; it's a complex path of Bézier curves and points, exactly as if you had carefully drawn the character with the Bézier tools.

You should have noticed that when you applied the "Text to Box" command, an outline (graphic) version of the character was created but the type itself remained on the page. If you want to, you can simply delete the original type.

7. Save the file in your **Work in Progress** folder and name it "Complex Type Practice.QXD".

8. Pull on several of the points and play around with modifying the character. This is something that artists of old simply couldn't do; to accomplish this type of effect they would have had to draw the character. When you've finished experimenting, choose File>Revert and click OK when asked if you're sure.

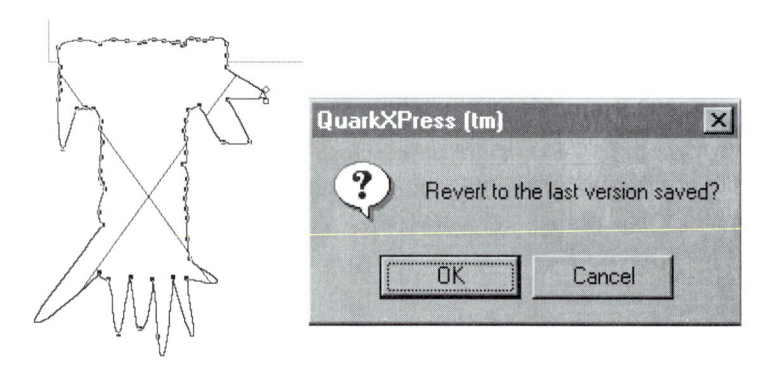

100 CHAPTER 5/COMPLEX TEXT ELEMENTS

9. Remember the letter "I" that you turned sideways? Highlight it with the Content tool and convert it to a graphic element (Style>Text to Box). Do the same to the letters "ropical".

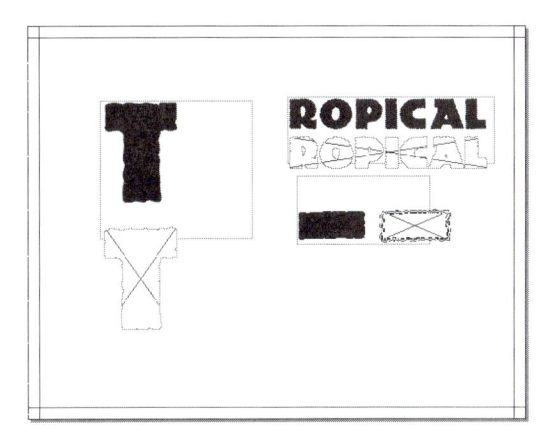

10. Select and delete the original text elements so that all that remains are the graphic elements.

11. Select the letter "I" and duplicate it twice so that you have three copies.

12. Move one of the vertically-oriented "I" elements near the capital "T" so that it actually overlaps and essentially extends the cap of the "T".

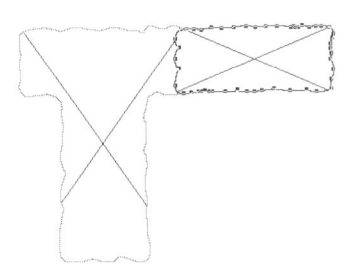

13. Shift-click the letter "T" and select Item>Merge>Union. This will turn the two elements into one letter "T" with a big overhang.

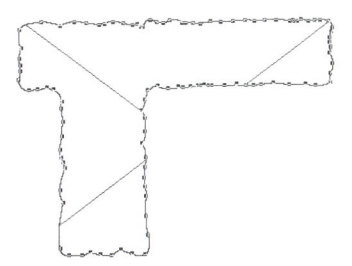

14. Slide the letters "ropical" into place underneath the overhang.

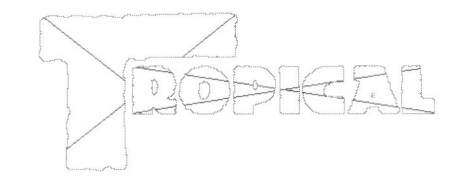

15. We need a little more overhang. Drag the other sideways "I" elements into place until you have the logo balanced.

16. Shift-click all the components of the "T" and merge them to a Union.

17. Select the modified "T" and the letters "ropical" and merge them (Item> Merge>Union) into one big picture box.

18. Using the Item tool, double-click the element and use the Modify>Box dialog box to build a mid-linear blend inside the picture box. Set the Box color to Magenta, the Blend style to mid-linear, the angle to 90 degrees, and the second color to Blue.

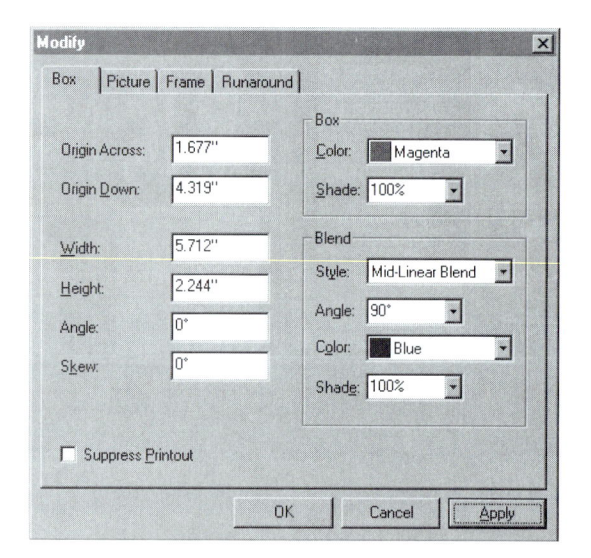

19. Click OK. The entire collection of modified and normal type elements have been converted into a single, custom-designed colored box.

20. From Item>Content, convert the box to a content of None.

21. Choose Save As... from the File menu. Save the file in your **Work in Progress** folder under the name "Final Tropical Logo.QXD".

Putting Type inside of Character-based Graphics

Another variation on this same theme is to use a type character as a text box for imported copy files. This is another one of those techniques that were so very difficult to achieve in pre-computer days that QuarkXPress makes possible with a few (well, maybe more than a few) mouse clicks. Even though this is an advanced technique, it's not that difficult to master.

The example we're going to use in this hands-on exercise is hardly an award-winning design; it was put together to give you an idea of the amazing range of possibilities available to you when you're approaching your own assignments.

Creating Text Boxes in the Shape of Type

1. Create a new document, letter-sized, with no automatic text box, and 0.25 inch margins.

2. Draw a text box. Click in it with the Content tool and enter the letter "L". Press Command-A (Macintosh) or Control-A (Windows) to select the letter. Set its attributes to ATC Monsoon, 300 pt.

3. Select Style>Text to Box and create an outline version of the character. Delete the original type element. Move the graphic character into the upper left corner of the page.

4. Create another text box about 5.5 inches wide. Enter the letters "ures" and set them to ATC Monsoon, 96 pt. Position and resize the box until it's slightly to the right of the foot of the "L" and spells out the word "Lures".

Chapter 5/Complex Text Elements 103

There are many examples of putting type into shapes in magazine layouts and advertising design. The ability to convert any type character into a text box is a unique and powerful technique. As we often recommend, you might consider going to a magazine stand or bookstore to find examples. Additionally, most design associations have contests, both locally and nationally, and publish the results in beautifully illustrated books and magazines. Creative Arts is one of these publications, and there are many more. You might ask your teacher to recommend some sources of good design that you can look at to find examples of techniques that you can adapt to your own work.

5. If your rulers aren't showing, press Command-R (Macintosh) or Control-R (Windows) to turn them on.

6. From the 4-inch mark down, fill the page with a rectangular text box.

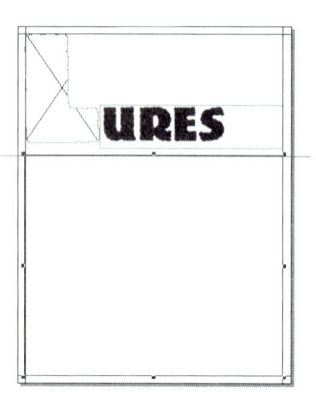

7. Using the Item tool, double-click the bottom text box. Click the Text tab and set the number of columns to 3, with a Gutter Width of 0.25 inch.

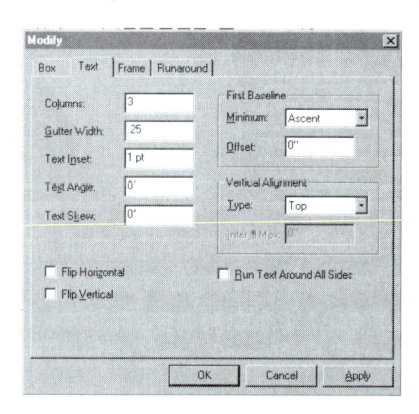

8. Click OK. Select the Graphic Letter "L" in the upper left of the page. Choose Item>Content>Text.

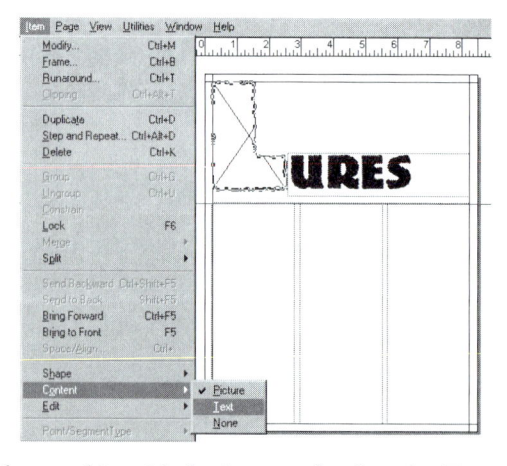

9. Double-click the graphic with the Item tool, select the Text tab, and set the text inset to 6 pt. Select the Frame tab and create a 1 pt. black frame around the graphic. Click OK when you're done.

104 CHAPTER 5/COMPLEX TEXT ELEMENTS

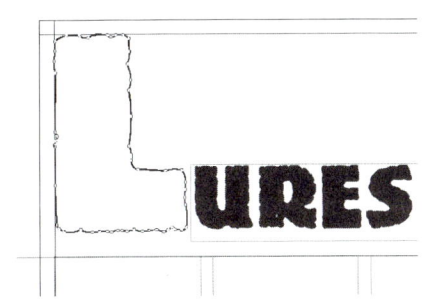

There are many different changes that you might consider making to this mechanical to refine and detail it. One good example would be to format the type so that the first paragraph fits perfectly into the graphic "L." You might also try moving some of the anchor points to change the wrap of the copy within the shape.

10. Click in the "L" graphic with the Content tool. Choose Get Text from the File menu or press Command-E (Macintosh) or Control-E (Windows). Navigate to the **Book Building** folder within the **SF-Adv QuarkXPress** folder and find the file named **Lures.TXT**. Double-click it and it will flow into the shape.

11. Select the Linking tool. Click on the "L" graphic and then on the large three-column text box. The type will flow from the graphic into the other text box.

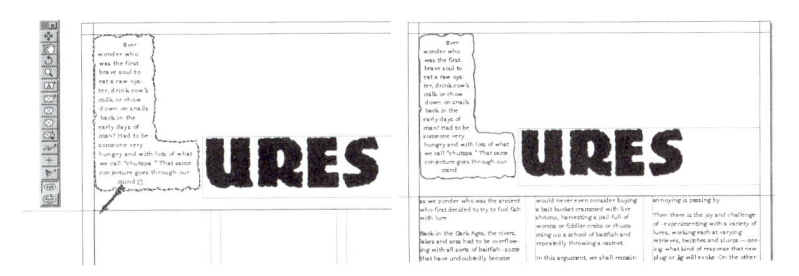

12. Save the file in your **Work in Progress** folder and name it "Lures.QXD". Close it when you're finished.

Combining Text and Picture Box Characteristics

You can also combine the characteristics of type and picture boxes. For example, you can convert a type character into a graphic yet cause it to remain inside the original box, which can contain either type or graphics. In other words, you can mix and match the contents of a box.

This is a variation on the Item>Text to Box function with a slight difference. The best way to demonstrate what we're talking about is to perform a short exercise.

CHAPTER 5/COMPLEX TEXT ELEMENTS 105

Combining Graphics and Picture Boxes from Text

1. Create a new document, letter-sized, with no automatic text box and 0.25 in. margins.

2. Somewhere around the center of the page, draw a text box. Using the Measurements palette, make it 3 inches square.

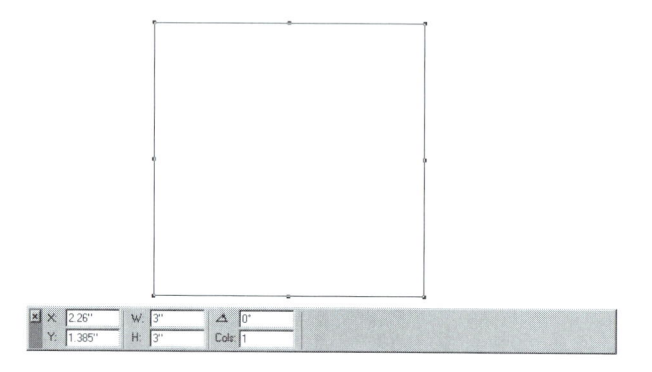

3. Click in the box with the Content tool and enter a capital "O". Select it and set its attributes to ATC Gulf Stream, 200 pt. Center Align the character from the Measurements palette.

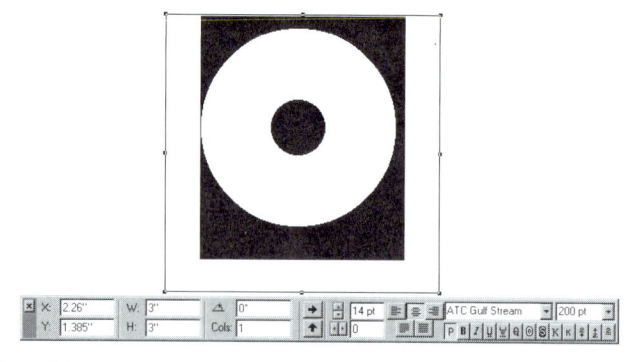

4. While it's still highlighted, hold down the Option key (Macintosh) or Alt key (Windows), and while holding down the key, select Text to Box from the Style menu. The character will be converted into a graphic but will remain within the original text box as an in-line graphic.

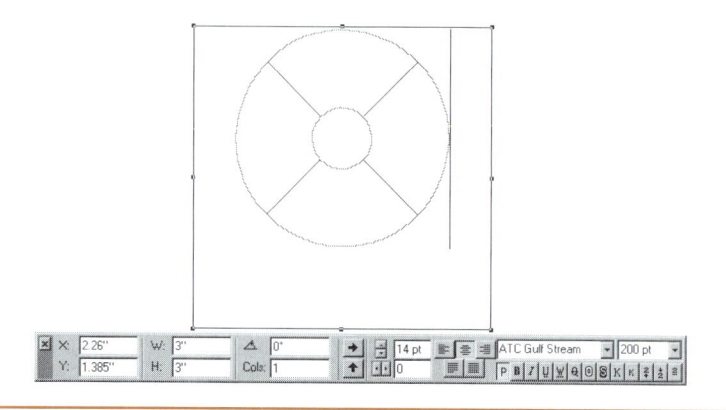

When you add the Option (Macintosh) or Alt (Windows) key to the Style>Text to Box command, the converted type elements remain connected to the original text box. Without this modifier key, a duplicate of the character is created, and the original, native type character(s) remain unaffected.

106 CHAPTER 5/COMPLEX TEXT ELEMENTS

5. Using the Content tool, select the "O" graphic. Press Command-E (Macintosh) or Control-E (Windows) to activate the Get Picture command. Navigate to your **SF-Adv QuarkXPress** folder and double-click the file named **Type Case.TIF**. It will be imported into the letter "O" graphic.

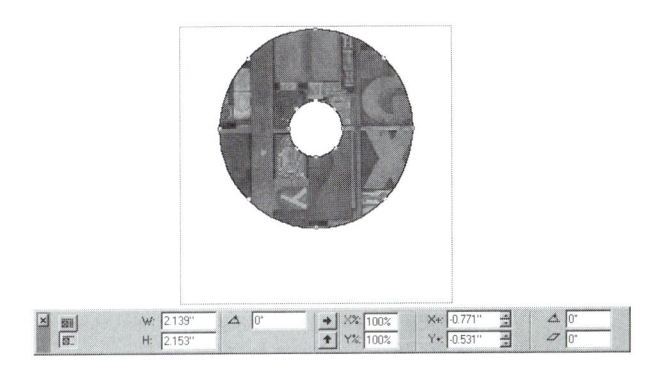

6. Let's try something different now. Enlarge the entire text box to reach from margin to margin and position it at the top of the page.

7. Using the Content tool, click in the text box. Look at the Measurements palette. The type style is still set to 200 pt. ATC Gulfstream. In the Measurements palette, change the alignment to Left Aligned, change the type to ATC Colada, the point size to 18 pt., and the leading to 20 pt. Press Return (Macintosh) or Enter (Windows) and type "ften, designers forget how exciting type can be. Rather than experiment with the use of type as a design element, they stick to conventional treatments."

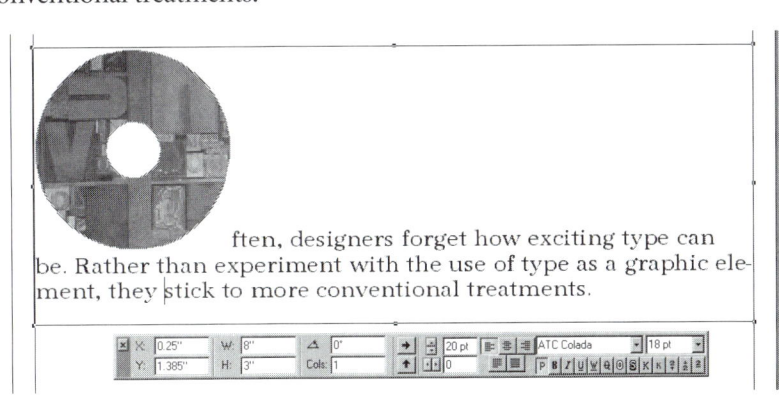

8. Save the file. Name it "Images in Type.QXD".

Text on Paths

Another advanced and popular method of using type elements as graphic objects is the use of type on paths. Since you have an extensive arsenal of drawing tools, you can create paths in almost any shape, which allows you to add text to these paths in a wide variety of fashions.

Besides the ability to create text boxes of almost any imaginable shape, you can also place type on three different types of lines: a straight line, a freehand line, or a Bézier curve (including circles, ovals, or fragments of each).

We could fill this entire course with examples of using text elements converted into graphic or text boxes. On your own time, you should try to come up with five or more examples. If you can find any in professional or commercial work, try to duplicate the effect on your own, adding your own ideas and details. Remember, professionals have a lot of experience having worked through hundreds of real-world problems. Nothing takes the place of time and experience working with the tools you have available. You're only limited by your imagination.

The best way to get a sense of using type on paths is to experience the techniques firsthand. Naturally, the more you use these techniques, the easier it will be for you to come up with your own design applications. For now, let's just explore some of our options.

Exploring Text on Path Options

1. Create a new document, letter-sized, with no automatic text box, and 0.25 in. margins.

2. Select the Orthogonal Text-Path tool and draw a straight line about three or four inches long.

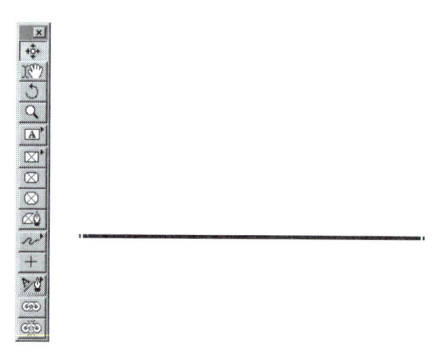

3. A text cursor appears on the line. Type the words "FOR SALE" in uppercase.

4. Press Command-A (Macintosh) or Control-A (Windows) to select all the copy. Set the attributes of the type to ATC Nassau, 36 pt., and click the Center Alignment icon in the Measurements palette.

5. Since the type is on a rule, you can use any line or rule attributes that you could with a no-content rule. Type is now fixed to the line, but this doesn't mean the line's attributes are locked in any way. Choose the Item tool. As soon as you do, the Measurements palette will show the line's attributes. Using the Measurements palette and the Colors palette, change the weight (width) of the rule to 12 pt. and the color to Magenta.

This is one of those techniques that isn't difficult to find in commercial work. Examples abound in advertising and publication work, logos, and other types of projects. Technical drawings, blueprints, and illustrations also make use of this technique. Once again, the better you can recognize techniques in the work of others, the easier it will be to apply those techniques when called upon to solve specific problems in your own work.

6. When you use this technique to lock type onto a rule, the vertical alignment of the type relative to the rule can create some interesting effects. Using the Item tool, double-click the rule. The Modify dialog box will appear. Select the Text Path tab.

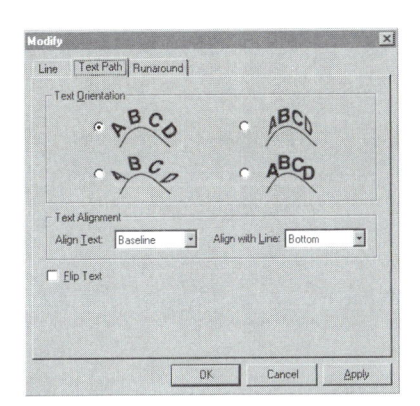

7. With the Align with Line menu set to the bottom, click on the Align Text menu and change the alignment to Ascent. Click Apply.

8. Try changing the alignment to Center.

9. Experiment with various alignment options. You can also simply use the Content tool to change the copy.

10. Try using the Rotation tool to adjust the slope of the line.

Chapter 5/Complex Text Elements 109

You can import an image into any type element that has been converted into boxes, as we did when we imported the Type image into the letter "O" in the last exercise. The possibilities with these various type and graphic options are endless.

11. Highlight the type and choose Style>Text to Box. Using the Item tool, position the graphic element so that the black type shows slightly underneath (like a shadow).

12. Experiment with putting different blends into the type objects. You can adjust the angle of the blend to match or complement the angle of the type elements.

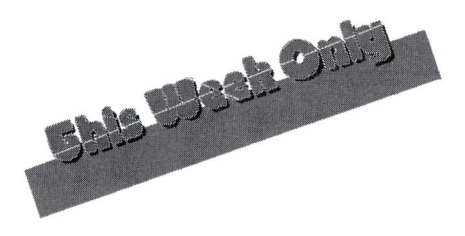

13. If you want to save the file for more experimentation, do so. Otherwise close the file without saving.

Text on Curved Paths

Placing text on curves and circles is one of the staples of modern design. There are so many examples of text on paths, curves, and inside and around the edges of circles and ovals that you don't have to look far for examples.

As you've seen in the last exercise, using only a straight line, there are many design options available. Both the text and the line can have their own attributes, and each can be changed and modified independently. You can even apply paragraph- or character-based styles to text elements that are attached to lines and rules.

Your options aren't limited to putting type on straight lines. You can also use the Bézier and Freehand tools to create lines meant to hold text.

Working with Curved Text Paths

1. Create a new document, letter-size, with 0.25 inch margins. Select the Bézier Text-Path tool and create a gentle curve.

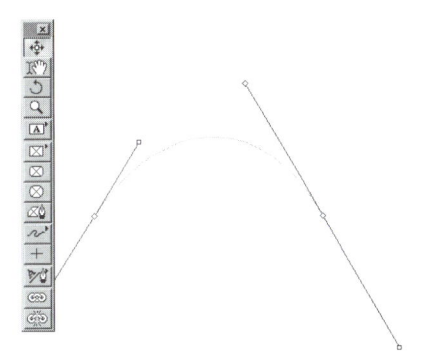

2. Click the Content tool. Type the words "Across the Continent" on the curve. Set its attributes to ATC Colada, 18 pt. (check the sidebar about the size of the type).

3. Zoom out by pressing Command-0 (Macintosh) or Control-0 (Windows) to fit the page in the available monitor space. Use the Item tool to grab the type and move it onto the pasteboard to either side of the page.

4. Draw a picture box that fills the top half of the page. Press Command-E (Macintosh) or Control-E (Windows) to activate the Get Picture command. Navigate to your **SF-Adv QuarkXPress** folder and double-click the file named **Speedy.TIF**. Position the athletic tortoise in the middle of the picture box (Command/Control-Shift-M).

If you don't draw exactly the same curve we did, you might have to adjust the size of the type to make it fit the line in approximately the same relative size and position.

CHAPTER 5/COMPLEX TEXT ELEMENTS   111

5. Drag the curved type path onto the picture. Position it so that the left anchor point is close to the point where the left side of the turtle touches the ground. Press F5 to bring the path to the front.

6. Use the Content tool and select all the type. Change its color to White so that it is easier to see.

7. The objective here is to fit the path to the shape of Speedy's back. We'll need to add a few anchor points on the path. Once we get it to fit, we'll continue to work with the type. Using the Content tool, Option-click (Macintosh) or Alt-click (Windows) in the middle of the curve to add another anchor point. The cursor becomes a square when you use it to add anchor points.

When drawing Bézier shapes, the fewer points you add, the cleaner the curves will be, resulting in a less complicated drawing. It's always preferable to create a shape with two points rather than three or four.

Please keep in mind that we don't consider ourselves to be great designers by any stretch of the imagination. We've trained many talented designers though, and we know what they need to learn to accomplish their various artistic visions. So if you think the turtle, or any of our designs aren't nearly as cool as what you could come up with, you're right. That's because you're a designer and we're courseware developers. We hope that you can see possibilities in the techniques we're teaching, because that's what's really important.

8. Pull the point up until it's slightly above the top of the shell. You can see that we'll need points in between this center point and the two end points.

9. Add anchor points between the left point and the center point, and between the center point and the right side of the path, if needed. Pull them into place until the path fits the shell.

10. Format the type to fit the shape. First, Center Align the paragraph by selecting all of the type (if it's not already selected) and pressing Shift-Command/Control-C. Change the point size to 60pt. and the tracking to –10 (by pressing Command/Control-[), or whatever size best fits the path you created.

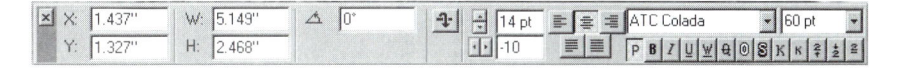

CHAPTER 5/COMPLEX TEXT ELEMENTS   113

11. By "detailing" the shape of the curve and the fit and size of the type, you can achieve some pretty cool effects.

12. Close the file without saving.

Text on Circles or Ovals

There are many times when designs call for type in and around circular paths. This practice is common in logo design, retail "splash" messages (sometimes called *bugs* in the design world), technical illustrations, and many other types of visuals containing type and graphics.

There are many ways to place type on circles, and many designers use illustration programs to achieve their desired effect and then import these elements as graphics. If you choose, you can create such elements directly into QuarkXPress.

Creating Circular Text Elements

1. Create a new document, letter-sized, with no automatic text box.

2. Draw a circular text box 3.5 inches in diameter. If you need to, adjust the size using the Measurements palette.

3. While the circle is still selected, use the Item menu to change the shape to a freehand path.

114 CHAPTER 5/COMPLEX TEXT ELEMENTS

Whenever you're creating type on a circular path you should consider using all uppercase. It often looks and reads better than upper and lowercase. Remember, no rule is fixed in stone, so you'll have to experiment with each design, but uppercase often works more effectively in this type of application.

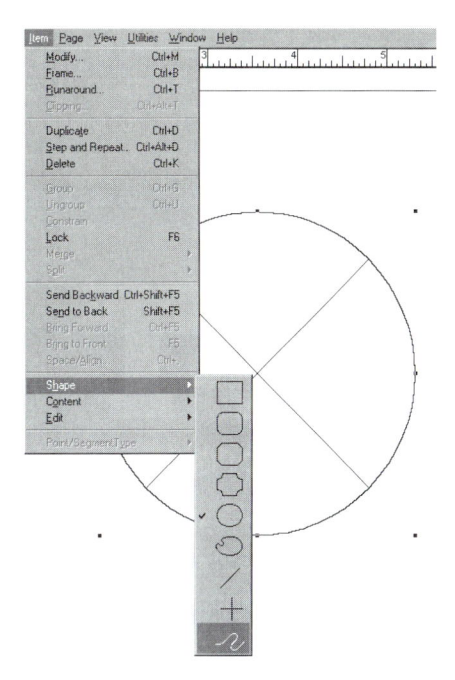

4. Once you've converted the box into a freehand path, you can use the Item>Content menu to convert its content to Text.

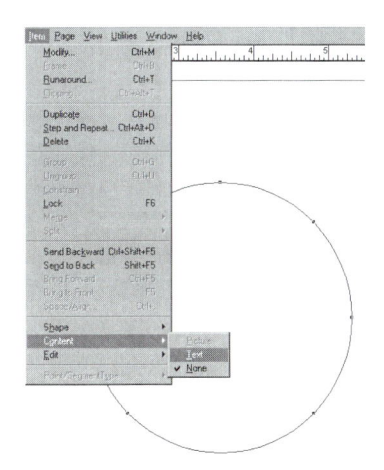

5. Choose the Content tool. The text cursor will appear at the bottom of the circle. Type "EARTH FRIENDLY HERBAL PRODUCTS".

6. Press Shift-Command-C (Macintosh) or Shift-Control-C (Windows) to center the type at the top of the circle. Press Command/Control-A to select all the type. Set it to 36 pt. ATC Colada. It should fit just fine. If you need to, adjust the tracking.

Even though QuarkXPress offers powerful tools for creating complex text effects, there are times when it might be a better choice to create certain elements in dedicated illustration programs and save them as Encapsulated Postscript (EPS) files. If they're going to be used often, and within many different applications (such as word processors, page layout programs, painting programs, or other dedicated applications), EPS might be a better choice since it's more universally recognized by independent programs. If the item is going to be used repetitively only in QuarkXPress documents, you can create the element and store it in a QuarkXPress library. Then you can simply open the library and drag the element into a picture box.

7. Select the circle with the Item tool and press Command/Control-M to access the Modify menu. Choose the Text Path tab, set Align Text to Descent, and Align with Line to Bottom. Click OK.

8. Select the circle with the Item tool. Change the weight of the line to 40 pt. It will appear to cover the type.

9. Select the Content tool again. Click in the circle and select all the type. Change its color to White.

10. Close the file without saving.

Dingbats and Type Paths

There are so many options for placing type on paths that it's impossible to cover all of them in a single course. With every project you work you on will uncover new and interesting uses for these powerful tools. One example is using dingbats or character fonts on paths. Here's a simple example using one called MiniFishes:

116 CHAPTER 5/COMPLEX TEXT ELEMENTS

Remember to continuously look at the work of professional commercial artists, thinking about ways to apply various features and tools of QuarkXPress to achieve your own creative masterpieces. Have fun and always remember that type is one of the most important and critical design elements that you have in your considerable arsenal of tools.

Complete Project B: Recipe Book

Notes:

Review #1

Chapters 1 Through 5:

In Chapters 1 through 5, you learned how QuarkXPress can be customized to fit your specific production needs. You learned how to manage images and text; how to use templates; how to properly structure your layouts; how to use the Color Management System (CMS); how to work with QuarkXPress's drawing tools to create custom shapes for holding imported text or graphic components; and you learned QuarkXPress's advanced text handling features. Through this series of discussions, extensive hands-on activities, and projects, you should:

- Know the differences between Application and Document preferences and how to customize them for your specific job requirements. You should be comfortable with the functions of the Application dialog box — the Display Interactive, Save, and Xtensions tabs. You should understand the functions of the Document Preferences dialog box; know how to customize the Toolbar; understand how to use Templates; and know how to manage images and image types.

- Know how to properly plan and construct a job from start to finish. You should understand how to use non-printing girds; how to build grids; how to use text boxes to create custom grids; understand how to manage Styles and Baseline Grids; how to apply Baseline Grids to Styles; understand the "color" of type; and understand H&Js.

- Understand Complex Merging and be comfortable with merging different types of shapes to create designs. You should know how to apply Blends to Merged objects. You should be comfortable with advanced Bézier tool techniques and understand the different Bézier tools and their functions.

- Be comfortable with the advanced text element handling features inherent within QuarkXPress such as typographic controls, style features, and type management functions. You should realize that QuarkXPress delivers the most most advanced text management tools available in any page layout program in the design industry.

Chapter 6

Text And Graphics Living Together

Chapter Objective:

To learn QuarkXPress's controls for combining text and graphics on a page, including the ability to position text with graphics or objects drawn in QuarkXPress. You will also learn how to use imported art or other text boxes to define runarounds, wrap text, and color text and text boxes. In Chapter 6 you will:

- Learn how to create transparent text boxes, which gives you the ability to place text over imported art or another text box.
- Exercise in changing backgrounds.
- Learn how to create runarounds, which will allow you to wrap text around the shape of an image.
- Learn about clipping paths, a valuable feature for controlling images. Clipping paths allow you to correctly mask an image on your design.
- Learn about the different types of runarounds.
- Learn how to adjust hyphenation and justification of runarounds.
- Learn about kerning and tracking of runarounds.
- Learn about anchored objects.

Projects to be Completed:

- Gym Ad
- Recipe Book
- Tropical Suites Brochure
- Staying Alive Newsletter
- Automation Booklet
- GASP Newsletter

You can select any color in the Document Preferences to be the default text and picture box color, although it's a good idea to leave them set to White. Double-clicking a tool will let you edit the tool's default behavior.

Text and Graphics Living Together

QuarkXPress has powerful controls for combining text and graphics on a page. You can position text in nearly every imaginable way in combination with graphics or with objects drawn in QuarkXPress such as polygons or Bézier paths. You can use imported art or other text boxes to define runarounds, or the wrapping of text relative to another object, and you can color text and text boxes in a number of different ways.

Coloring Text and Text Boxes

One of the essential features of QuarkXPress is the ability to place text over imported art or over another text box by creating transparent text boxes. Initially, new text boxes have a background color of White. You can make them transparent by changing the background color to None in the Colors palette.

Changing Backgrounds

1. Create a new file, letter-size, with no automatic text box.

2. Double-click on the Text Box tool to display the Document Preferences dialog box.

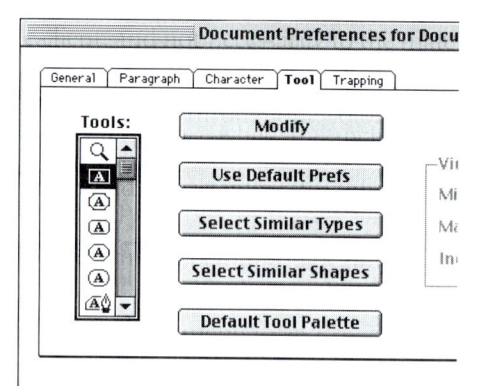

3. Click Modify; this displays the default behavior of a new text box.

   Click the Runaround pop-up menu and set the Type to None.

4. Click OK, then click OK again to close the Preferences dialog box.

122 CHAPTER 6/TEXT AND GRAPHICS LIVING TOGETHER

When the runaround of a text box is set to None, the box will default to a background color of None. This may be changed by changing the color of the box after the runaround of None is defined.

The only reason to set a text box to a background color of None is when its text will overlay the text of another box or will overlay a graphic.

Filling a text box with a tint will not show any items behind it; the only color that allows this is None.

5. Draw a 3 inch × 1.3 inch text box and type the words "Will that be one lump, or two?" Set the text to ATC Flamingo Bold, 36 pt., Aligned Center.

6. Draw a slightly larger text box and type "TWO". Set the type to ATC Flamingo Bold, 72 pt., Horizontal Scale of 150%, Aligned Center. Set the Vertical Alignment to Center from the Modify>Text dialog box.

7. Select the word "TWO" and click the Text Color icon on the Colors palette. Change the color from 100% Black to 20% Black with the Tint pop-up menu.

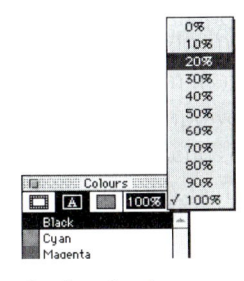

This produces a gray-tinted color for the text.

8. With the Item tool, move the text box containing "TWO" on top of the first text box.

9. The contents of the background box appear through the foreground box.

CHAPTER 6/TEXT AND GRAPHICS LIVING TOGETHER   123

You can place colored text over any other object in QuarkXPress, such as pictures, other text boxes, or anything else you create or import into the document. Be certain that the text color is legible after you place the text over another object.

Press Shift-F5 to send the transparent text box to the back.

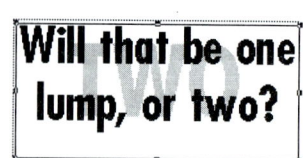

10. To add visual interest to a text block, you can add color to the background and to the text. This color can be solid (100%) or tinted (less than 100%).

    Select the background text box and give it a background fill of 100% Magenta. Change the Foreground text color to 100% Yellow.

11. Close the file without saving.

Runarounds and Clipping Paths

Runarounds, sometimes called "wraparounds," allow the wrapping of text around the shape of an image. Sometimes these wraps are to a rectangle or oval picture box, in which case they are generally referred to as "simple wraps." More complex text wraps to the shape of the image itself require additional treatment, often the introduction of a clipping path from within the graphics program.

Runarounds

A runaround controls text behavior in relation to an imported image, another text box, or any type of frame created in QuarkXPress. It's called a runaround because it controls how text runs or flows around other objects. Normally, the default status of new picture boxes, text boxes, and other objects is to have runaround turned On. Objects that will create a runaround must be in the foreground on top of a text box before the runaround will affect the text flow.

A simple runaround (wrap)

124 CHAPTER 6/TEXT AND GRAPHICS LIVING TOGETHER

Clipping Paths

A clipping path is a Bézier path that determines which parts of an image will view and print on the page. Anything inside the path will show and print; anything outside the path won't. QuarkXPress generates clipping paths for objects for certain types of runarounds, or they can be created and saved in applications such as Photoshop. Clipping paths are valuable in image control: You can place a clipped image over any other object in QuarkXPress and only the portion inside the path will show. Anything outside of the path will be invisible and anything behind the clipped image will show through the outside of the path if the background color of the picture box containing the clipped image is set to None.

Clipping paths are important for correctly masking an image. You cannot simply import an image and set the picture box background to None because this only affects the parts of the picture box that are not filled by the image; for example, if your picture box is larger than the image. Setting the background to None can also cause the visible parts of the image to show jagged edges when printed. QuarkXPress picture boxes should always have a fill of White or 0% Black for this reason except in two cases: images with clipping paths, and images that are black-and-white line art or 1-bit images. Picture boxes containing these two types of images can effectively use a background color of None.

Examples of the usefulness of clipping paths are shown below.

- This shows one image in front of another. The objective is to make the white background disappear so that the kids' heads appear to float over the image behind the foreground picture box.

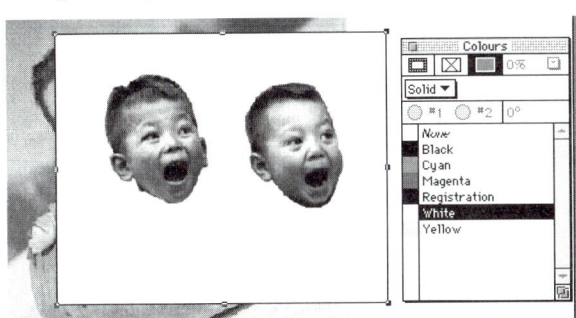

- Setting the background color to None only makes the unfilled areas of the picture box transparent.

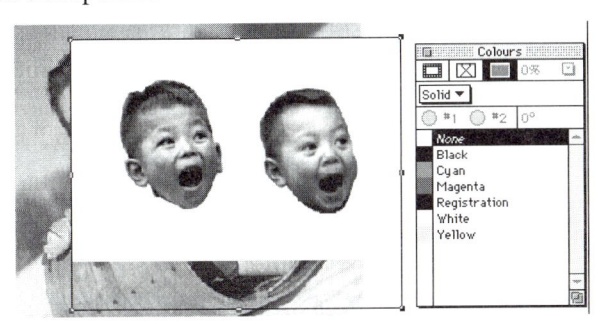

Clipping paths can be created in many other applications such as Photoshop, FreeHand, Illustrator, and CorelDraw!

CHAPTER 6/TEXT AND GRAPHICS LIVING TOGETHER   125

- To eliminate the white background in the image, we must create a clipping path around the heads. Here's what the page looks like after clipping paths are drawn for both of the little heads:

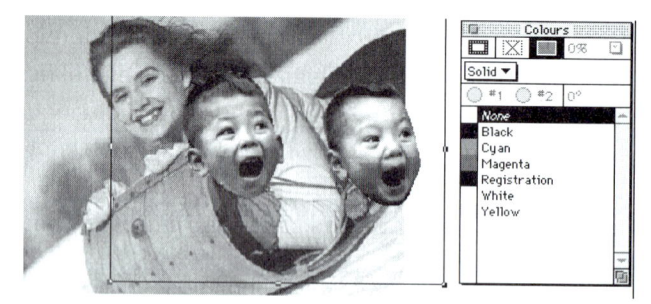

- Only the area inside the path shows. Now you can move or resize the picture box as desired.

- This is a crude way of altering a photo, but it works for this example.

There is a type of image that does not work well with a clipping path: the vignetted photo. Vignettes are areas of color that contain a gradient of tone, similar to a blend created in QuarkXPress. A vignetted photo has soft edges that typically fade to white.

This edge isn't well-defined and is unsuitable for use with a clipping path. It's not that critical since the photo can be used as is, assuming that what you see is really what you want to show. But if you want to place a vignetted photo over another image, you will need to create a composite of the two images in Photoshop to achieve the desired effect, because if you were to place a vignetted photo over another image or a solid fill and set its background color to None, the white background would still show.

Example of a vignetted photo composited in Photoshop

Creating Runarounds

There are several types of runarounds available in QuarkXPress, and they can be used according to the type of image you're placing over a text box.

Making a Basic Runaround

1. Open the file **Dsouls.QXD** from the **SF-Adv QuarkXPress** folder.

2. Draw a 2 inch square picture box between the two columns.

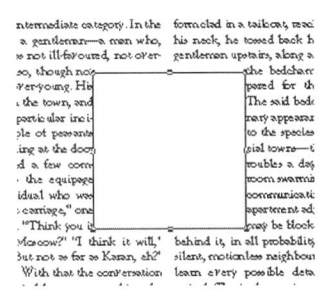

See how the text automatically moves around the box? This is the runaround, which you can adjust.

3. Import the image **Girl.TIF** into the picture box. Move the image to a pleasing position.

CHAPTER 6/TEXT AND GRAPHICS LIVING TOGETHER   127

4. The text is too close to the sides. Adjust the spacing by pressing Command-T (Macintosh) or Control-T (Windows) to display the Runaround dialog box.

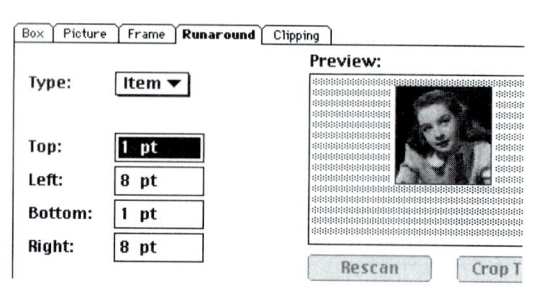

5. Change the Left and Right settings to 8 pt. and click OK.

6. The spacing is OK now. Leave the file open.

Runaround Types

You can select the Runaround Type with the Type pop-up menu.

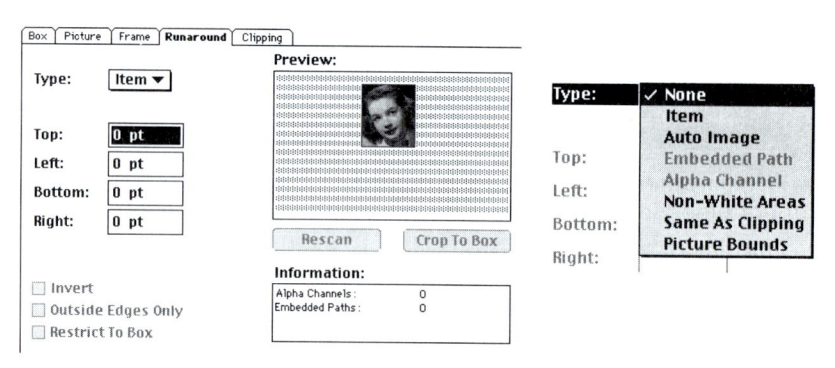

You can specify that new picture boxes have a runaround of None, or a Runaround Type that suits you as the default behavior of the Picture Box tool by double-clicking on the tool's icon.

Item

The most basic type of runaround is Item, which uses the edge of the picture box and allows you to specify in points the amount of white space around the image.

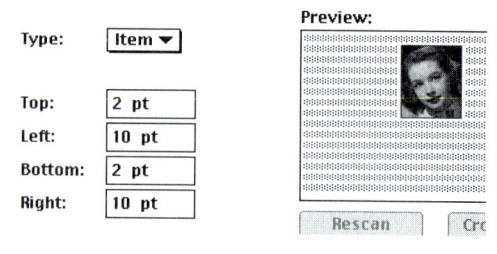

128 CHAPTER 6/TEXT AND GRAPHICS LIVING TOGETHER

These runaround settings produce this runaround:

By default, text in a single column (we've used an image that straddles two columns for prior examples) will only wrap around one side either to the left or right of an image with a runaround.

Single-Column Runarounds

1. In the open file, change the shape of the picture box from a rectangle to an oval.

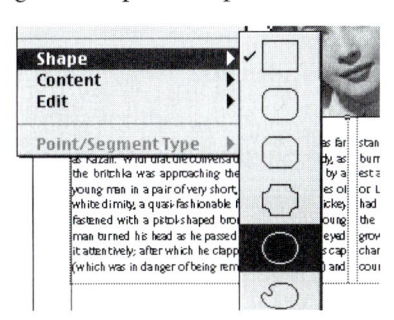

2. Use the Item tool to move the image to the middle of the left column. What happens?

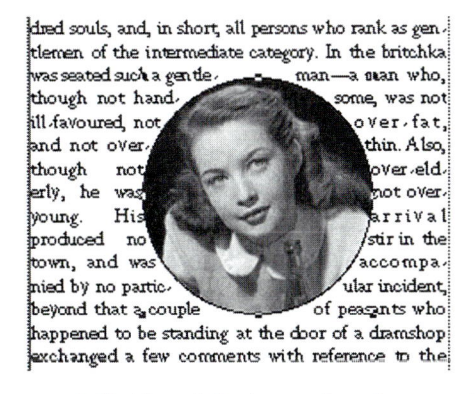

The text wraps around all sides of the image, but the wrap is very close.

3. Select the text box and press Command/Control-M to display the Modify dialog box. Click the Text tab to display the Text dialog box.

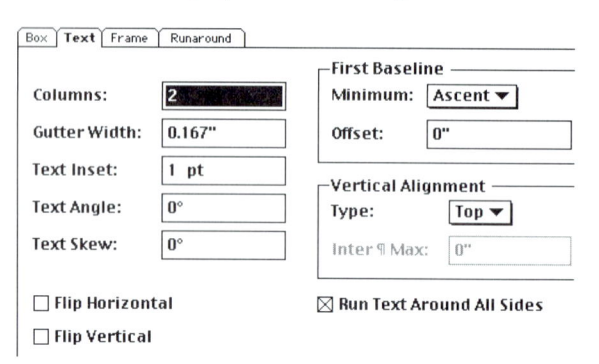

4. The little box next to Run Text Around All Sides is unchecked by default, but it was checked when this document was created. Uncheck it and click Apply to view the default. Recheck the box and click OK.

5. Let's put more space around the picture box. When rectangular boxes are converted to oval boxes they take the runaround from the top, which was only 1 pt. Change it to 8 pt.

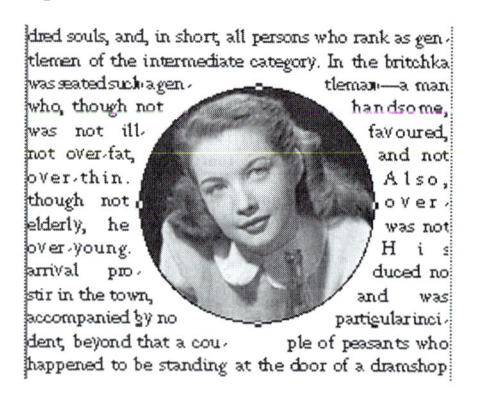

The hyphenation and justification of the text has changed noticeably; this is one of the drawbacks of using a runaround, but we will cover the steps needed to further adjust the hyphenation and justification in this section.

6. Leave the file open.

Adjusting Hyphenation and Justification of Runarounds

The image's interaction with text is unattractive and most clients would reject it. The problem is that there's not enough space on either side of the image to allow the type to justify properly. There's not much you could do to fix the word spacing. Use runarounds with care and don't try to force an image into a column of text that's too narrow for it to fit into comfortably. If you have a multi-column layout, consider straddling the image between columns.

Since the text in each column only has to wrap around one side of the image, the letterspacing is much more even.

In many cases you will need to adjust the hyphenation and justification for a paragraph or two. An easy way to do this is to make a new H&J setting, then make a copy of the paragraph's style sheet and change the style's H&J to the new H&J or simply override the style's H&J with another. This retains all the formatting, but only with different H&J settings.

Here's a runaround that exhibits a little too much word spacing, even though the image straddles two columns.

To adjust the H&J for this paragraph, choose Edit>H&Js… .

A river is excessive white space in a column of text caused by poor justification, bad hyphenation, or both.

Click New to display the default H&J settings sheet.

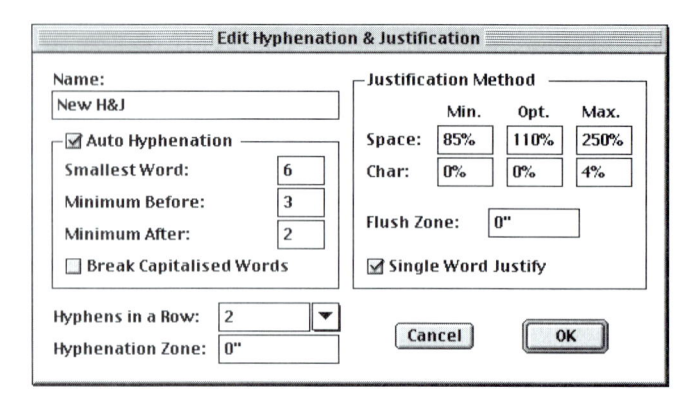

You could change the Space settings to allow tighter word spacing and change the smallest word size in Hyphenation to five (meaning words of less than five letters won't be hyphenated) for example. Your choices here are quite broad and you should experiment with these settings to achieve H&Js that will result in a color of type that appeals to you and your clients. Some clients don't care about rivers while others may be much more typographically demanding.

These settings for the new H&J sheet are effective in this case for tightening up the words on either side of the runaround.

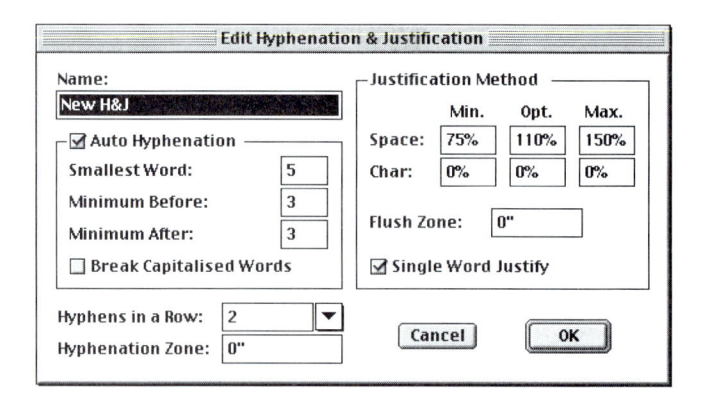

This produces a more legible flow of type around the image, though it could stand to be fine-tuned.

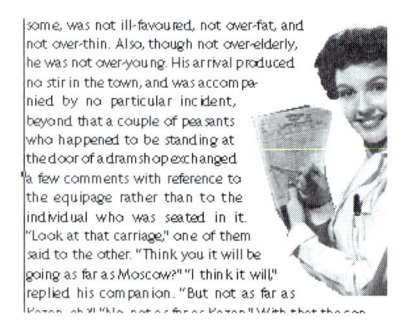

There aren't any hard and fast rules for hyphenation and justification settings. The optimal settings will vary according to the typeface used, any tracking or kerning applied to the text, the column width, and you or your client's standards.

132 CHAPTER 6/TEXT AND GRAPHICS LIVING TOGETHER

Kerning and Tracking in Runarounds

Kerning and tracking should be used sparingly in cases of excessive white space. Apply tracking to entire paragraphs; tracking only a line of type will make it stand out like a sore thumb. Use tracking for small blocks of type such as sidebars or headings to achieve a typographical color. Use H&Js to control word and letterspacing in body copy where possible. You can apply tracking or character kerning to text affected by runarounds in some cases.

Here's an example of a Bézier picture box with an Item runaround and some text. The text is too wide to fit beside parts of the image and is forced down.

We'll track the lines that moved to make them tighter. Select the text to be tracked, and type in a negative (for tighter spacing) or positive value (for looser spacing) in the Measurements palette.

A value of −10 is a good start. This moves the lines up to where they should be.

Unfortunately, the first two lines look a lot looser than the last two. Here's a way to balance tracking in a paragraph so that the change isn't obvious: Reduce the tracking value until the text rewraps. If the text rewraps at –6, enter –7 in the Measurements palette. Now select the untracked text and track it at –7 as well. If the lines reflow somewhat you can use the "new line" character to force the lines down if you like. The little angled arrow after the first "milk" is how QuarkXPress displays a new line character if you have Show Invisibles turned on.

Now all the text is tracked to the same value.

Auto Image

When Auto Image is selected, QuarkXPress examines the image to determine an edge, if any, upon which to base the runaround, and then creates a visual runaround. This works OK on images with clearly defined edges and a light background, but works poorly on images without defined edges, such as a vignetted photo. Remember, you only want a runaround and not a clipping path that will affect the image.

In the example below the Runaround Type is set to Auto Image.

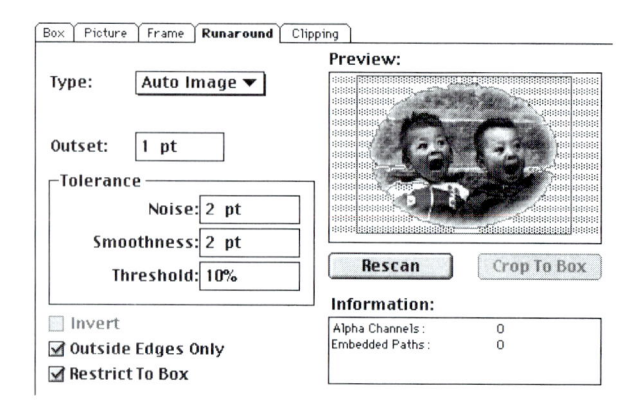

You can see that the clipping path generated is fairly rough. In this next example, the background text box has been assigned a color to magnify the poor results of the Auto Image runaround.

The smooth edges of the vignette are gone and the clipping path intrudes into the image. Not a good idea.

In cases like this, it's always better to use the Item runaround with a picture box that is shaped to the image. Here we can use an oval-shaped picture box to create the runaround.

This creates a proper runaround and doesn't ruin the image.

Non-White Areas

With this type of runaround, QuarkXPress examines the image for a white background and creates a runaround based upon a clipping path it will generate. This can be useful in some situations, but as with our example of the Auto Image method, it can produce undesirable results. In most cases, a runaround of Non-White Areas will produce the same results as Auto Image.

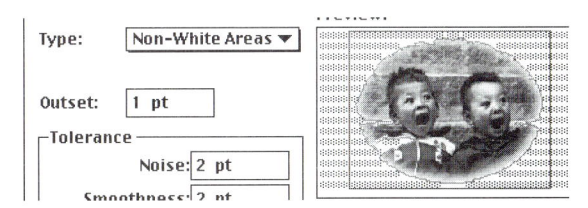

CHAPTER 6/TEXT AND GRAPHICS LIVING TOGETHER   135

You can see that the clipping path generated by Non-White Areas is as poor as the one made by Auto Image. Non-White areas works best with line art, or art that is only composed of solid black-and-white areas.

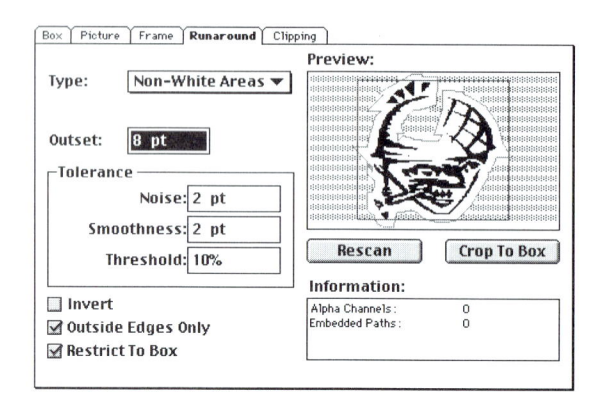

The runaround for this image will print out fine since there are obvious differences in the contrast areas, and the clipping path will not intrude into them. This is a reliable way to make custom runarounds with line art.

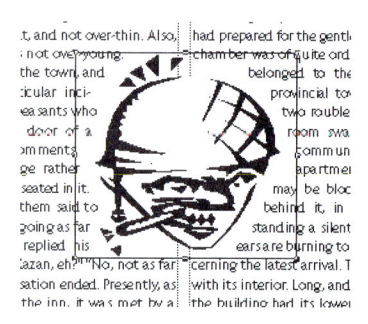

Embedded Path

This type of runaround requires an image that already has a pre-drawn clipping path, such as a path created in Photoshop.

Runaround with an Embedded Clipping Path

1. In the open file, use the Item tool to delete the picture box containing the girl's photo.

2. Draw a new picture box that straddles both columns, about 2.5 inches square.

3. Import the image **Nurse.EPS** and position it as below.

4. Click the new image with the Content tool and press Command/Control-T to display the Runaround dialog box.

5. Select a Runaround Type of Embedded Path. Specify an Outset of 6 pt. to give some breathing room around the image and click OK.

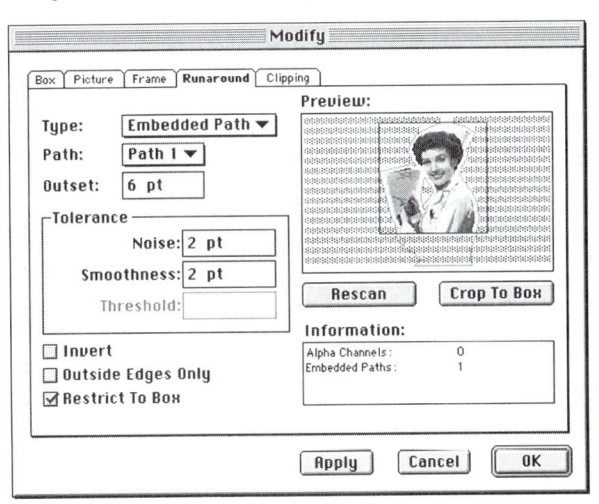

6. The resulting runaround looks good, but there's a problem.

See the word "by" between the nurse and her chart? This happened because the clipping path has a large enough gap in it to allow room for type. If QuarkXPress sees room, it will attempt to flow type into any available space. This obviously isn't the desired effect you want.

7. The easiest solution is to use QuarkXPress's built-in tools. From the Runaround menu, make certain that the Outside Edges Only box and the Restrict to Box checkboxes are checked.

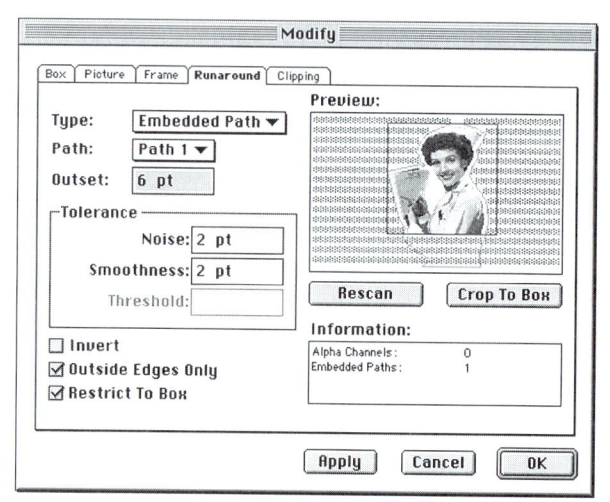

Notice that the thumbnail view shows how the image will look with and without these boxes checked. Check them and click Apply. Uncheck them to compare the thumbnail view. With both boxes checked, click OK.

8. Another solution would be to create a custom-shaped picture box with a Bézier path. Leave the document open and go on to the next exercise.

Creating Runarounds When There Is No Clipping Path

Sometimes an image will not have a clipping path, and you may not have the time to go into Photoshop and create it. When this is the case, the best and easiest solution is to create a custom-shaped picture box using the Bézier Picture Box tool.

1. Delete the Picture box in the open document, the draw a rectangular picture box approximately two inches square. From the **SF-Adv QuarkXPress** folder, import the file **Nurse.EPS**. We're going to treat the image as though it has no embedded path. Resize it to 50%, and make certain that the entire image is showing in the picture box.

2. Select the Bézier Picture Box tool. Draw a picture box approximately the shape of the image by tracing over the existing picture box.

138 CHAPTER 6/TEXT AND GRAPHICS LIVING TOGETHER

You can edit the shape or change the Outset value at any time to make the text wrapping a little tighter or looser around the image.

3. Close the picture box. The image seems to disappear because the default fill color for new picture boxes is White.

4. Select the Item tool, and while holding down Command-Option-Shift/Control-Alt-Shift, click on the new picture box. This key-click combination selects items from behind. Now the rectangular box is selected, even though you can't see it well.

5. With the Content tool selected, press Command/Control-C to copy the image, then press Command/Control-K to delete the old picture box.

This leaves the new Bézier picture box.

CHAPTER 6/TEXT AND GRAPHICS LIVING TOGETHER   139

6. Select the Bézier box with the Content tool and press Command/Control-V to paste the image into the new box. Align with the Grabber hand tool as desired.

7. Leave the file open. This is a good method of creating irregular runarounds, when there is no clipping path embedded in the image.

Picture Bounds

This type of runaround uses the entire size of the image as the boundary of the runaround. For example, you can place an image into a picture box that's smaller than the image. The actual size of the image, including parts masked by the picture box, is used to determine the runaround. We can't think of many situations that would require this.

The preview shows the outline of the picture bounds, which is the portion hidden by the picture box. This type of runaround is the same as Item, except for the Restrict to Box check box. Unchecking it causes the picture bounds to be used for the runaround.

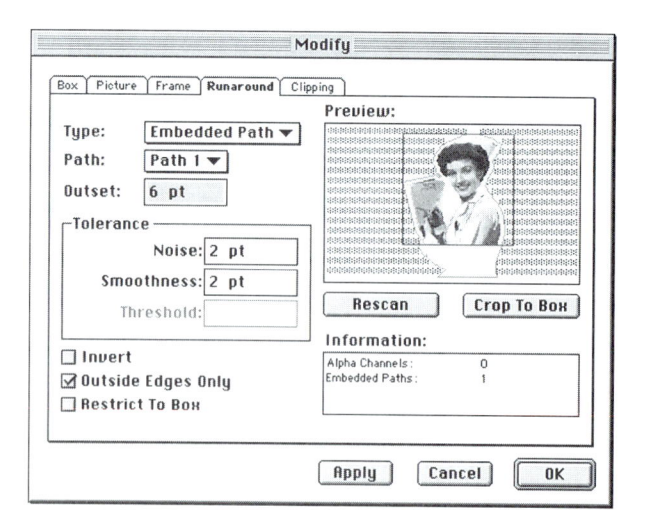

The results aren't attractive, but you may have a potential use for this type of runaround.

Alpha Channel

This type of runaround uses a mask that is saved into a TIFF file. A mask in Photoshop is similar to a clipping path except that it uses more of a stencil-like approach.

An Alpha Channel (mask) in Photoshop

Alternatives to Automatic Runarounds

As we've seen in these examples, QuarkXPress doesn't do an effective job of handling anything other than basic runarounds, except with images containing embedded clipping paths. We've shown you ways of getting better runarounds that don't compromise the image, such as using shaped picture boxes or boxes drawn with the Bézier Box tool and using Item runaround. This will produce better results than relying on the automatic generation of a defective clipping path. This is a known deficiency in QuarkXPress 4 and should be addressed in future releases of the program.

Few TIFF files have Alpha channels embedded in them. When a layer mask is created in Photoshop, the mask is applied to the image when the file is saved in the TIFF format, simulating a clipping path.

"Sneak" clipping paths can be a real problem when converting QuarkXPress files created by older versions of the program. After converting an older QuarkXPress file, be certain to check each picture box for unwanted clipping paths and adjust runarounds as necessary by creating Bézier picture boxes.

QuarkXPress 4 Clipping Paths — Avoid

The runaround examples proved that the built-in clipping path generation capability in this version of QuarkXPress is poor. You would not want to rely on these types of clipping paths for high-quality output due to their lack of precision. Given this deficiency, we are going to commit a bit of heresy and tell you not to use these features because we believe that they are unsuitable for professional design purposes. If you need a clipping path in an image for placement over another object, you should create it in Photoshop, or in many cases you can recreate the effect of a clipping path with a well-drawn Bézier picture box. Given the power of the Bézier picture box, there's little need for using QuarkXPress's automatic clipping paths.

Beware of "sneak" clipping paths. Depending on the type of image, QuarkXPress will sometimes create a clipping path without your knowledge when you import it. You can check for this problem by examining the Clipping Path dialog box. Press Command-Option/Control/Alt-T or choose Item>Clipping… to display the dialog box.

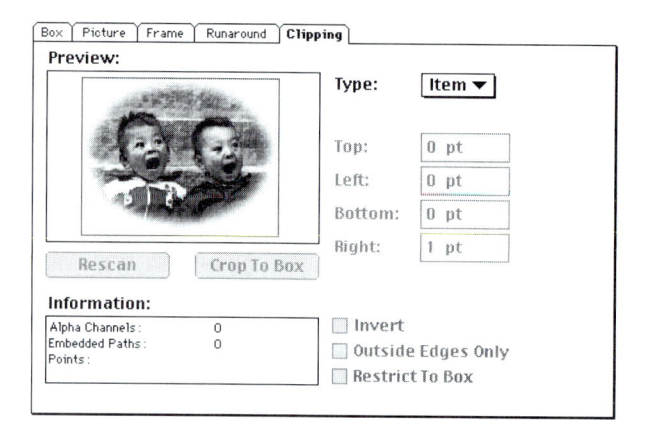

Clipping paths of the Item type are safe. In fact, they aren't really clipping paths, but simply define the bounds of the picture box, as you can see in the above preview. Any other type of QuarkXPress-generated clipping path is risky, and should be changed to Item.

Running Text Inside a Picture's Contours

QuarkXPress's generated clipping paths are useful to create a boundary into which you can flow text that conforms to the shape of a picture's outline or contour. This works well with pictures that are placed against a white background, so that the clipping path generated is usually fairly accurate.

Inverted Runarounds

1. With the document still open, delete the Nurse.EPS photo. Expand the text box to the bottom margin.

2. Create a picture box with a width of 3.3 inches and a height of 7.5 inches. Position it in the first column of text. Import the image `Chef Silo.TIF` from the `SF-Advanced QuarkXPress` folder.

You can enlarge the image as much as you like because we're not going to be printing it; instead we'll be using it as the basis for the runaround. This time, though, leave it at actual size.

3. Press Command-Option/Control-Alt-T to display the Clipping dialog box.

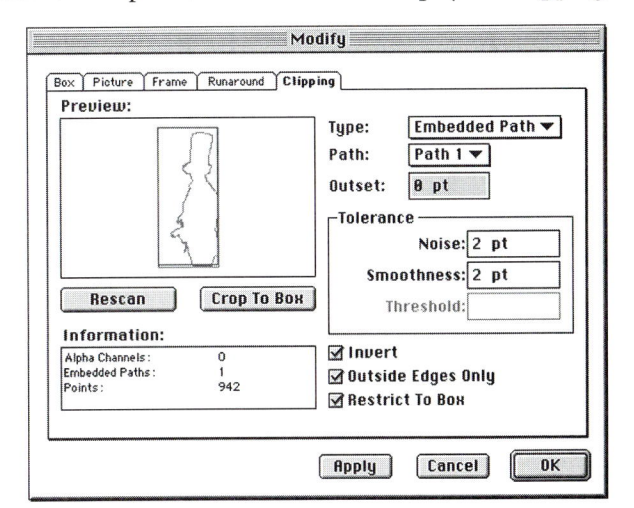

This is an interesting effect, but one that should be used carefully to avoid readability problems.

Imagine "filling" a wine glass or milk bottle with type. These are applications that are often used to good effect in today's advertising typography.

CHAPTER 6/TEXT AND GRAPHICS LIVING TOGETHER 143

4. Select Embedded Path and make certain that the Invert box is checked. Click Apply to show the new path.

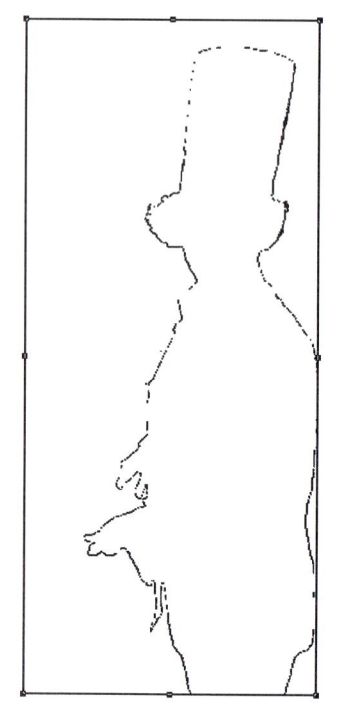

You can see that there is a slight amount of edge showing around the clipping path. You can deal with this in several ways: specify an Outset for the path; adjust the clipping path manually; or use the Modify dialog box (Command/Control-M) to suppress picture printout. We'll assign an outset of 2 pt.

5. Press Command/Control-T to display the Runaround dialog box. Specify Same as Clipping for the Runaround Type and click OK. The preview shows approximately how the text will flow. You can see that text will flow inside the path and outside of the picture box. To make the text flow only inside the picture box, make the text box smaller than the picture box.

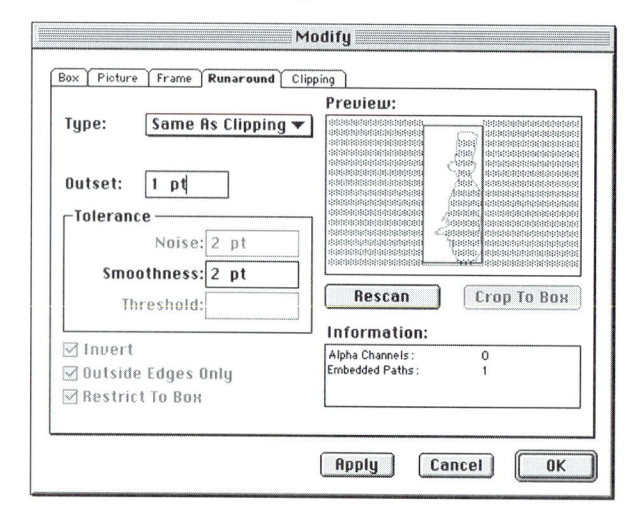

6. Reduce the text box to a width of 6.75 in., and be sure the picture box covers the width of the first column. Here's the result. You may need to force the screen to redraw to see the effect (zoom in or out to redraw the screen). You can adjust the paths or outset to fine-tune the run-around and to hide any visible edges of the picture. Use H&Js to adjust the text flow.

7. Close the file without saving.

Anchored Objects

QuarkXPress lets you copy and paste any object except for grouped items in-line with text inside a text box. You can also anchor an object in text on a Bézier path. The object then becomes part of the text flow and can be formatted or positioned much like a character. You can also adjust the position of the object relative to the text or resize it with scaling, but you can't rotate or otherwise transform an object while it is anchored. You can change the runaround of the text relative to the object with the same runaround options we've already seen. If you add or delete text, the in-line graphic reflows along with the rest of the text. This is useful for documents that may undergo a number of revisions, so you don't have to manually reposition other objects that need to move along with the edited text. Large objects may cause text to reflow to the following page. Just like a word or a character, you can simply press Backspace to delete an anchored object, or you can select it and Cut.

Anchoring an Object

1. Open the file **Dsouls.QXD** from the **SF-Adv QuarkXPress** folder.

2. Draw a picture box and import the file **Ghoul.EPS** from the **SF-Adv QuarkXPress** folder.

3. Holding the Shift key, resize the box to about one inch square. Press Command-Option-Shift-F/Control-Alt-Shift-F to scale the image proportionally to the picture box.

4. Select the Item tool, select the picture box, and press Command/Control-C to copy it to the clipboard.

5. Select the Content tool and click an insertion point before the first word in the story, "To".

6. Press Command/Control-V to paste the object into the story.

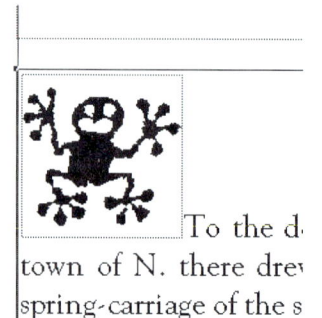

7. Press the Delete/Backspace key once. What happens? An anchored item is treated in some respects like a large letter, and you can delete, center, justify, or put it in text on a path. Press Command/Control-Z to undo the delete.

8. Adjust the object. Click on the object with either the Content or Item tool. A new option appears on the Measurements palette — the Align with Text icons.

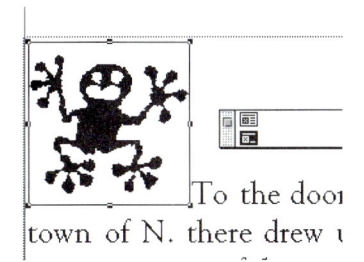

The upper icon adjusts the object relative to the ascent of the character on the object's right; the lower icon adjusts the object relative to the baseline of the line to which it is anchored and is the default setting for newly anchored items.

Click the upper icon to adjust the object to the ascent of the "T".

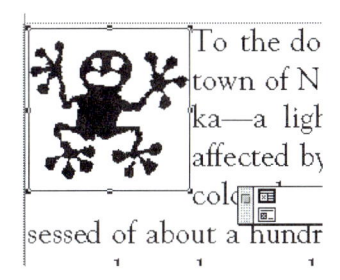

Click the lower icon to reset the baseline of the object to the first line.

9. You can adjust the offset of a baseline-aligned object to move it up or down.

Select the object and press Command/Control-M to display the Modify dialog box. Click the Box tab.

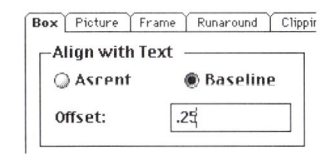

Enter a positive value in the Offset field to move the object up, or a negative value to move it down. Type 0.25 and click OK.

CHAPTER 6/TEXT AND GRAPHICS LIVING TOGETHER

10. Reset the image to Ascent. Resize the image by dragging the lower-right corner point diagonally downward.

11. Select the image and press Command/Control-T to display the Runaround dialog box. Try to change the Runaround Type with the pop-up menu.

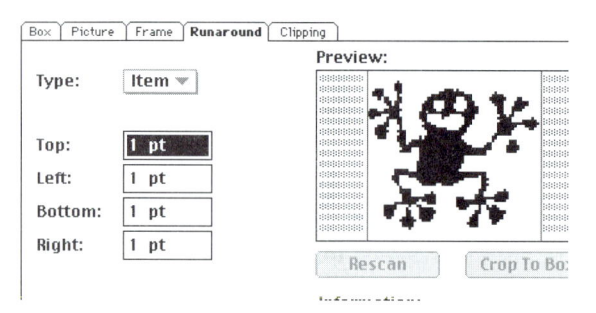

    You can't change the Runaround Type once you've anchored an object; you can only alter the spacing around the edges. Click Cancel.

12. Anchored objects behave as if their picture boxes were rectangles only. Select the image, choose Item>Shape, and change the shape of the picture box to an oval.

    The runaround is unaffected by the new shape. To use a picture box's shape for a runaround, you can't anchor it, but must instead cut the anchored image, paste it outside of the text box (using the Item tool), and move it to the desired position.

13. Select the image with the Item tool and press Command/Control-X to cut it. Click outside the text box and press Command/Control-V to paste it. The image is now un-anchored and you can adjust the runaround. For now, just move the image to approximately the same place where it was before.

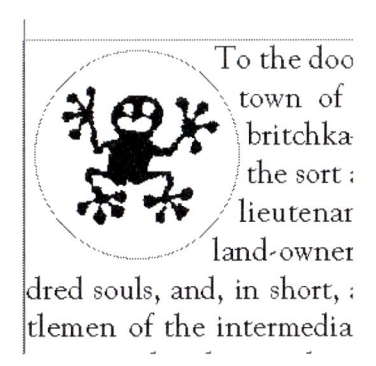

Now the runaround follows the shape of the picture box.

14. Close the file without saving.

Complete Project C: Tropical Suites Brochure

Notes

Chapter 7

Advanced Styles

Chapter Objective:

To learn about Editorial Priority and how it relates to style sheets. You will learn how to create highly-structured editorial priority with the use of Paragraph and Character styles. You will learn about first-level headlines and subheads. In Chapter 7 you will:

- Learn how to create a Default Style document.
- Learn how to append styles from another document.
- Learn to append Default styles and append styles within the current document.
- Become familiar with the importance of styles and workflow.
- Use tagged text files and the Next Style feature.
- Learn about widow controls.
- Learn how to create and apply Character styles.
- Learn how to delete styles from the Default document.

Projects to be Completed:

- Gym Ad
- Recipe Book
- Tropical Suites Brochure
- **Staying Alive Newsletter**
- Automation Booklet
- GASP Newsletter

Many people feel that the use of style sheets is best reserved for long documents such as technical publications (like this course book for example) or magazines and other publications that must retain the same format from issue to issue. That's just not true. In this chapter we're going to talk about something called editorial priorities, which basically states that all documents share similar styles, whether they're single-page display ads or a book spanning hundreds of pages.

Advanced Styles

Many professional designers and publication artists don't make use of style sheets despite their power and ability to improve productivity and consistency of design. Whether this is because they feel that style sheets limit their "creativity" or that it takes too much time to build them, these thoughts couldn't be more wrong. Style sheets allow for a separation of editorial functions from design. While writers and editors determine the text and the heirarchy of elements in a document, the designer or artist determines how it will appear. Style sheets provide the versatility to alter a number of elements document-wide with just a few key strokes.

Editorial Priority

What exactly is editorial priority? It's a term that describes the relative importance of a given piece of copy. We've been using the term for a long time, and we must admit that we don't know who taught us the idea. Since we work on series of books, it's very important that we use consistent styles and formats from book to book; however, priority is something we think about in every project on which we work. And we think that all artists and designers who work with documents that contain both text and graphics should keep the idea in mind as well.

The Against The Clock course material you're using is an example of highly-structured editorial priority organized with Paragraph and Character styles. The first thing that we do when we begin a book is to determine the chapters that will be included in the course. These are selected based on what skills we think are important to cover. Each chapter becomes a first-level headline — something we normally call Heading 1. The below screen shot is from Microsoft Word, which we use to develop our outlines before moving them into QuarkXPress.

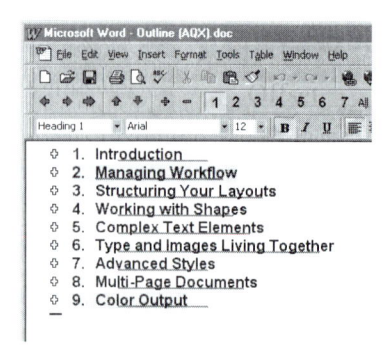

Once we've decided on the primary content of each chapter, we determine what the second-level heads will be; these are often called subheads by designers, copywriters, and artists. We call them Heading 2 (probably because we have even lower levels and want to avoid terms like sub-sub-subhead).

```
⇩ 8. Multi-Page Documents
  ⇩ 8.1.        Importance of Structured Approach
      ▫ 8.1.1.      Building and Testing a Master
      ▫ 8.1.2.      Using the Master to Build the Book
      ▫ 8.1.3.      Changing the Master
      ▫ 8.1.4.      Applying the Changes
  ▫ 8.2.        Creating a Book
  ▫ 8.3.        Sections
  ⇩ 8.4.        Managing Chapters
  ▫ 8.5.        Page Numbering
  ▫ 8.6.        Running Headers and Footers
  ▫ 8.7.        Lists
```

This chapter assumes that you already know how to create both Paragraph and Character styles, and will teach you more about actually using and applying styles to your work. The more structured your approach, the more effective you'll be as a designer. That's not to say that all your documents should look alike — many designers rebel at that thought. A structured approach to your work is different than structuring all your documents to be the same.

You should note that this isn't a writing course, although developing your ideas from an outline will often result in a more cohesive first draft, besides improving the structure of your work. We want to look at how styles affect every document you work on, whether you use them or not.

Once we've put together the outline for the book, we use QuarkXPress for the layout. The styles that we use in Microsoft Word are imported directly into the QuarkXPress document; but the real formatting, style editing, and creation takes place in the page layout application; it's there that we create new styles. For example, a style that automatically centers and aligns images is called, appropriately, "Images". Another set of styles we create are called "Task Heads" (the hands-on activities throughout the course with the colored double-rules above and below the paragraph) and "Task Items" (the outdented, numbered activities themselves). We also have styles set up for sidebars, and Character styles set up for all boldface and italicized copy throughout the course.

Again, this is a long document, so it might seem to make sense to use styles. What about a display ad, though? A quick look at almost any design shows that there are, in fact, headlines (Heading 1), subheads (Heading 2), body text, captions, decks, pull quotes, and so on. Documents often have more than one level of copy; those levels, and which style takes visual as well as editorial priority, define how the document looks, reads, and is put together.

In theory, all documents that you work on should have a Heading 1 style, a Heading 2 style, a Body Text style, a Caption style, and any other styles that you can name that will (normally) be used in any work you do. That way you can change the attributes of a style instead of carefully selecting and manually editing attributes one paragraph, line, or word at a time.

CHAPTER 7/ADVANCED STYLES   153

Building Styles

Let's say you work in an agency, or work alone as an independent, freelance artist. Or maybe you're part of a team of designers and copywriters who work each month (or day) to put together a magazine or newspaper. If you could immediately begin all new projects with a set of predefined styles, all you would have to do is edit the styles to apply your design to new work.

To do this, you need to create a default template that carries several common styles into all your new documents.

Creating a Default Style Sheet

1. Launch QuarkXPress if it's not already running. Before you create a new document or open an existing publication, let's make some changes to the Default styles. Select Edit>Style Sheets or press Shift-F11.

You don't need to call your styles Heading 1, Heading 2, Heading 3, and so forth. Use whatever names are useful or descriptive in your own environment. The reason we use Heading 1, Heading 2, and Heading 3 is because we use Microsoft Word as the starting point for our writing. Its built-in outline feature, which allows us tremendous flexibility in moving and shifting items within headings, reserves these names as special objects. Rather than wrestle with workarounds in Word, we simply use the styles provided by the outlining feature and let them carry over into QuarkXPress.

2. When the Style Sheets dialog box appears, there are two styles: a default Paragraph style and a default Character style. While both are called Normal, they have different icons to let you know which is which. For now, we're going to work with the default Paragraph styles. Notice that the dialog box is titled "Default Style Sheets." The program knows that you're changing defaults since no document is open right now.

3. Look at the default Paragraph style — the one called Normal. Select it (if it's not already selected). It's attributes are listed in the scrolling box below the main window.

In this exercise we're working to change the Default styles for all new documents. Whenever you change an attribute without a document being opened, those changes become the default attributes for that item. If you have an open document, changes you make to styles, line widths, and other standard settings apply only to that document, without changing defaults.

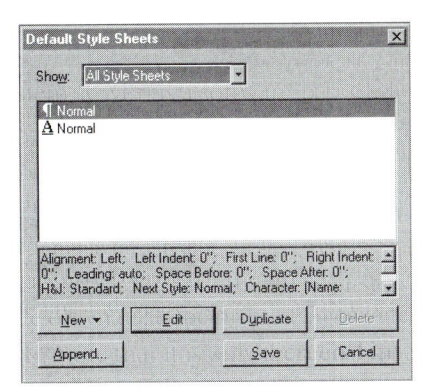

4. We're going to create a Default style for all headlines which include all the necessary paragraph attributes as well as font characteristics. Click the New button and select Paragraph from the pop-up menu. Using the General tab, name the style Heading 1 and assign it a keyboard equivalent of the Control key and the number "1" from the numeric keypad.

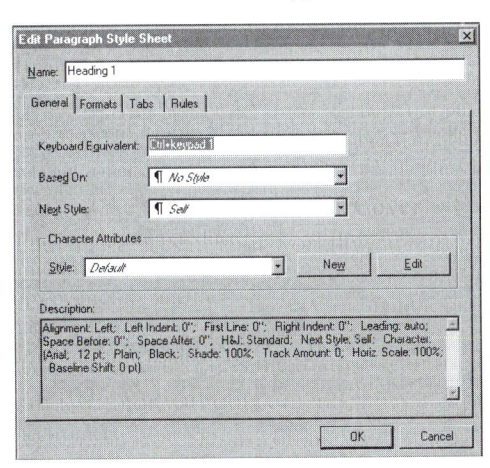

5. Return to the General tab. Click the Character Attributes>Edit button. Leave the pop-up menu set to Default. This is the default Font style for this Paragraph style only, not the entire document. The Normal style can be edited to change your default document font. Set the Character styles as shown below (ATC Cabana Heavy, 18 pt. with –3 tracking). Click OK.

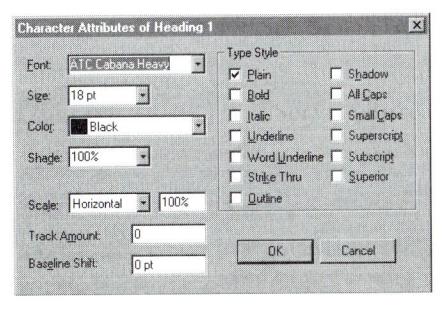

6. Click the Formats tab, set the Space After to 0.25 in., Alignment Centered, Keep All Lines in ¶ Together, and Keep with Next ¶. You don't need to access the Tabs or Rules tabs yet. Click OK.

CHAPTER 7/ADVANCED STYLES 155

When considering editorial priorities, you should realize that we're mostly talking about paragraph priorities such as headlines, sub-heads, captions, an so on. Character formats could also be prioritized, but they wouldn't have the same affect on the construction of the design. The best way to think about editorial priority is to put yourself in the shoes of a copywriter — one working with a pencil and piece of paper. A copywriter will usually label each component of his or her text to indicate what goes where. That's the idea of editorial priority; using default and common styles is a dramatically effective way to make a connection between the writers and designers in your environment, no matter where you work or how many people you work with. It's a matter of creating effective workflows.

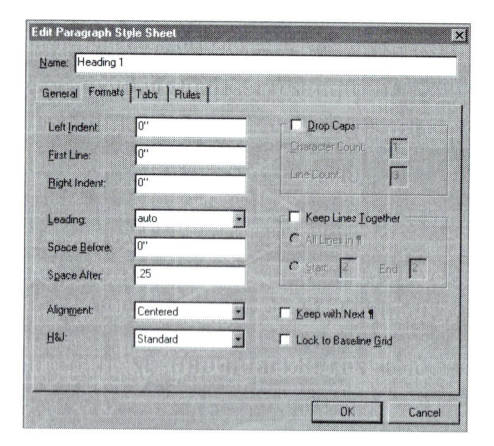

7. Click Save to add the Paragraph style Heading 1 to your defaults.

8. Start a new document with the default settings. Press Shift-F11 and look at the styles in the document. You can see that the document contains the new Default style that we created (and will keep that style until you decide to change it).

Appending Styles From Another Document

There are many times when using the styles from an existing document can save considerable time when building a new mechanical. You can copy all the style sheets from one document to another using the Append Styles command.

As we've already mentioned, we approach almost all new projects with some idea of editorial priority; we know that there will be at least be one headline and some body text in every document we create. The more complex the copy elements, the more styles we're likely to require. Over the years we've developed a selection of five or six styles that we keep as defaults for all of our work. No matter what the document or project, it contains style definitions for:

Heading 1	Reserved for headline, titles, or primary chapter heads.
Heading 2	Used for subheads in lengthy text documents. If the outline for the project is particularly detailed (such as a book project, for example, we might have a third Heading style named Heading 3. We rarely, if ever, use more than three Heading styles. If the outline is more complex than that, we simplify the job.
Body Text	This represents the primary body copy in our work. It's normally indented slightly (we don't use tabs at the beginning of any paragraph except for special-purpose tables). We sometimes create a duplicate of this style called "First Paragraph", which is used after subheads to avoid a choppy look. It's OK not to indent the first paragraph in this case.

Bullets   Bulleted or numbered paragraphs are ones like this one, where a bullet, number, or label is hanging out in the left margin while the body text is indented along a specific vertical line. The hands-on sections of this course are another example of Outdented, or Bullet styles.

Captions   Used for pictures and illustration titles.

We suggest that you analyze the type of work you do, and start with our simple list of Default styles. Create a document that contains all your Master styles, save it, and use it as the template from which you make future changes to your defaults. When you need to modify the Standard styles in new documents, simply make the changes to your styles master and append them into your Default styles.

Appending Default Styles

1. If it's not already running, launch QuarkXPress.

2. Choose Edit>Style Sheets or press Shift-F11.

3. Click the Append button.

4. Navigate to the **SF-Advanced QuarkXPress** folder and select **Master Styles.QXD**. Double-click the file. The Append Style Sheets dialog box will appear.

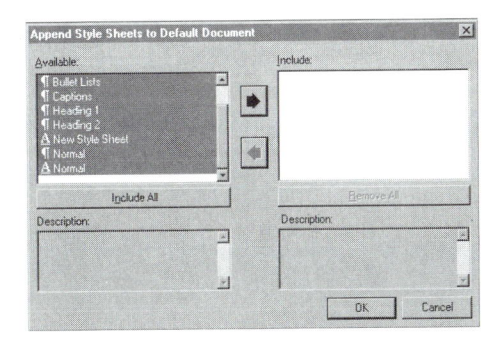

If you're creating a Default style (or any style, for that matter) from scratch, you will need to create a Character style to accompany it. If you're creating a style from an example, by first doing all the formatting and then creating a new style, the Paragraph style will contain whatever character formatting you completed before creating the new style. We're reviewing the creation of both character and paragraph formatting at the same time.

CHAPTER 7/ADVANCED STYLES

On a Windows system, the default normal character font is Arial, while on a Macintosh it's usually Times Roman. Listed below are the default settings for the Normal styles on one of our machines (before we did this exercise):

Alignment: Left

Left Indent: 0"

First Line: 0"

Right Indent: 0"

Leading: auto

Space Before: 0"

Space After: 0"

H&J: Standard

Next Style: Normal

Character: (Name: Normal; Arial; 12 pt.; Plain; Black; Shade: 100%; Track Amount: 0; Horiz. Scale: 100%; Baseline Shift: 0 pt.).

5. Highlight the styles on the left side of the dialog box and click the right arrow, or click the Include All button. This will move the styles from the disk-based existing document to the default document (which will apply to all new documents). Click OK.

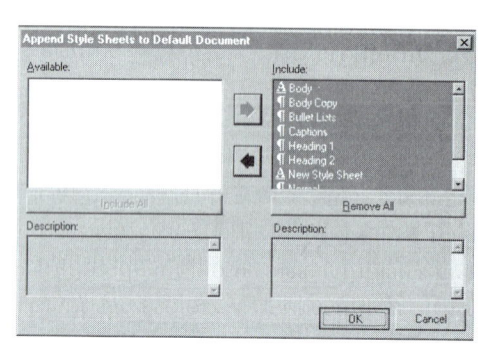

6. If you try to append styles into a document that already contains styles with the same name, you will be given the opportunity to decide what to do on a style-by-style basis. For this exercise, use New for all styles except Heading 1; use Existing for Heading 1.

7. You can choose to rename the Incoming style, auto-rename it (QuarkXPress assigns numbers to the ends of the style names), override the Existing style (Use New), or let the Existing style stand (Use Existing).

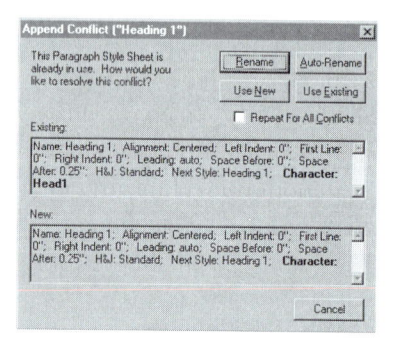

The styles that were already contained in that document now become part of the standard settings for the workstation that you're using.

You're not limited to using the Append command to change your QuarkXPress defaults. You can also use Append to change the look of a live document — one you're working on at that moment. Let's try this technique to show you how it works.

158 CHAPTER 7/ADVANCED STYLES

While managing style sheets, using tagged copy or styles defined in a word processing program will improve your ability to quickly format text on the page (according to your design specifications); it's only one step in proper communication between editors and designers. The best designs are those that arise from a close relationship between these two functions. We know people who write their own copy and do all their own layout; but in the real world, you, as a designer, must learn to talk to and work with your copywriters.

Appending Styles into the Current Document

1. Create a new letter-sized document with margins set at 0.25 inch, an automatic text box with three columns, and a Gutter Width of 0.25 inch.

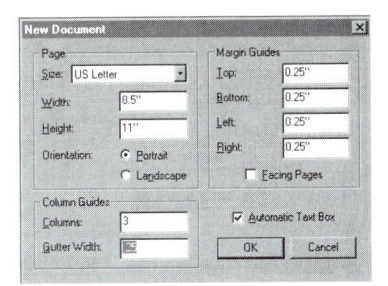

2. Move the top of the text box down to the 2.5 inch mark on the vertical ruler. Create another text box that extends from the top margin to the 2 in. mark, and extends the width of the page between the margins.

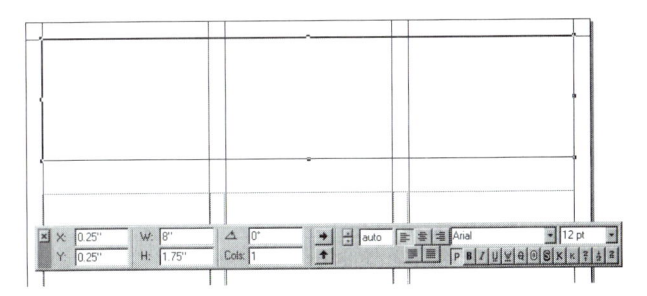

3. Click the Content tool in the upper text box. Navigate to the **SF-Advanced QuarkXPress** folder and get the text file named **Meeting.TXT**.

4. Link the two text boxes together.

5. Activate the floating Style palette by pressing F11 (if it's not already showing; if it is, this command will turn it off). Press Command-A to select all the text. Press F11 to activate the floating Styles palette. With all the text selected, click on Body Copy. This will change the entire article to one type style.

CHAPTER 7/ADVANCED STYLES 159

6. Place the cursor in the first line, the one that says "Having Effective Meetings". Assign the Heading 1 style to it by pressing Control-Keypad-1.

7. Move down the page to the sentence that says "The Importance of Structure". Make it Heading 2 by clicking the cursor in the line and using the floating Styles palette.

8. Continue working through the document; assign the Heading 2 style to all the subheads. The next one is called "The Agenda"; after that there's "Who's in charge of this thing"; and then "The Facilitator at work". After that comes "Getting real results"; "Three minutes left"; "We do that, don't we?"; and "Where to go from here".

9. Press Shift-F11 to access the Styles dialog box. Click the Append button, and navigate to the **SF-Advanced QuarkXPress** folder. Double-click the file named **Newsletter Styles.QXD**. Select all the styles on the left side of the dialog box and click the right arrow to move them into the current document. When you click OK, you'll have to choose what to do with the conflicting style names. Select New (overriding the Existing styles), click the Repeat For All Conflicts box and click Save. The document will reformat itself using the Imported (Appended) styles.

10. Zoom in to the top of the document. You'll notice that the Heading 1 style uses an offset rule and baseline shift to put the headline type over the rule itself. Put the cursor in front of the first word of copy following the headline.

11. Press Enter to move the copy to the next box (the main one on the page).

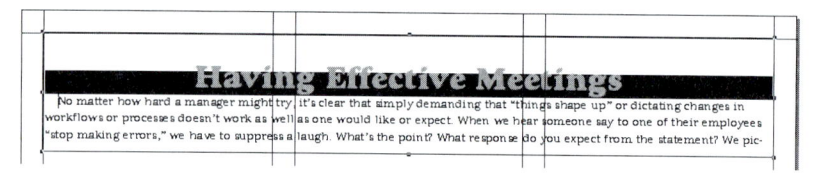

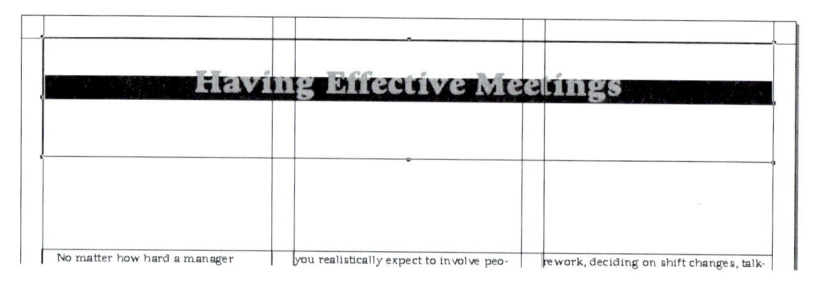

12. Assign the "First Paragraph" style to the first paragraph and any paragraphs that immediately follow the Heading 2 style. This is an example of not indenting the first paragraph after a subhead. You can see that it's more pleasing visually not to have an indent on those paragraphs.

13. Go to the end of the document and select all the pull quotes (they're at the end of the entire story.) Assign the Pull Quotes style to them.

As you're working through these style exercises, think about ways that you might apply these techniques to your own work. We certainly didn't cover every style that you might need in your own documents. Want a good example? Numbers and tables come to mind. If you're designing menus, price lists, or financial information (such as annual reports), you'll need styles that contain tabs, so that imported text lines up properly as soon as it is brought into the page.

14. Save the document to your **Work in Progress** folder. Name it "Styles Practice.QXD".

If we were going to actually build a newsletter we would be able to use these pull quotes to help us fit copy into the article. We would create text boxes at appropriate places in the text and cut and paste individual pull quotes into place or run the pull quotes in line with body text. This is a common and very effective way to detail and fit final copy in text-intensive documents.

We would also have included some styles detailing such as checking "Keep Lines Together" commands and "Keep with Next ¶" commands.

Styles and Workflow

We'll return to editing and modifying styles, and explore some of the more intricate uses of style sheets, but before we do, we are going to discuss workflow. In this instance, workflow refers to the processes whereby the components of your projects come together on your desktop system.

In many professional graphic arts environments, the people who are writing the copy for ads, publications, and projects aren't the same people as the artists and designers responsible for putting the pages together. Managing the relationship between these two groups is challenging, and style sheet management can be used to help smooth out the process of getting type into well-designed mechanicals and layouts.

When editorial priority effectively combines with design it is a beautiful (and highly productive) accomplishment. The best way to do this is through tagged text. That text may be generated through supported style sheets in a word processing program such as Microsoft Word or Corel Word Perfect, or the tags may be typed or generated by macros. Tagging refers to the insertion of style labels directly into the copy that is being written. When you import a tagged file, the styles in place in the QuarkXPress document are automatically applied to the incoming text.

In this situation, the editorial group decides the priority of an element (Heading 1, Heading 2, and so on) and the design group decides how each element will look. Styles are defined and automatically applied when the text is flowed in. It's almost like magic.

Using Tagged Text Files

1. Create a new letter-size document with margins of 0.25 in., and a 1-column automatic text box.

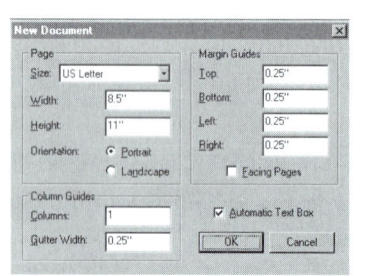

2. Select the Content tool and press Command-E (Macintosh) or Control-E (Windows) to access the Get Text dialog box. Navigate to the **SF-Advanced QuarkXPress** folder and select **Tagged Copy.XTG**. This is a special type of text file that contains style descriptions in text format. Make certain that you deselect the Include Style Sheets option.

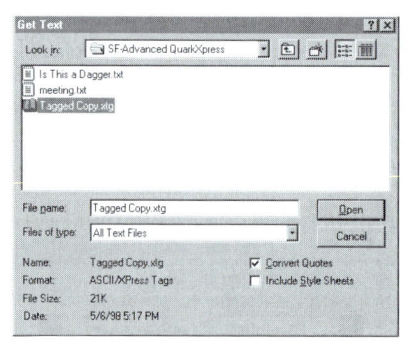

3. Look closely at the text and you'll see that the copy is exactly the same as the file we were working on in the last exercise. The code represents plain text descriptions of styles: which styles to associate with each paragraph of text.

4. Press Command-A (Macintosh) or Control-A (Windows) to select all the copy. Press the Delete or Backspace key to remove it from the document.

5. Select Get Text again. This time, check the Include Styles box. Now the copy comes in automatically formatted. Tagging the copy in the word processor eliminated all the steps that we had to go through in the last exercise to get the file into this nearly finished state. Close the file without saving.

Style tags are case-sensitive. "Body Copy", "Body copy", and "body copy" are seen by QuarkXPress as three separate and distinct styles. It's all in the details.

Tagging text files is easy. Although you're looking at a lot of confusing code, to associate copy with predefined styles all you have to do is place an @ sign, the name of the style, and a colon (:). Like this:

@Heading 1: blah blah blah blah.

@Body Copy: more blahs and senseless copy.

We're certain that you get the idea.

162 CHAPTER 7/ADVANCED STYLES

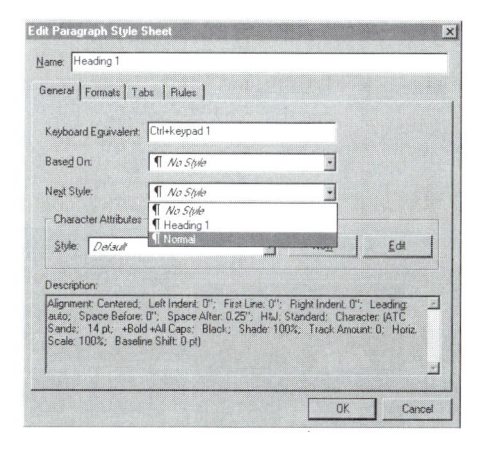

Whether you're writing classified ads or a technical publication, Next Style will save you a lot of time. Any primary heads, subheads, or other Inter-copy styles should always have a Next Style associated with them. Changing from one style to another is very common; rarely if ever would a headline or subhead have another head or subhead follow immediately afterward. Usually something like the First Paragraph style that we used in the last exercise comes next.

Next Style

If you are in a position where you must enter copy into QuarkXPress, styles can be used to speed up the task of changing from one format to another. A good example is the use of the Next Style feature. Let's say you had to enter a listing such as those found in a classified ad where each head was bold and centered and each paragraph of copy had to be justified in a serif typeface. The Next Style feature is found in the Edit Paragraph Style Sheet dialog box.

Using the Next Style function

1. Navigate to the **SF-Advanced QuarkXPress** folder and open the file named **Classifieds.QXD**. Activate the Style Sheets palette by pressing F11.

2. Click inside the first column with the Content tool. Control-Click/Right-Click the Heading 1 Style. Select Edit Heading 1 from the menu. Alternately, you could Command/Control click on the style name and choose Edit from the Style Sheets menu.

3. When the Edit Style dialog box appears, use the pop-up menu to change the Next Style field to Normal.

CHAPTER 7/ADVANCED STYLES 163

We meet many artists and designers who don't think that using techniques like the one we're showing here really saves them any time. We disagree. This small example of autoformatting copy as it's entered shows how productive and effective these kinds of style-based tricks are. If you counted the mouse clicks, dialog boxes, and OK buttons you had to go through to format rows of copy like this it would prove to be much more time-consuming. Again, the less time you spend on drudge work (like selecting each line one at a time and setting the font and paragraph attributes), the more time you'll have to create award-winning designs and layouts.

4. Click OK and Save to close out the dialog boxes and complete the change. Now edit the Normal style so that the Next Style field is set to Headline 1.

5. Select the Headline 1 style and type Item 1. Press Return (Macintosh) or Enter (Windows). The next style is automatically set to Normal. Type some nonsense copy (like jkhsadhj hjkashdkj hjdh h hkjsahdkjh jjh hj hdsajk). Make certain that you hit the Space bar a few times in between randomly pressing the keyboard. Press Return/Enter again. Type Item 2, Return, and some more nonsense. Get the idea?

6. Close the file without saving.

Widow Controls

Another function available from the Style Sheets>Formats (Paragraph Attributes) dialog box that can help with workflow efficiency is the ability to keep lines together, or to keep a specific style (such as a subheading) with the copy that follows.

In the last example, if one of the items came close to the bottom of a text box, the item title might end up at the bottom of one column, while the copy might be moved over to the next. This is both unsightly and makes the copy harder to read, making it more confusing to associate the copy with its title.

The more you work with and refine your styles, the easier life is — particularly if you're working on documents containing more than a few pages. Even jobs as small as a set of business cards can benefit from styles. Each name, title, address, and component could be styled, the cards set six or eight "up" (on one page), and font changes, sizes, spacing, and more could be accomplished with fewer mouse clicks.

If, however, you modify the Paragraph formats for the Heading 1 style, you can force each head to stay with the paragraph that follows. Simply put the cursor in the style and choose Edit Style (QuarkXPress shows the actual name of the style in the pop-up menu if you have the Content tool within the text). You can also simply press Shift-F11 to access the Edit Styles dialog box and pick the style from the list.

Click the Format tab; one of the choices is "Keep with Next Paragraph."

Turn this attribute on; the Heading 1 style will "stick" the following paragraph:

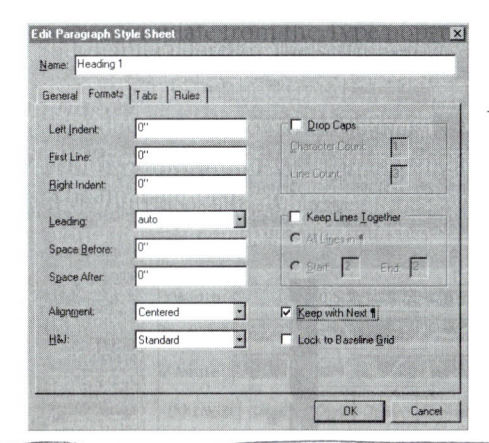

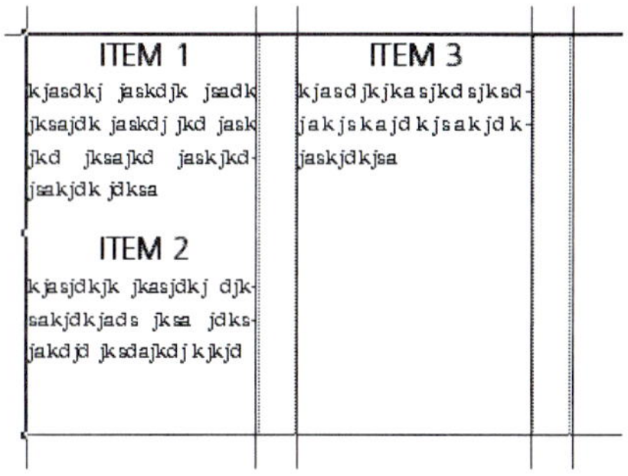

Another feature that keeps the lines you want together and avoids strange breaks is the Keep Lines together function, which is in the same dialog box. If you select All Lines in ¶, all the lines in that paragraph must fit in that column or text box. This is wonderful for headlines and bulleted copy; and also for body text. You can also specify a number of lines in each paragraph that must stay together. This number is usually two or three.

Reasonably, a style sheet may have the following parameters:

Body Text: Keep Start 2 and End 2 lines together.

First Paragraph: Keep Start 4 and End 2 lines together.

Subhead: Keep All Lines in ¶ together; Keep with Next ¶.

Creating Character Styles

QuarkXPress also allows you to create Character styles, which in certain cases can be very productive and save you time and mouse clicks. You could find many examples in technical publications, courseware, and other types of documents.

If you have used too many Keep with Next Paragraphs and Keep All Lines in ¶ together, you may create a situation where it is impossible to import the text. If you flow your text onto one page and all you see is a text overflow box, go to Body Text or Normal, and make certain that these elements are not checked.

CHAPTER 7/ADVANCED STYLES   165

Character styles aren't meant for simple text formatting such as applying italics to text; they're better suited for situations such as when a line of text contains characters with completely different attributes such as lists of items where the first words are in a different typeface altogether or contain a number of style changes such as size, weight, and color.

CATTLEYA SKINERII: First identified in shipments from Brazil in the late 19th century, the Cattleya is also known as the "Corsage" orchid because of its popularity among prom-goers. There are over 150 species of the spectacular wildflower. Since it's a favorite among hybridizers, you can find them from small to large in every color of the rainbow.

VANDA HYBRID: Another very popular species, the warm-growing orchid is found in the old-world tropics: places like Vietnam, Thailand, New Guinea, and Australia. It is often grown in slatted wooden baskets, which closely mimic its natural habit of growing in the "crotches of large trees" with its roots hanging in the air. This plant was grown in Florida.

In this example, the first words (the names of the orchids) are small caps, Minion Black, 10 pt., PMS 186. The body text is Myriad Roman, 9 pt. on 11 pt. of lead. To make the changes to the first line, you would have to press or click about six or seven times to select the face, change the point size, and so on. Character styles can automatically apply these font-specific attributes at the click of a button or a quick selection from the floating Styles palette. If you have to work on dozens of these paragraphs, you can see how it could save a great deal of time. Another consideration is if you decide to change the look of this style, you can do so globally throughout the document without changing them one at a time.

Creating and Applying Character Styles

1. Create a new document, letter-sized, with an automatic text box, 1 column, and no facing pages.

2. Click in the text box and press Command-E (Macintosh) or Control-E (Windows) to get a text file.

3. Navigate to the **SF-Advanced QuarkXPress** folder and select the **Orchid Copy.TXT** file. It will pour into the text box.

4. Create a new Paragraph style called "Descriptions" with 2 inch right and left indents and 9 pt. of space after. Select Justified for the alignment.

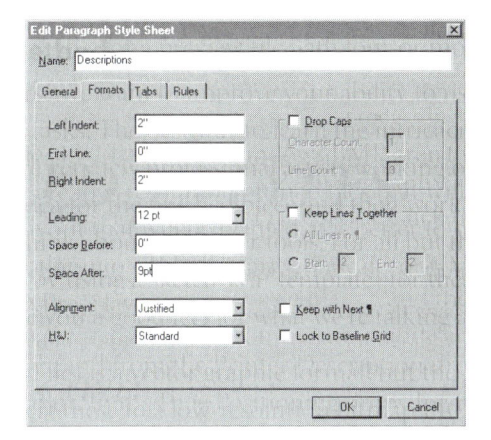

5. Apply the Style to the text. Examine the copy:

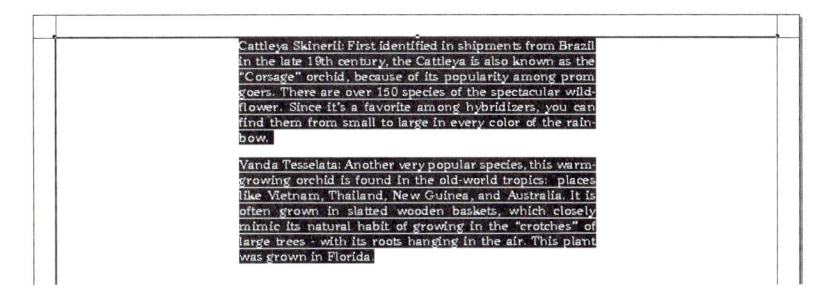

6. Create a Character style named Labels; format it as shown below.

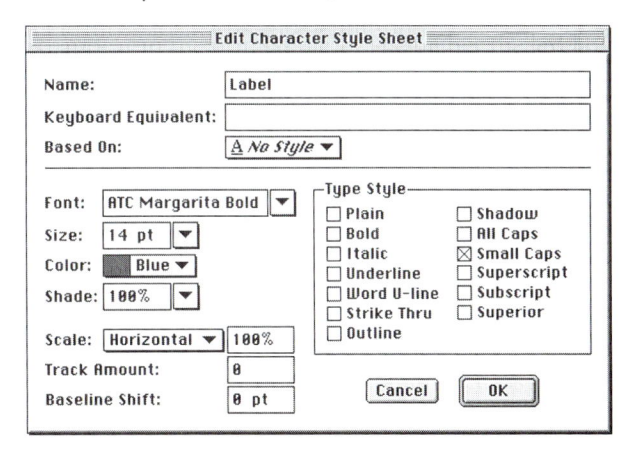

7. Apply it to the labels in each paragraph. Examine the results. <u>Try Control/Right-clicking the style's name in the bottom half of the floating Styles palette (press F11 if it's not showing) and editing the color or some other attribute</u>. When you click OK, the labels will change without affecting the rest of the paragraph.

This is a very productive technique and one that you should consider using if you are ever called upon to design and layout directories, lists, or other documents where a certain range of characters needs to be styled differently than the text in which it's contained.

Because we don't really want to include all those styles we imported earlier in this chapter in every new document we create, we're going to delete them from the default style sheet.

Deleting Styles from the Default Document

1. With all documents closed, open the Default Style Sheets menu (Shift-F11).

2. Shift-click on all the styles and click the Delete key. All styles except the Normal Paragraph style and the Normal Character style will be removed. Click Save.

Complete Project D: Staying Alive Newsletter

Chapter 8

Working With Long Documents

Chapter Objective:

To learn how to create, edit, and manage long documents. You will learn the importance of creating well-designed, highly-structured documents and publications. You will understand how to create superior designs with continuity and consistency. In Chapter 8 you will:

- Learn the importance of creating a document master that contains certain attributes for consistency in a long document.
- Create and use Templates.
- Learn how to achieve efficient management of long documents by using QuarkXPress's Book Creation feature.
- Create and edit chapters; and build a book.
- Making global style changes using the Master document.
- Understand Lists, types of Lists, and how they work.
- Generat a Table of Contents.
- Understand the Index palette.
- Exercise building the Index.

Projects to be Completed:

- Gym Ad
- Recipe Book
- Tropical Suites Brochure
- Staying Alive Newsletter
- **Automation Booklet**
- GASP Newsletter

While not all artists find themselves working on long documents, knowing how to build multi-page publications like booklets, annual reports, magazines, and similar projects will prove very valuable over the long run. In the real world, most artists and designers are called upon to create a wide variety of materials for their clients. Today it might be a simple display ad; tomorrow it might be a 200 page technical manual. You just never know. Long documents require a different approach and more advanced skills than single-page or two-sided projects.

Working with Long Documents

In this chapter we're going to explore the creation, editing, and management of long documents. As we mention in the sidebar, even if you're not working on long documents right now, the need will almost undoubtedly arise at some point in your design career.

The Importance of Consistency

One of the key issues we have stressed over the course of these lessons is that proper structure will enhance your creativity, not restrict it. The creation and management of multi-page documents is probably the best example of this that we can provide. Many awards are given to well-designed, highly-structured documents and publications.

All the structure tools that we have discussed focus on the minutiae of single-page document design — consistency in type, in elements, colors, and so forth. On a global scale, however, QuarkXPress allows you to create templates of styles and appearances for multi-page documents that can carry through groups of documents, and that is what we're going to focus on in this chapter.

Long documents lend themselves well to the use of templates. The importance of this "templatability" cannot be overestimated: designers know that each client has a unique style and deserves to have his or her work reflect that uniqueness. However, uniqueness applies to the client, and not necessarily to the materials they use. There should be some continuity that carries across the pieces of their design work: A logo should be used in a consistent manner throughout; color usage should employ the same themes; type styles should be consistent from piece to piece; and layout structures of individual projects should consistently reflect those preferences and styles.

All of the foregoing can be determined before you begin creating a group of related pieces by using templates of grids, style sheets, and master pages (such as we have done previously with single-page documents).

Starting with a Primary Master Document

In a perfect world, whenever you had to start a new multi-page project, you would begin with a tight "comprehensive" sketch and complete specifications (about type styles, editorial priorities, margins, contents, placement, image size, and many other attributes). In most cases, however, you start with a relatively good idea of what you want, and make changes to individual pages as the need arises.

The best way to start a long document is to create a "master" master — a document that contains certain attributes that aren't likely to change for a long publication.

Don't get the impression that templates are limited only to long documents; let's say your ad agency routinely places ads in a specific magazine. Since each publication publishes mechanical requirements relative to size, bleeds, and colors, and offers a variety of sizes, templates can be created for each ad size for each publication where your work is placed. If you need to create an ad of a certain size, these templates can be used, eliminating the need to set margins, guides, and other attributes.

If you use templates and locked files, you should open them and immediately save them under their new name. This way you can start using the regular Save command while you're working.

These attributes include margins, page size, trims, bleeds, and perhaps placement grids. This primary master would then be used whenever you need to add pages, chapters, or create another project with the same (or similar) requirements. This template would then be opened, saved under a new (and appropriate) name, and you would get to work modifying, importing, positioning, detailing the individual pages, running headers and footers, and other chapter, section, or publication-specific attributes.

There's nothing special about a template except that when you double-click it or open it from within QuarkXPress the original remains intact and the program opens a copy named "Untitled," exactly as if you had started a brand new document. If you make any changes, and then try to save or close the document, you'll be prompted for a name and location. It's sort of like using Save as to make a new version of an existing document.

There are basically two ways to create a template. The first is to lock or change the file at an operating system level so that it is a "read only" file. Read only means just that: you can open it, but you can't save it.

The second way to create a template file is directly from within QuarkXPress. We'll examine both methods. Creating the template from within QuarkXPress creates a specific type of file that you can recognize from its name or icon. In some environments, however, network managers may be empowered to keep templates in a special place on the server and lock them there; it depends on your situation. If you're working alone or in a small group, it's probably better to use the template function from within QuarkXPress.

Locking Documents from the System

The ability to lock a file from the operating system level dates back to the earliest days of computing. It's slightly different on Macintosh and Windows systems, but the concept is the same.

In the MacOS Finder, you can select your document and Get Info (Command-I, or File>Get Info). In the bottom of the window there are two check boxes: Locked and Stationery Pad. Checking either one will produce similar results, but they have different purposes: Both will prevent you from saving changes to the original document. You can perform a Save as from an application and overwrite the original. If the file is locked you can't do this. Template files created within QuarkXPress can be overwritten as well.

If you're working on a Windows system, the ".qxt" extension is automatically applied to the file name, even if you don't type it into the name. On a Macintosh, you have to include the extension, which you should do if you ever intend to move the file to a Windows system. Windows uses these three-letter extensions to identify a specific file type with the application that created it. If a file doesn't have an extension, it will display a generic icon and, if you double-click it, the system will ask you what application you want to use to open the file.

Here's the Info window from the Macintosh:

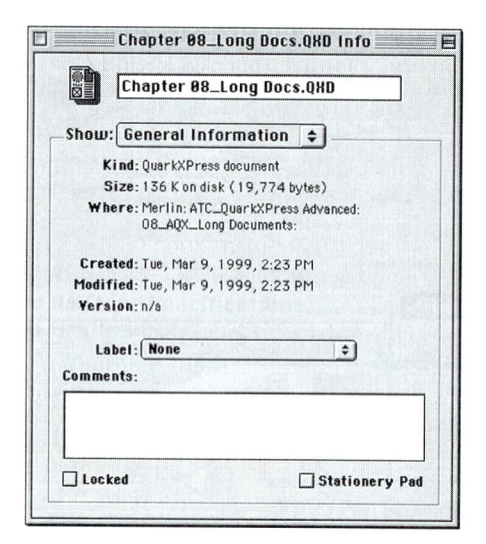

On a Windows system you would right-click the file's icon and select Properties. When the Properties dialog box appears, you would select Read Only: This will lock the file. There is no Stationery option on a Windows system.

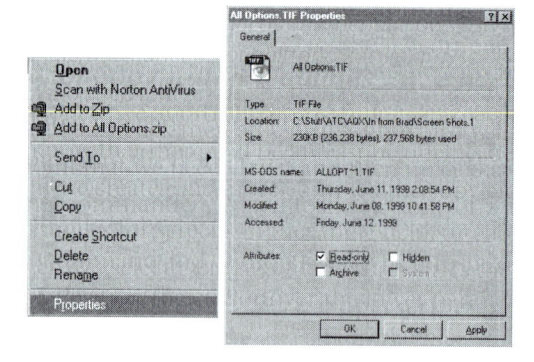

Although locking a file from the system level is simple, and will protect an original document, the recommended method of creating template files is from within the QuarkXPress application.

Creating and Using Templates

1. Open **Book Design.QXD** from within the **Book Building** folder, located inside the **SF-Advanced QuarkXPress** folder.

2. Choose File>Save as. Navigate to the your **Work in Progress** folder. Using the pop-up menu at the bottom of the dialog box, choose Template and save the file as "Book Design.QXT".

172 CHAPTER 8/WORKING WITH LONG DOCUMENTS

The reason we always name our files with 01, 02, 03, and so on (when we're building books or long publications) is so that they will sort properly when viewed by name. If you name a file Chapter1, Chapter2, and so on, once you get to Chapter 11, it appears in the list after Chapter 1. Putting the extra 0 in front of the first nine numbered files is called "padding," and will ensure that files will be listed in the proper order (01, 02, through 10, 11, and so on).

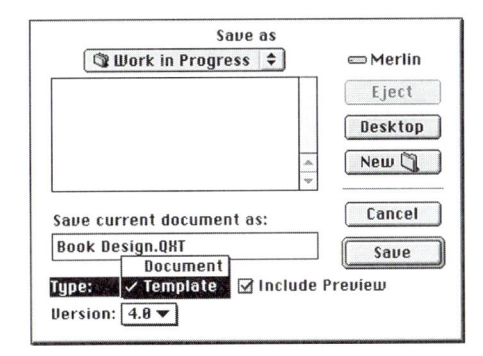

3. Close the document.

4. Now open the document by either double-clicking on its icon or by using the Open command. Notice that the file opens with the generic name "Document1" (actually, it might be named Document2, 3, or whatever, depending on how many documents you've opened or created in any session).

5. If your Document Layout palette isn't showing, activate it by pressing F10 (Macintosh) or F4 (Windows). If you examine the file, you will see that it has three different master pages: one for the first page of each chapter, a blank page, and the main publication pages.

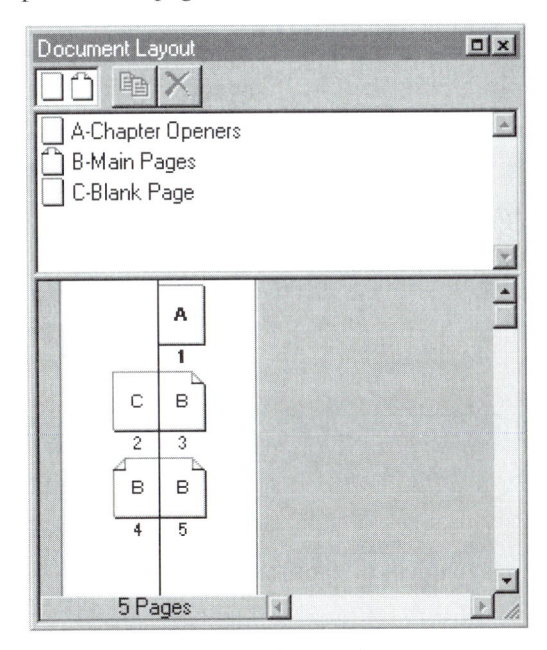

6. Choose File>Save and make certain that you're in your **Work in Progress** folder. Name the file "Fishing01 (Intro).QXD." Close the file. Open the Template file again (**Book Design.QXT**). Save this one as "Fishing02 (Lures).QXD". Close it, open the Template again and save it this time as "Fishing03 (Flats).QXD". Close the file. You now have three chapters for your new book, all with perfectly consistent settings and attributes.

CHAPTER 8/WORKING WITH LONG DOCUMENTS   173

We continue to stress that Macintosh users should consider adding a three letter extension to their files (like .qxd for document, .qxt for template files, and .qxb for books). Many of you are Macintosh users (an overwhelming majority, actually), and may revolt at the thought of using this naming convention. We have both Macintosh and Windows users working on the same projects, so this extension issue is important to us, as it is to anyone working in an environment where both operating systems are in use.

Books

When you're working on a long document, you're faced with two basic choices: either build an incredibly huge, single file that contains every component and maybe a few hundred pages, or build the document out of a collection of individual QuarkXPress files. Then you can link them all into a single, document known as a "Book." QuarkXPress supports Book creation, and this can result in much more efficient management of long documents. For one thing, if you create a single document, it starts to get unwieldy and slow. It also might (heaven forbid) become corrupt. If it's one, big document, you're in trouble. In a book, corruption will only affect a single chapter.

We're going to use the Book command to put together the three chapters you already created from the original `Book Design.QXT` template file. First let's make some minor changes to each of the three chapters.

Creating and Editing Chapters

1. Open the first file, `Fishing01 (Intro).QXD`. On the first page (the Chapter Opener), click the Content cursor in the text box and change the "99" to a "1". We used "99" as a positioning-only element, designed to be changed for each chapter.

2. Now change the chapter name to "Introduction". The first page of Chapter 1 is now complete.

3. Go to page 3. Click the Content tool in the text box and press Command/Control-E to Get Text. Navigate to the `SF-Advanced QuarkXPress>Book Building` folder and select the file named `Introduction.TXT`. Double-click the file. It will flow into place onto the pages of the chapter.

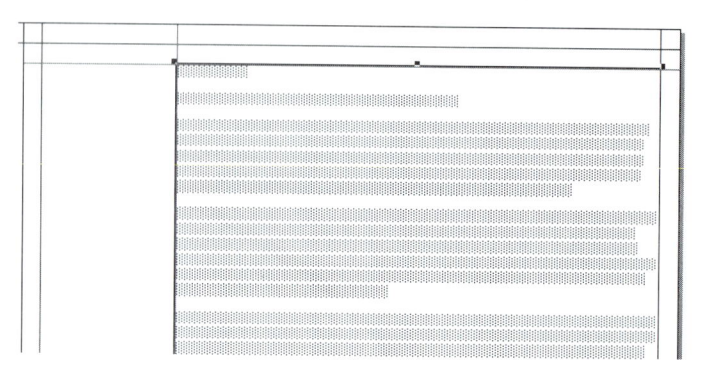

174 CHAPTER 8/WORKING WITH LONG DOCUMENTS

4. Delete any blank pages (you may need to turn on View>Show Invisibles or press Command/Control-I). Save the file. Open the second and third chapters, change the type on the first page, and import **Lures.TXT** into Chapter 2 and **Flats.TXT** into Chapter 3. When you're done, save them; you'll have three chapters with their text in place and their numbers and titles correctly modified.

While this is a simple example of throwing together the chapters of a book, in the real-world you would naturally have done a great deal more detailing, setting type attributes, styles sheets, and applying other global settings. Actually, using the Book command will allow you to make global changes to these items; so for now we'll just leave the text alone. This is a workflow issue. In some environments, the styles are set before the copy is written; in others, the editors just want to see raw copy set roughly into the space available, and want to leave the type formatting until later when they know how much space is available.

Building a Book

1. If you have any documents open, close them. From the File menu, choose New>Book. Name it "Backwater Fishing.QXB" and click Create to save it in your **Work in Progress** folder.

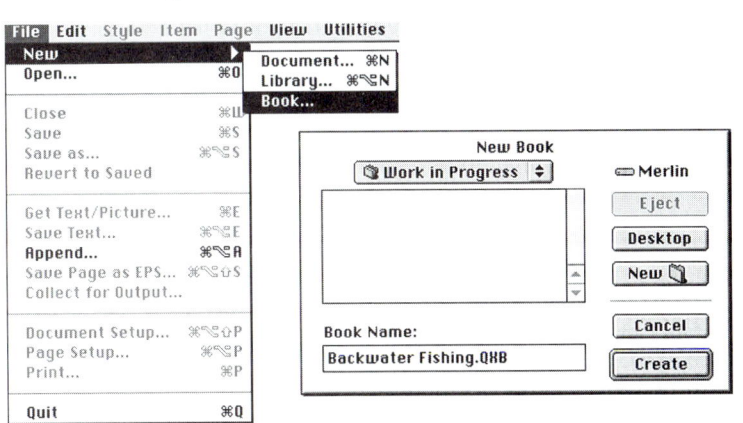

2. The Book dialog box will appear. You will be able to build and modify books composed of dozens of documents here. If you click the little Book icon in the upper left corner, you can add documents to the list. Look at it for a moment.

You should always view document management from the aspect of efficiency, security, and logic. For example, try to build entire chapters and avoid making one chapter in a book out of ten parts. On the other hand, you shouldn't put all your eggs (content) in one basket. The Book command is a much more secure method to work with in the event of a system failure or a corrupt file. Keep your chapters in individual files if possible.

CHAPTER 8/WORKING WITH LONG DOCUMENTS   175

3. Click it now. A dialog box will appear that lets you add chapters to the book. Add the first chapter, **Fishing01 (Intro).QXD** from your **Work in Progress** folder.

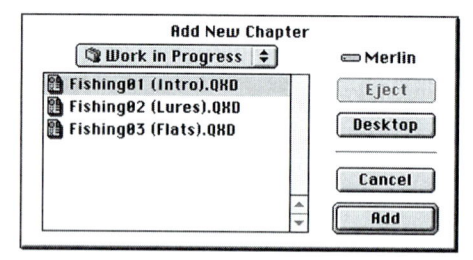

4. Add the next two chapters. Look at the dialog box; it shows the chapters in order, with the first chapter boldfaced and with an "M" alongside it in the left column. It also shows that the files are available under the Status column.

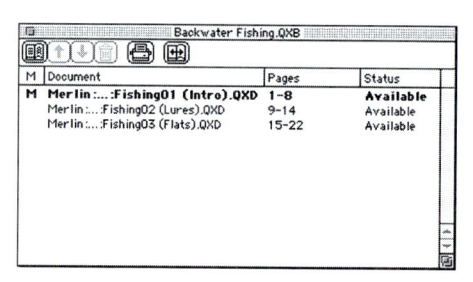

5. Double-click the first chapter. It will open, and the Status column will change to reflect your updates.

6. Close the documents and the book for now.

More about the Book Palette

In the first column, the Master Chapter is designated with an "M". The second column lists the individual chapters (QuarkXPress documents) that comprise the book.

The third column lists the pages in each chapter. Later, we'll discuss Sections, which can cause changes to occur in page numbers, their styles, or formats within a specific range of a document. Right now the command is simply numbering the pages from 1 through however many there are.

The last is the Status column. The Status column is your window into what is happening with your book. This is a key column, as more than one person can have a particular book open at the same time. You have five possibilities here: Available, Open, (UserName), Modified, and Missing. Available means that the chapter is just that: available for you to work on. Open means that you have the document open on

---

In these exercises, we're calling the components chapters, but you can link together any type of QuarkXPress document using these techniques — even ones with different page sizes and orientations. This can be very useful for building complex books and publications.

your computer. (UserName) means that person (UserName) has that chapter open on their computer (on a network). Modified and Missing are similar to "modified" and "missing" in the Picture Usage box: the chapter was modified or moved and needs to be updated.

To prevent someone else from working on your chapter, move the chapter from its location to a subfolder/subdirectory. The Book palette will show it as missing, and if any of your coworkers are working on the same book, their Book palettes will show the chapter as missing. Your palette should show it as missing, too. Return your edited, now-beautiful chapter to its original place with the book. Double-click on the name of the chapter and in the resulting Navigation box, relink to the revised chapter. The Book palette will update to show that the chapter has been modified. Reopen the chapter through the palette, and all will be right with the world (or at least the palette).

Master Documents

The first chapter in a book has the "M" in the column because it serves a special function. Once you add a document to the list, all subsequent documents that you add are "synchronized" to that chapter. That includes style sheets, line and rules, and H&J settings. Document setup, page sizes, margins, guides, the positioning of master page items, and other document-level elements aren't affected by changes to the master.

If you do make changes to the master, they're not automatically applied to existing chapters in the book unless you use the Synchronize command.

This provides the designer with a great deal of flexibility in globally changing a document's attributes without having to open each chapter and making changes one at a time. This master book document is sort of a style master for the entire book.

Making Global Style Changes Using the Master Document

1. From your **Work in Progress** folder, open **Backwater Fishing.QXB**.

2. There are three chapters in the book right now. With no chapters highlighted, click the Add Document icon (the book in the upper left corner of the dialog box). Navigate to the **SF-Advanced QuarkXPress** folder, open the **Book Building** folder, and add the original **Book Design.QXD** file to the list.

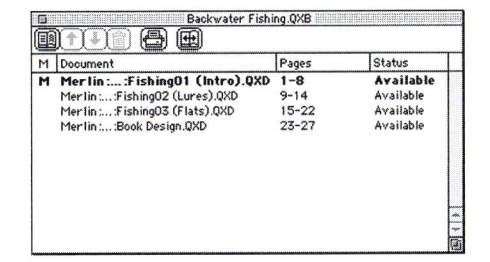

```
Backwater Fishing.QXB
M  Document                              Pages   Status
M  Merlin :...:Fishing01 (Intro).QXD     1-8     Available
   Merlin :...:Fishing02 (Lures).QXD     9-14    Available
   Merlin :...:Fishing03 (Flats).QXD     15-22   Available
   Merlin :...:Book Design.QXD           23-27   Available
```

3. Double-click its name in the list to open it.

4. Choose Edit>Style Sheets. Double-click the Paragraph style named "Chapter Titles".

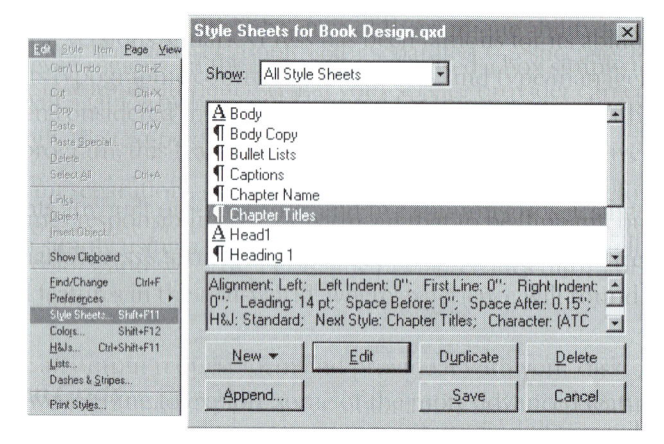

5. Click the Edit button under the Character Attributes section of the Edit Styles dialog box.

6. Change the horizontal scaling to 100%.

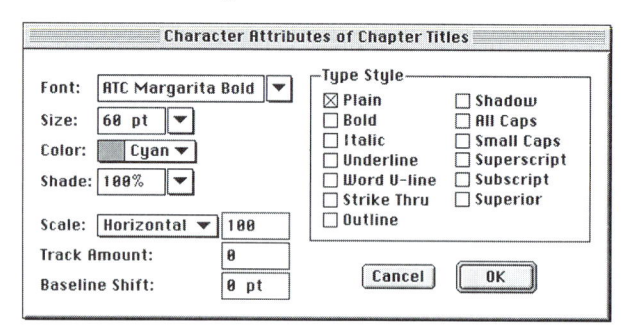

7. Using the same process, change the color of the Chapter Name style to 50% Cyan. Save the document to your **Work in Progress** folder when you're done.

8. If the new chapter did not appear at the top of the list, use the Up arrow in the Book Dialog box to move the Book Design chapter to the first position in the list. As you can see, even though the chapter is at the top of the list, it isn't the Master Document. This attribute remains attached to the first document you imported into the book.

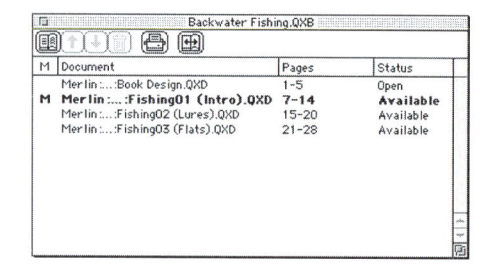

9. Click in the left column next to the **Book Design.QXD** file. It will now be the Master Document in the list.

10. On the right side of the icons in the Book dialog box is a book with two arrows spreading across the pages. This is the Synchronize command. Click it and a warning will appear. Click OK.

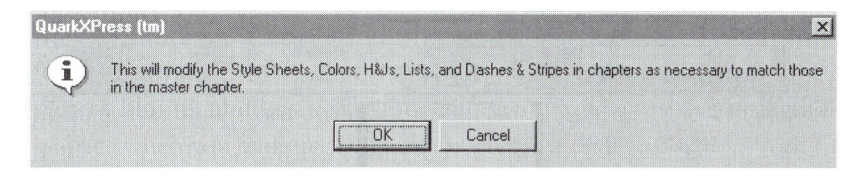

11. The styles that we modified in the master have now been applied to all the documents in the book. Open one of the chapters and check it out. When you're done, close the book (it will save automatically) and all the chapters that might be open, saving them as you go.

Sections and Page Numbering

If you've been paying close attention, you've noticed that you can see that when you added the **Book Design.QXD**, its pages were added to the list, and the book is now numbered from the first page of that chapter instead of the first chapter of the book, which is the **Fishing01 (Intro).QXD** document.

Since we're using the first document (**Book Design.QXD**) simply to use its styles, we don't want it counted in the total number of pages in the book. This is also true in many real-world instances where a book contains a front section or other materials that shouldn't enter into the book's numbering scheme. For an example, just look at this book; it has a front section containing a bunch of legal stuff, introductory materials, a walk-through, and a table of contents. Yet the actual chapters start at page number 1. This is accomplished using the Section command.

Any document can have various sections, and each section can have its own unique style of page numbers, and you can use the Section command to change or modify the numbering in part or all of a book.

Creating Section Breaks

1. Open the **Backwater Fishing.QXB** book file.

2. Double-click the second file in the list, **Fishing01 (Intro).QXD**. If the Document Layout palette isn't open, press F11/F4 to display it.

3. Click on the icon for the first page. Select the Page menu and choose the Section option.

4. The Section dialog box will appear. Click the Section Start box and change the Number field to 1.

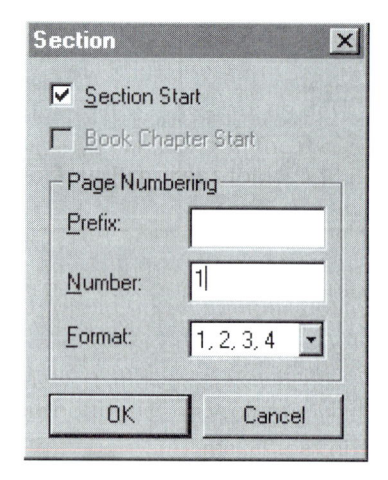

5. Click OK and save the file. Look at the Book dialog box; it's renumbered the pages for the whole book.

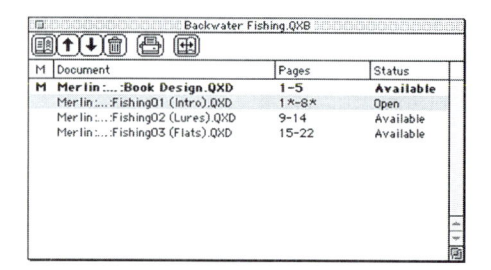

6. Close any open files and the book.

180 CHAPTER 8/WORKING WITH LONG DOCUMENTS

There are times when you're building a book and find that you need to rearrange chapters. This can easily be done in the Book dialog box. Just grab the chapter you want to move and either use the arrow keys to move it up or down or drag it to where you want it to be. When you're done, issue the Synchronize command again to fix the page numbers.

When you reference a specific page, there are two ways to do it: by paginated location or by absolute location. If you specify page 1 to print you will get the first page of the section in which your cursor is located. This is referencing by paginated location. On the other hand, if you precede the page number with a plus sign "+", you will get the absolute number, and the first page of the document will print.

Lists

Organizing information helps in two ways — you, as designer, can understand how your work is fitting together and can double-check it to make certain that you are still on track, and your audience can have an overview into the work you are creating. The best way to organize your structure is to create a list of the points that you deem relevant to your creation. Recognizing that, the lists feature is QuarkXPress's way of gathering user-specified information from throughout a document and bringing it all together in one place.

Types of Lists

A list can be a Table of Contents, an index of advertisers, a list of illustrations and so on. It all depends on what you choose to highlight for a list, how you indicate it, and the placement of the list within a document.

The Table of Contents could almost be the outline you created when you originally organized your book — usually it is your chapter names and section headings. As you can imagine, it is best to start with your Table of Contents and wait until you have finished your book before you generate your index. While you can generate your index at any time, if you have revisions that cause text reflow or repagination, you will have to regenerate the list. Depending upon how highly-formatted the list is, this could be an arduous chore.

How Lists Work

While you could just type in your Table of Contents, it is easier to simply designate one or two styles, usually your Chapter Head and Subhead styles. When it's time, you tell QuarkXPress to search for the text that is in those styles. You'll get a list based on those styles and the pages they are on.

Once you are reasonably satisfied with your book (it's preferable to do this once the book is finished, but it's OK to do it beforehand, depending on the amount of revisions you think you might have — you don't want to spend as much time revising your TOC as you do creating your document!), you can begin the Table of Contents.

A word or two about the Edit List box: Like the Book palette, it is designed for efficiency. On the left is a list of your available styles; on the right, your selections. Between them are the Add and Remove buttons. In the Styles in List box you have the name of your selection, what level the style will fit into the hierarchy of the list, how you want the pagination to show, and the format of the text in the list itself.

Setting up a Table of Contents

1. Open the file **Backwater Chapter01.QXD** from within the **Making Lists** folder in your **SF-Advanced QuarkXPress** folder. Save it to your **Work in Progress** folder as "TOC Practice.QXD".

Chapter 8/Working with Long Documents 181

You can delete a Section break by selecting the page, choosing Page>Section, and unchecking the Section Start box.

When you use set the page numbers on the Master Page, make certain that you only use the automatic page number character (Command-2, -3, or -4). You do not have to type in any preface with the automatic page number character; these settings can be specified in the Section dialog box, which will put that into place.

2. The first thing that must be done is to give your Table of Contents elements styles of their own. We're going to create three new styles: TOC-Chapter, TOC-H1, and TOC-H2 as follows:

    TOC-Chapter   ATC Sands, 12 pt. on 14 pt. leading, 7 pt. Space After. Keep All Lines in Paragraph Together. Right Tab at 6.208 inches with a fill of [space] and [period (.)].

    TOC-H1   Based on TOC-Chapter. Left indent 0.167 inch.

    TOC-H2   Based on TOC-Chapter. Left indent 0.333 inch.

3. Select Edit>Lists and click New.

4. In the Name box, assign "TOC" as the name for the list.

5. From the available styles, select Chapter Names, then click on Add (alternately, you can double-click on the name of the style).

6. Add Heading 1 and Heading 2. You may select additional styles up to a maximum of 32 style sheets (if you're using more than four in any given list, the list may become somewhat cumbersome).

7. Click on the Chapter Name entry and select the following from the drop-down menus: Level- 1, Numbering- Text…Page #, Format As- TOC-Chapter.

8. Select the Heading 1 entry and assign it: Level- 2, Numbering- Text…Page #, Format As- TOC-H1.

9. Select the Heading 2 entry and assign it: Level- 3, Numbering- Text, Format As- TOC-H2.

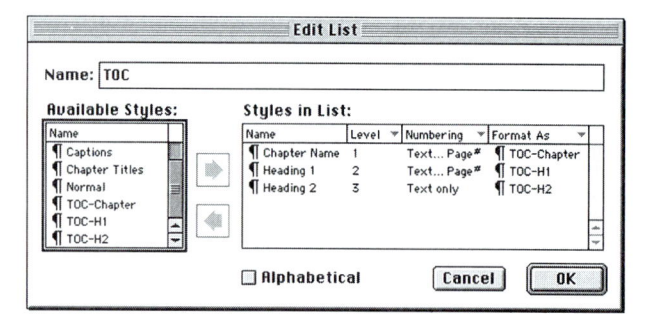

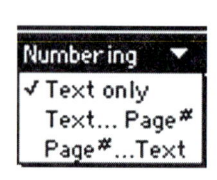

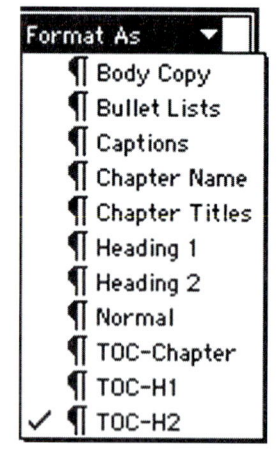

182 CHAPTER 8/WORKING WITH LONG DOCUMENTS

10. If you want the list to be alphabetical, click on the Alphabetical box; this could reasonably be used for a list of advertisers in a publication.

11. Click OK and save the list. Leave the document open for the next exercise.

Generating the Table of Contents

Now that you have specified the parameters for QuarkXPress, you will need to generate the list that will become the Table of Contents.

1. Apply the Chapter Name style to the name of the chapter (the second line on the chapter title page) in the open document.

2. With the **TOC Practice.QXD** document open, select View>Show Lists.

3. In the Lists palette, select Current Document as the Show List For: option.

4. In the List Name box, select TOC if it doesn't come up automatically. You'll see a thumbnail of your Table of Contents in outline form.

5. Drag a B-Main Pages master page before the A-Chapter master page. Position the Content tool in the text box.

6. Click on the Build button. This will flow the text in the list into the box. The styles you set in the Format As column are automatically applied.

7. Save and close the file.

Note: The list will flow into whatever text box is selected; therefore it is critical that the desired box is selected, otherwise the TOC will disappear into a text box buried somewhere in the document, and you will probably waste considerable time attempting to find it.

When you "Build" your list, QuarkXPress searches through your document to see if a list with that name has already been generated. If it finds a list with the same name, you are alerted to it, and you can either click Insert to create a new list wherever your insertion point is located or Replace to replace the text. However, if you have tweaked the list for proper formatting or content, QuarkXPress will **not** maintain those changes; you will have to repeat tweaking the text to your desired format. So it's best to try to save list-generating as one of the last things that you do.

Now that you've seen how to generate a list for a single chapter, let's create a list for an entire book.

Generating a TOC for a Book

1. Open the file **Final Formatted Book.QXB** from within the **Making Lists** folder in your **SF-Advanced QuarkXPress** folder.

2. Double-click on the Master Chapter (**Backwater Chapter01.QXD**) and apply the Chapter Name style to the second line of the Chapter Opener page, as you did before. Leave the chapter open. Open Chapters 2 and 3, and apply the Chapter Name style, then save and close them. (This is something that happens often; designers will experiment with major headings and forget to assign the style to them after they work with them. The only time this has serious repercussions is when you use the styles to build a list.)

3. From Edit>Style Sheets, append the three TOC styles from **TOC Practice.QXD** in your **Work in Progress** folder to the book.

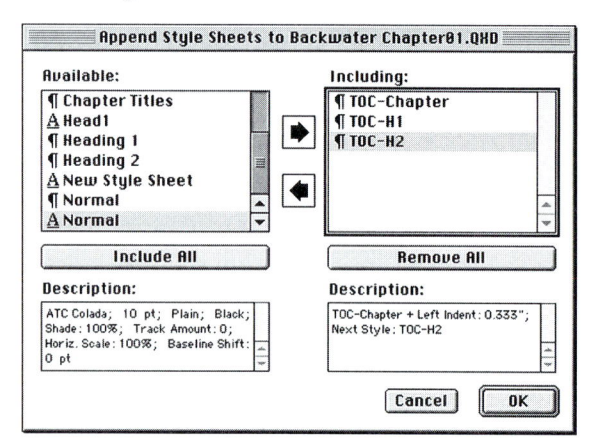

4. From Edit>Lists, create a new list and name it TOC. Follow the same steps as you did in the Setting Up a Table of Contents exercise.

184 CHAPTER 8/WORKING WITH LONG DOCUMENTS

5. Synchronize the book.

6. Select View>Show Lists.

7. In the Lists palette, select **Final Formatted Book.QXB** as the Show List For: option.

8. In the List Name box, select TOC if it doesn't come up automatically. Click Update to preview the Table of Contents.

9. Drag a B-Main Pages master page before the A-Chapter master page. Position the Content tool in the text box.

10. Click on the Build button. This will flow the text in the list into the box. The styles you set in the Format As column are automatically applied.

11. Close and save the file as "Backwater with TOC.QXD" to your **Work in Progress** folder. Close **Final Formatted Book.QXB** and the Lists palette.

Index Creation Prep

To create an index, you must have the Index XTension loaded. To ensure that it is loaded, use XTensions Manager, which is located under the Utilities menu. If it is not loaded, click in the Enable column in front of Index, then quit QuarkXPress. When you reopen QuarkXPress, the XTension will be active.

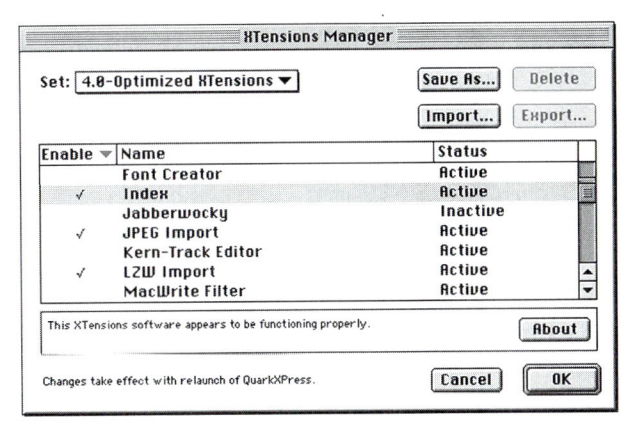

There are two different styles of indexing, and you need to decide which one to use before you start: Run-in or Nested. When you have a Nested index, the entries are listed alphabetically with up to four different levels of reference, all separated by line breaks (similar to an outline). When you have a Run-in index, the references are not separated by breaks, and "run-in" together as one paragraph.

One warning: As you tag entries in your text for the Index, the markers are only visible while the Index palette is open.

It is important to be aware of how the marker is displayed. When you select a range of text as an index entry, a bracket appears around it. When you click into the text and insert the marker, a small box appears at the end of the word. It's important to note this to avoid mistaking either marker as typographical errors.

The Index Palette

When you open the Index palette (Utilities>Build Index), you have several options:

The top part is the Entry area, where you specify the options for the Index Entry. The Text field is where you type in the actual text you want QuarkXPress to find. The Sort As field gives you the option to revise the location of the entry; that is, if you want to include numbers (for instance, the 2nd floor in a house-building manual), you can use numerals as the index entry and spell out the number in the Sort field (Second floor). This will sort your term in the alphabetical order of the Sort Entry (in the S's of your Index). The Level pop-up menu lets you specify which level the entry will be in. First Level Entries show up in the lower portion of the palette. For Second, Third, and Fourth Level Entries you must specify which First Level Entry it goes under. You do that by clicking in the left column next to the First Level Entry in the palette.

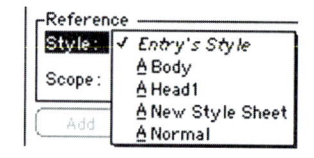

The middle area of the palette is the Reference area; this is where you can specify the entry's type style, scope, and cross-references. The Style is available through the Style pop-up menu; it picks up from the style sheets that already exist in your document.

186 CHAPTER 8/WORKING WITH LONG DOCUMENTS

The Scope pop-up menu allows you to specify the range of the text covered by the entry (if your indexed subject spreads over more than one page) and any cross-references. The options here are Selection start, which only lists the starting page number of the reference; Selection text, which surrounds your text with index brackets; To Style, which lets you specify from the opening bracket of your marker to the first appearance of a particular style sheet, specified in a sub-pop-up menu; To End Of, which carries to either the end of the story or the document; Suppress Page #, which does not list page numbers (for instance, you index "Referee" as the reference term, but want specific instances of "Umpire", "Official", and "Judge" listed with page numbers); X-Ref, which is the cross-reference, giving you the option of redirecting your reader to a different entry in the index (for instance, you index "Referee" and want the reader to "See Also" and "Umpire", which lists references to famous umpires).

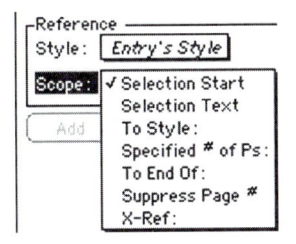

Beneath the Reference area are the specifics for each entry. The Add button adds your selection to the list of entries at the bottom of the palette. The Find Next button goes to the next index marker in your text. The Delete button deletes the highlighted entry; the Edit button lets you edit the entry.

The Entries area of the palette shows you the entries you have specified. To the left of your Index Entry there are several symbols that can appear. An arrow will specify which Main Entry a sublevel will go under. A triangle will flip open the entry to show you the page numbers and any specified cross-references. The Occurrences column shows you the number of times the particular entry shows up in the document.

Picking your Index:

1. Open **Backwater Fishing.QXB** from your **Work in Progress** folder and then open **Fishing02.QXD**.

2. Open the Index palette (View>Show Index).

3. Beginning with the first page of text, go through the document and highlight each phrase that you think is key to the document (such as "Lure"); as each highlighted phrase shows up in the Index palette, click on Add. If you use QuarkXPress's Find function, it will take you through the entire document one word at a time. You can then determine whether or not you want that instance of the word included in the index.

4. Select the First Level from the Level pop-up menu.

5. Choose an option from the Scope menu. For the word "lure" choose the To End of: Story option.

6. With the Index palette open, find "bait" and add it as a First Level index item.

    Now we're going to build Second Level index items.

7. Click in the arrow column next to "bait". That establishes "bait" as the main level for the head.

8. Using Find, search for all instances of the words "shrimp" and "baitfish". Add them as Second Level index items, with a scope of "Selection Text".

9. Place the arrow next to "lures" and add "plug", "jig", and "topwater" as Second Level entries. Add "Rat-Lure" as a Third Level entry below "topwater".

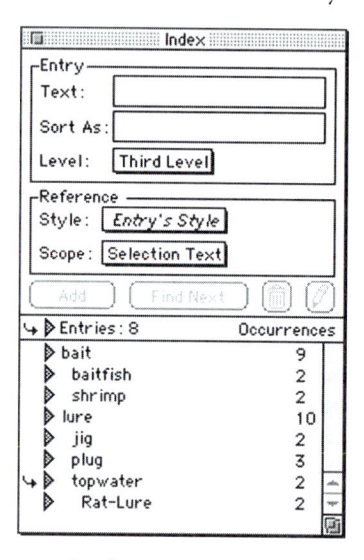

10. Leave the document open for the next exercise.

Cross-references are important and are created in a manner similar to a regular Index Entry. From our existing list, let's create one.

188 CHAPTER 8/WORKING WITH LONG DOCUMENTS

Cross-reference from Existing Index Entries:

1. Select a lure from the Entries list, and be certain that it is set to the first level.
2. Choose X-Ref from the Scope menu.
3. Leave the style at Entry's Style and select See also from the drop-down menu. Type in the word "bait".
4. Click Add.

New Cross-reference Entries

1. Find an instance of the word "artificial" in the text of the document.
2. Set the Sort As and Level controls.
3. Choose X-Ref from the Scope menu.
4. Select "See" and type "lure" into the Cross-reference field.
5. Click Add.

Establishing Index Preferences

Once you have gone through your text and specified your entries, you will have to generate (build) the index itself. The Index Preferences dialog box is your first stop.

1. Choose Edit>Preferences>Index.

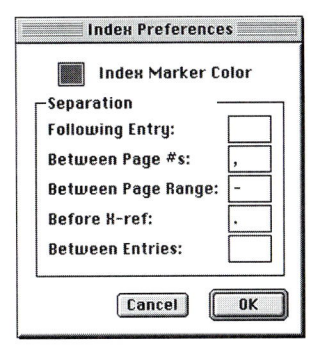

2. Enter the punctuation you want to use in the following areas:

    a. Following Entry, which is what comes immediately after the entry, but before the page numbers. Usually, it is a colon and a space.

    b. Between Page #'s, which is usually a comma and a space.

c. Between Page Range, which is usually an en dash.

   d. Before X-Ref, which is usually a period and a space.

   e. Between Entries is usually a semicolon for Run-in Indices. For Nested Indices, use the Between Entries character as the ending punctuation, usually a period.

3. Click OK.

Building the Index

From here, you now generate the Index. As with the TOC, we must first build style sheets for our index levels. We have three levels, so we'll need three style sheets.

1. Build the following style sheets:

   Index-1   ATC Colada, 10 pt. with 12 pt. leading and 0.56 inch space after.

   Index-2   Based on Index-1. Left Indent 0.167 inch.

   Index-3   Based on Index-1. Left Indent 0.333 inch.

2. Duplicate the master page B-Main Pages. From Item>Modify>Text, make each text box 2 columns with a 0.25 inch Gutter Width. Name the master page "D-Index". Because the index needs to flow from text box to text box across potentially dozens of pages, you need to specify a master page with an automatic text box.

3. Choose Utilities>Build Index.

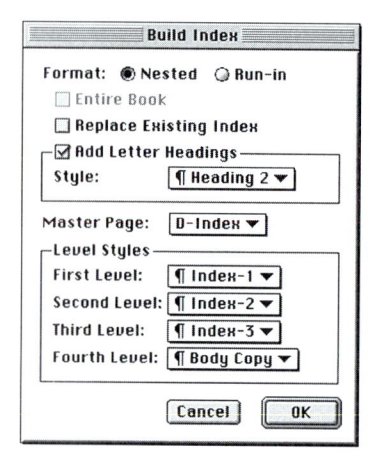

4. Choose Nested. This will create an outline form for the index. Choosing Run-in would run each sub-item into a single paragraph-like entry.

5. Leave Entire Book unchecked. We've only indexed the current document. If there is only a single document the option is grayed out.

6. Click on Add Letter Headings to specify Letter headings for each letter in the alphabet. Specify Heading 2 as the style to use.

7. Choose D-Index as the master page to base the layout of the Index.

8. Specify the style sheets for each of the levels.

9. Click OK.

QuarkXPress will now generate the Index and flow it into new pages at the end of the document, based on the master page set in step 5.

Tip: If you revise your text and have to re-index your document, you have a choice of either replacing the existing Index or creating a new one. This is an option in the Build Index box. Unchecking it will make a new index; checking it will make QuarkXPress replace the existing one. Just make certain that you get rid of the old one before you send your book on its way.

Complete Project E: Automation Booklet

Notes:

Chapter 9

Managing Output

Chapter Objective:

To learn about PostScript color output and how QuarkXPress's output tools will save you time, money, and headaches. You will become familiar with the workflow issues that are critical for proper output. You will also review Print dialog boxes. In Chapter 9 you will:

- Learn how to work with Print styles.
- Learn how to create, edit, duplicate, delete, and export Print styles.
- Learn about Separations and exercise Separated proofs.
- Learn about Tiling.
- Learn about halftoning.
- Learn how to use the PPD Manager.
- Understand how PostScript relates to QuarkXPress.
- Learn how to create an Output Request Form for your outside service provider.
- Learn about Trapping in QuarkXPress.
- Learn about Digital Imposition.
- Learn output tips and build an understanding of contract proofing.

Projects to be Completed:

- Gym Ad
- Recipe Book
- Tropical Suites Brochure
- Staying Alive Newsletter
- Automation Booklet
- GASP Newsletter

In this final chapter we're going to explore some of QuarkXPress's more advanced features relative to outputting (printing) your job. Since we don't know whether or not you have access to a high-resolution output device, we wrote this chapter with the goal of providing you with information about some of these features if and when you do have access to high-resolution output.

Managing Output

Most documents designed in QuarkXPress will eventually be output to a PostScript printer or imagesetter. A thorough understanding of PostScript color output and the output tools included in QuarkXPress will save you time, money, and headaches. In this chapter we will concern ourselves with the workflow issues to help your jobs run smoothly and give you control over the final quality of your printed pages.

Workflow Issues for Printing

There are a wide variety of settings available to you when you print one of your QuarkXPress documents. What settings are appropriate at a specific time during the life of a document can change dramatically; this is a workflow issue.

At the Design stage it may be appropriate to output black-and-white laser prints for establishing the publication's grid. Comps for presentation may be appropriately produced on a color printer, even if they contain only FPO art and greeking for text.

During Composition you might be outputting all the pages to a regular PostScript laser printer available on your office network or connected directly to your system. A number of copies will usually be generated during the production process, particularly whether the documents are book length or one page ads. It's necessary to plan to generate several proofs at this stage and to have the printed documents read by a proofreader.

Checking Color and color consistency is an important part of the design and production process. Since the per page cost of outputting quality color pages (even on a relatively inexpensive color printer) can be quite high, designers often wait until they're nearly finished with their work before using these devices. Other times, you might want to output a single page or range of pages in color to check things such as color matching and consistency in the layout and color selections.

Proofing for Clients may require that PDF files be sent so that the client can view them on-screen and attach comments, or print them to their own printer. This is especially useful in quick turnaround situations. Of course, clients may also be provided black-and-white or color paper proofs.

Proofing for the GASP demands that they receive *exactly* what will be output. If the document is to be color-separated, separated proofs should be sent. If the document is too large to fit on your printer's paper, it will be necessary to tile the output so that the service provider is able to view the document at actual size and not wonder whether or not you really want the image reduced to fit on an 8½ × 11 inch page.

Printing to High Resolution requires that still another set of parameters be considered, including the actual resolution of the document and how that relates to the line screen of the images included. Trapping and imposition issues are addressed at this stage, as well.

The default Print style can be edited but not deleted. You can create Default styles for the application, but not for individual documents. This means that the default Print style will remain the same regardless of the document that you have opened.

Print Dialog Boxes – a Review

Most likely, you're already familiar with the Print commands in QuarkXPress; after all, this is an advanced course. However, we sometimes do our work so mechanically that we forget about the details. In this section we're going to briefly review the dialog boxes found in the Print menu.

When you first issue the command to print a document (File>Print) or Command-P (Macintosh) or Control-P (Windows), the Print dialog box appears.

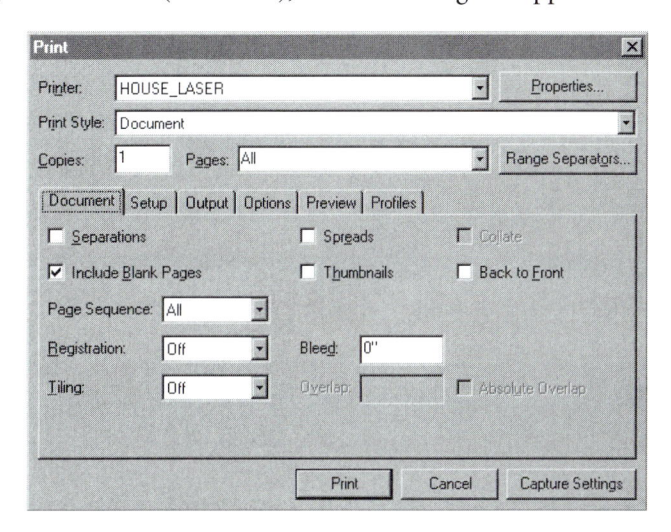

The Print dialog box displays the settings relative to the first "tab" (of which there are six), or the Document settings. These include the order in which the pages will print, whether to print "spreads" (for example, two facing 8½ × 11 pages printed to an 11 × 17 device).

The Setup tab displays yet another set of attributes relative to the page setup, including factors such as which printer the document is going to be sent to, enlargement or reduction factors, and the orientation of the page.

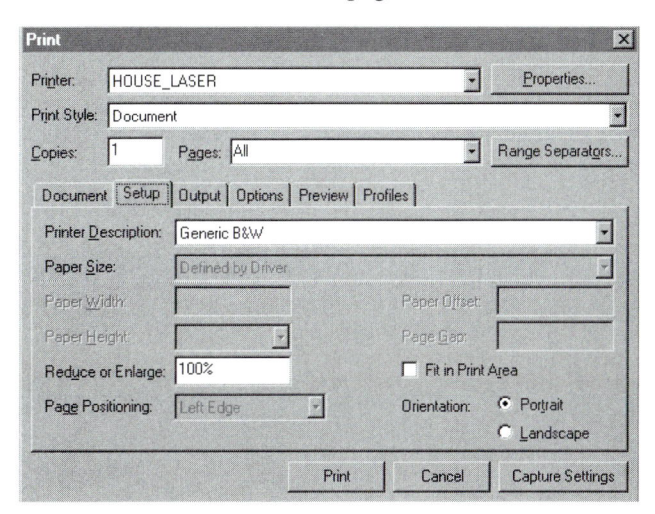

The Output tab contains information and data fields that tell the program about issues such as resolution, which colors are to print, halftoning information, the number of copies required, and which printer will be used (assuming there is more than one on the network).

Selecting Absolute Overlap will print your document off-center on the final tiled output. To ensure that your document is centered, leave this setting unchecked.

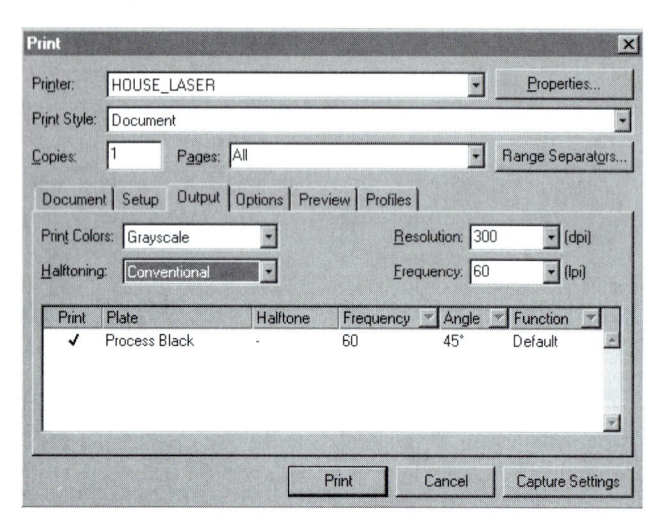

The Options tab contains a number of features often used by service providers. Pages may be flipped horizontally, vertically, or both; the page may be imaged as either positive or negative. Black in EPS files may be defined to overprint, even if it wasn't originally defined that way in the artwork. Here, too, are controls for picture output and instructions for use with OPI workflows.

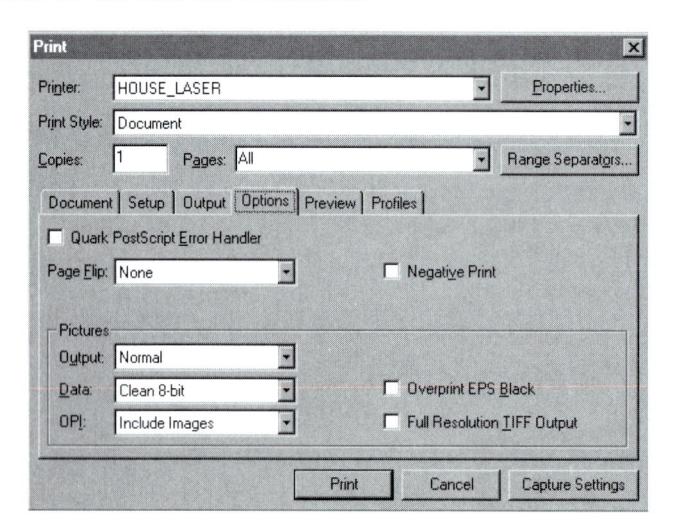

196 CHAPTER 9/MANAGING OUTPUT

Paper, ink, printing plates, and types of printing presses used all play a role in determining the quality of the final printed piece. Newsprint is coarse and absorbent. Dots printed on newsprint spread out as the ink is absorbed into the paper; this is called dot gain. When the lpi is high, dot gain can cause the space between dots to fill with ink and the image will lose its detail. This is why it is important to match the quality of the paper to the line screen being printed.

The Preview tab provides a view of the document in relation to the available print area or paper orientation and presents information about paper size.

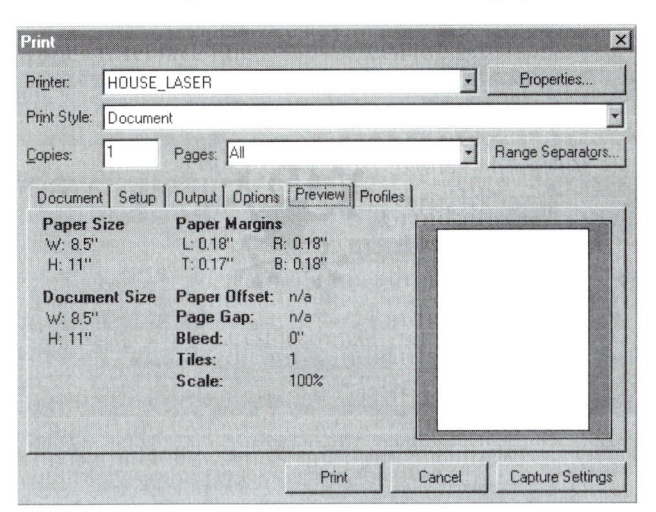

The last of the tabs in the Print dialog box controls Profiles. Profiles are descriptions of output devices and how they define specific ranges of tones. This ensures that what you see on your monitor will (roughly) match what you can expect from high-resolution output.

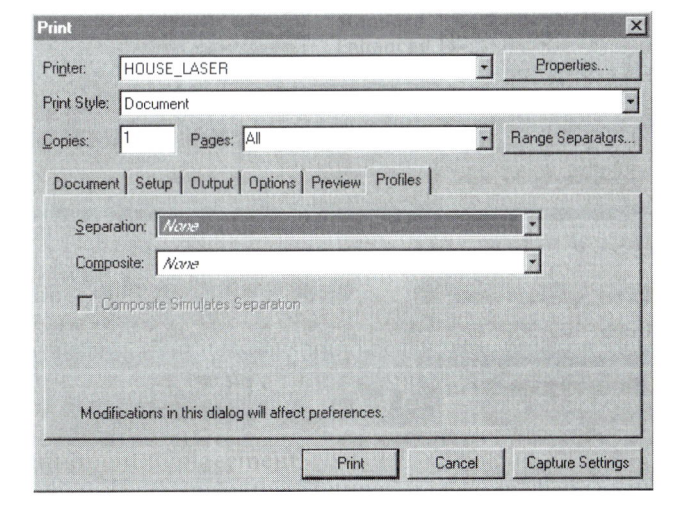

You can save printer settings for your documents using QuarkXPress's Capture Settings feature. By using the Capture Settings button you will save time and avoid selecting your document's printer settings a second time if you close the Print dialog box. The Capture Settings button is found in the lower, right side of the Print dialog box (Windows), or the lower center (Macintosh). This button allows you to close the Print dialog box without losing the printer settings that you have selected.

CHAPTER 9/MANAGING OUTPUT   197

PostScript itself is unable to reproduce certain screen angles and will print screen angles and frequencies as close as possible to those that you have selected.

Windows users must set up their printer to print to file by using the Printers control panel. You can have more than one printer setup for each PPD; this allows you to have one set to print directly to your device and another set to print a file. Refer to your Windows documentation for instructions on setting up printers.

Working with Print Styles

As you have seen, a normal workflow, especially in organizations with high-resolution output devices, will have several different print settings that can be regarded as "standard" because of the variety of output devices being used. Even a studio having only a laser printer may regularly use a standard output for simple pages, tiled output, and PDF. The Print Styles dialog box allows the definition of up to 1,000 print styles, which are always created for the application; they are not document-specific.

QuarkXPress allows you to create and manage multiple custom print styles through Edit>Print Styles. Print styles make printing to different output devices and under different conditions much more effective. Print styles assign settings to printers in the same way in which you use style sheets to format type. The Print Styles menu is located on the Print dialog box. If a PostScript printer is not selected under the printer setting, the Print Styles menu will appear gray, and you will not be able to select any print styles until you select a PostScript printer.

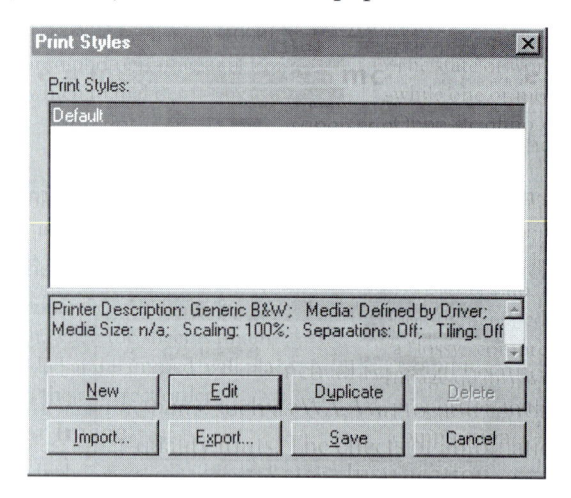

From this dialog box you can create new Print styles, delete existing styles, edit styles that you've already defined, import, or export Print styles to a folder for general use.

There are eight buttons along the bottom of the Print Styles dialog box. These buttons are used to create and edit Print styles.

Creating a New Print Style

Launch the Edit Print Styles dialog box from Edit>Print Styles, then click the New button. Name the style, then assign the parameters using the Document, Setup, Output, and Options dialog boxes. These are the same tabbed dialog boxes that appear in the Print Styles dialog box.

198 CHAPTER 9/MANAGING OUTPUT

Create a New Print Style

We're going to create a Print style for a color proofing device.

1. Launch Print Styles be selecting Edit>Print Styles. Click the New button.

2. Name the new Print style "Color 1" and make certain that the Include Blank Pages box is not checked.

3. Select the Setup tab, and from the Printer Description drop-down menu, choose Generic Color. In the Page Positioning drop-down menu, select Center.

4. Select the Output tab. Print Colors as Composite CMYK, Halftoning as Printer, and Resolution 300 (dpi).

5. Select the Options tab and leave everything standard except Overprint EPS Black, which should be checked.

6. Click OK to save the Print style and click Save to save and close the menu.

Editing a Print Style

You can edit a print style by highlighting its name in the Print Styles list and clicking the Edit button. This displays the Edit Print Style dialog box where you will select or change the settings for a Print style. Within the Edit Print Style dialog box you can modify an existing Print style's name and definition.

Duplicating a Print Style

You can create a copy of a Print style by highlighting its name in the Print Styles list and clicking the Duplicate button; the Edit Print Style dialog box will automatically open to allow you to edit and rename the copied style. This is especially useful for creating several styles that have many settings in common.

Deleting a Print Style

Selecting a style from the list and selecting this option will delete the style.

Exporting a Print Style

You can save Print styles as files that can be used by other QuarkXPress users. This allows you to define a printer setup for another QuarkXPress user so that they can supply you with PostScript files that you can print on your output device. This is also a quick way to set up several machines in the same office that use the same printer. (You will need to provide another user with your PostScript Printer Description [PPD] before they can create a PostScript file that will print correctly on your output device.)

To export a Print style, highlight its name and click the Export button. A dialog box will appear and prompt you to name and select a location to save the new file.

Depending on the size of the file documents that you're proofing, it may be necessary to turn Tiling on. If your printer supports at least 9 inch × 12 inch sheets of paper, you can proof a letter-sized document with crop marks. If not, then you need to check Tiling for letter-sized separated documents.

Importing a Print Style

You can import Print styles provided by other QuarkXPress users. This allows you to print PostScript files (provided you have the appropriate PPD) for output on someone else's PostScript printer without having to guess at the setup for their PostScript device.

You import styles by clicking the Import button in the Print Styles dialog box. The Import dialog box appears, prompting you to select a file for import.

The final two buttons are the Save and Cancel buttons. Clicking the Save button saves changes made to any Print styles and closes the Print Styles dialog box. Cancel closes the Print Styles dialog box, discarding any changes you have made to the Print styles it contains.

Separations

The design you create and how it will print determines how a service provider should separate your film. If you have designed a job with full color photographs or continuous tone artwork you will need Cyan, Magenta, Yellow, and Black (CMYK) separations. If you choose specific spot colors, based on a color matching system, you need spot separations. Pantone colors are the most widely used color matching system today. You need to discuss your project with your printer before you get separations. Process colors (CMYK) are more expensive than spot colors (because you're printing four inks) and the two in combination can be very expensive. Communicate first and save money.

Creating Separated Proofs

1. Launch Print Styles through Edit>Print Styles. Click the Default printer, then click the Duplicate button.

2. Name the new Print style "Separated Proof".

3. Make certain that the Include Blank Pages box is unchecked. Select Separations, and choose Centered from the Registration drop-down menu. Leave Tiling Off.

4. Under the Output tab, set the Resolution to the resolution of your printer. (300 and 600 dpi is available from the drop-down menu. Any other number may be typed in.)

5. Set the Frequency as appropriate to the printer. If your printer is 600 dpi or below, the default setting of 60 lpi is adequate.

6. Click OK to save the Print style and click Save to save and close the menu.

Tiling

You can print large documents to a printer with a smaller page size by tiling your output. This is an inexpensive way to produce printed proofs of large-format work. To print large documents in tiled layouts you must activate QuarkXPress's Page Tiling feature. The Document tab of the Print dialog box includes the settings for Tiling.

The Tiling drop-down menu provides three settings to control Tiling: off, manual, and automatic. Normally, Tiling will be set to Off.

If the document must be tiled because it is larger than the print area of the printer's media, the Tiling should be set to Automatic. QuarkXPress will then place marks on the page to assist in properly aligning the tiled document. The standard overlap is three inches, but that may be overridden, if desired. QuarkXPress will determine the number of tiles required based on the size of the printer's paper, the size of your document, the value entered in the Overlap field, and the absolute overlap selection.

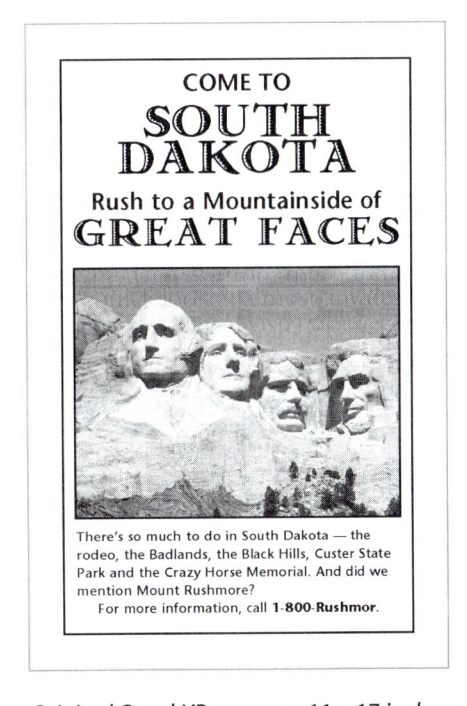

Original QuarkXPress page, 11 × 17 inches

CHAPTER 9/MANAGING OUTPUT **201**

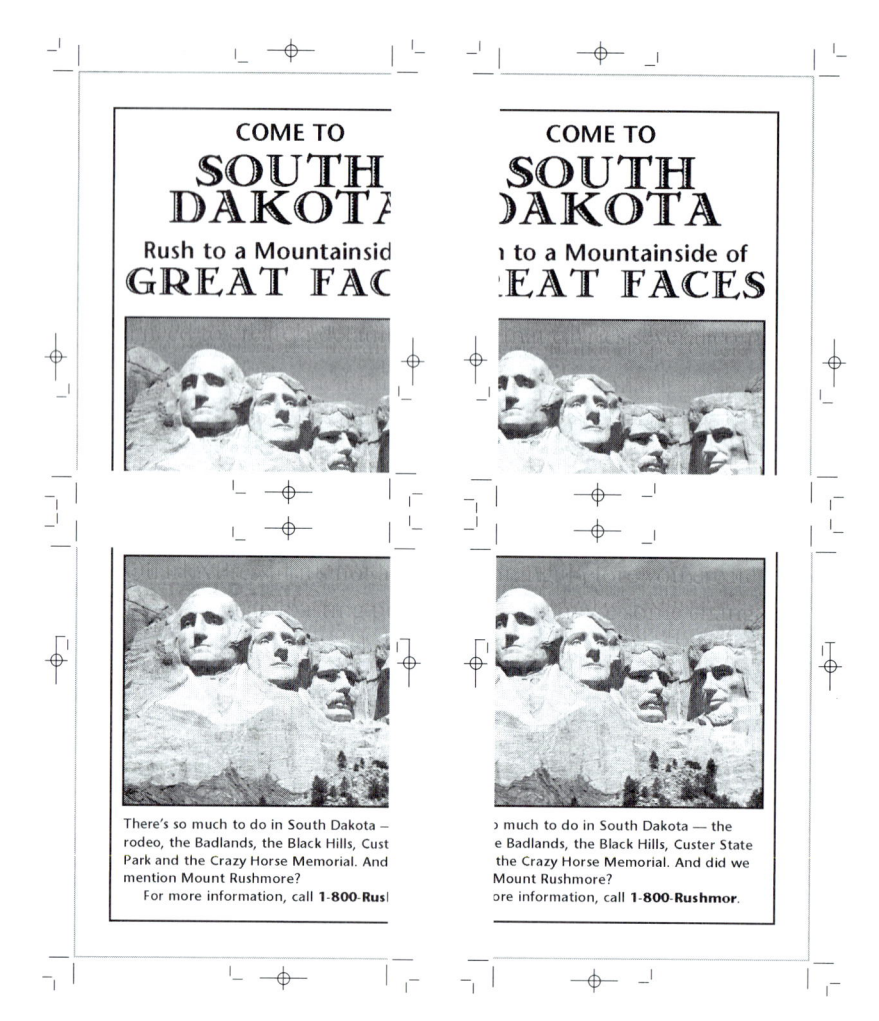

Tiled pages for the QuarkXPress poster

When you select Manual, you control page tiling by setting the ruler origin. Rather than tiling an entire page, this option is used when it is desirable to print only part of a page. The 0/0 ruler coordinate determines the upper-left corner of the first tile (which will often be the only tile).

Drag the 0/0 ruler coordinates to the upper-right corner of the area to be tiled, or cropped out of a page (above).
The results are the area where the tile began to the end of the page (below).

Halftoning

A printing press cannot print continuous tone art (such as a photographs) but it can print dots and line art. Before digital scanning devices and imagesetters, printers had to use glass or contact screens to reduce continuous tone art to thousands of tiny dots. These dots reproduce the illusion of continuous tone when printed. The resulting printed image is called a halftone. The screening technology built into imagesetters reproduces halftones digitally, without the use of a camera and halftone screen.

Digital and traditional screens are measured in lines per inch (lpi). The greater the lpi of a screened image, the finer the dot pattern used to print it. Higher line screens reproduce continuous tone images more faithfully, because the smaller dots are less visible to the naked eye.

You can set custom screening values for grayscale TIFFs in QuarkXPress. Use this feature to achieve a desired effect or to change the look of the final printed piece. Launch the Picture Halftone dialog box from Style>Halftone.

Be careful when using these specifications. You have a good reason to do so, especially if you are sending your document to a GASP for imaging. These functions override information in the Print Dialog Output menu, and the service provider has no way of knowing what you did to an image using the Picture Halftone Specifications menu.

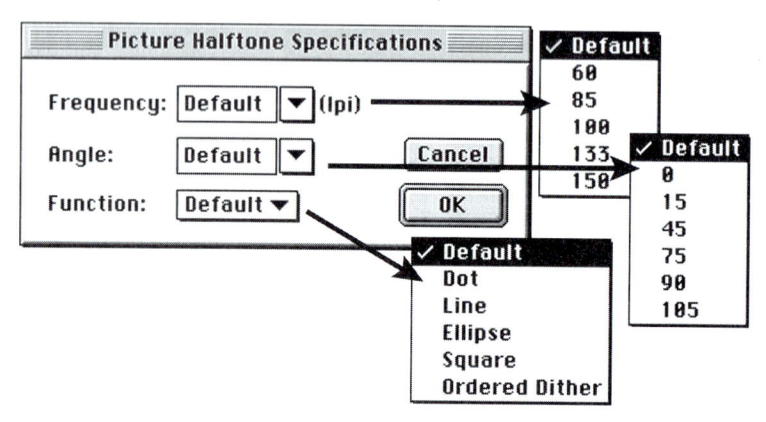

The Picture Halftone Specifications menu allows users to set Frequency, Angle, and Function of halftone dots in grayscale TIFF images.

Frequency allows you to set the lines per inch (lpi) value for the image from the drop-down menu or by typing into the field.

You can enter custom angles for screens in the Angle field, or choose from the drop-down menu. Whenever you select Default, QuarkXPress uses the values that are set in the Output tab of the Print dialog box.

You can choose from six preset screen patterns in the function field: Default, Dot, Ellipse, Line, Square, and Ordered Dither. Ordered Dither is used to achieve better results when the final print will be a laser printer or when a photocopier will be used to reproduce multiple copies.

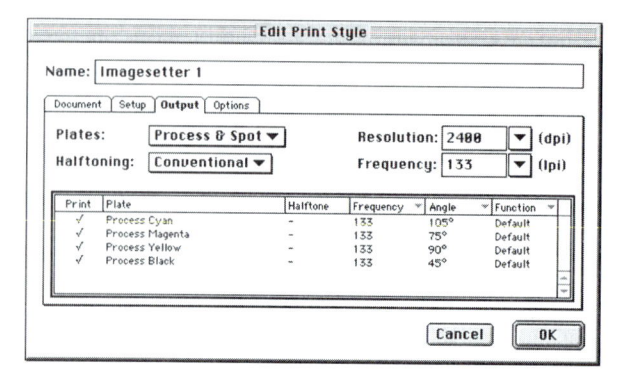

While the Print Dialog Output menu allows for determination of frequency for images, its function is overridden by the Picture Halftone specifications.

Using the PPD Manager

QuarkXPress uses PostScript Printer Description Files (PPDs) supplied by manufacturers to gain access to the features of PostScript printing devices. PPDs are accessed in the Print dialog box through the Printer Description drop-down menu in the Setup tab. If you have a lot of PPDs loaded in you system, this list can be very long. You will use the PPD manager to control which PPDs are displayed in the Printer Description list. A shorter list makes it easier to find your PPD.

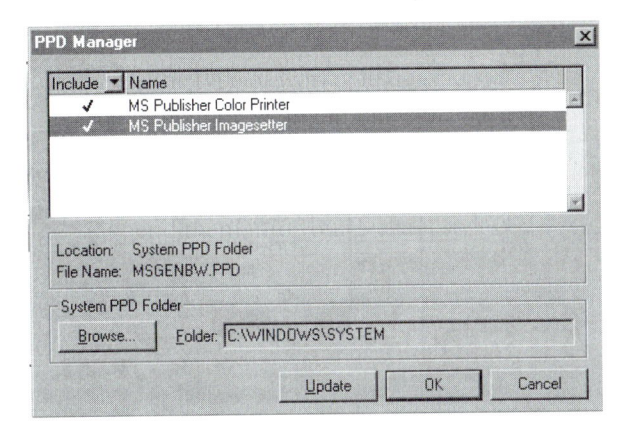

The PPD Manager dialog box appears when you click on the Utilities menu and select PPD Manager. You can select which PPDs will be displayed by adding or removing the check mark next to the PPD name that you want to include or exclude.

PostScript and QuarkXPress

When you are ready to output your QuarkXPress documents, you will most likely be printing to a PostScript device. PostScript language is the industry standard for desktop publishing and printing. Virtually all high-end output devices are dependent on PostScript. It is a page description language developed by Adobe Systems, Inc. that describes fonts, graphics, and other items in a page layout.

Service providers or commercial printers may want you to supply a PostScript file to them instead of your live QuarkXPress document. This way they don't have to generate the PostScript file or deal with missing fonts, graphics, and other problems that may arise when they try to print your file. You must be ready to assume all responsibility for film and other types of output (inkjets, paper, contract proofs) when you supply a PostScript file for output. If you are not comfortable creating a PostScript file, then don't. Mistakes can be costly and will drive up the cost of a project, reducing (or eliminating) your profit.

A PostScript file is created by printing to a file using the appropriate PPD for the device your file will ultimately be printed on. Under the File menu, select Print; the Print dialog box opens. Clicking the Printer button on the bottom of the screen opens the Print dialog box for the selected PPD. In the Print dialog box, check Print to File. Now when you are finished setting the rest of your print options, your file will print to a PostScript file and you will be prompted to name and choose a location for the file.

You can save individual page layouts in QuarkXPress as EPS (Encapsulated PostScript) files. EPS files can be imported into other QuarkXPress documents or applications. Under the File menu, select Save Page as EPS.

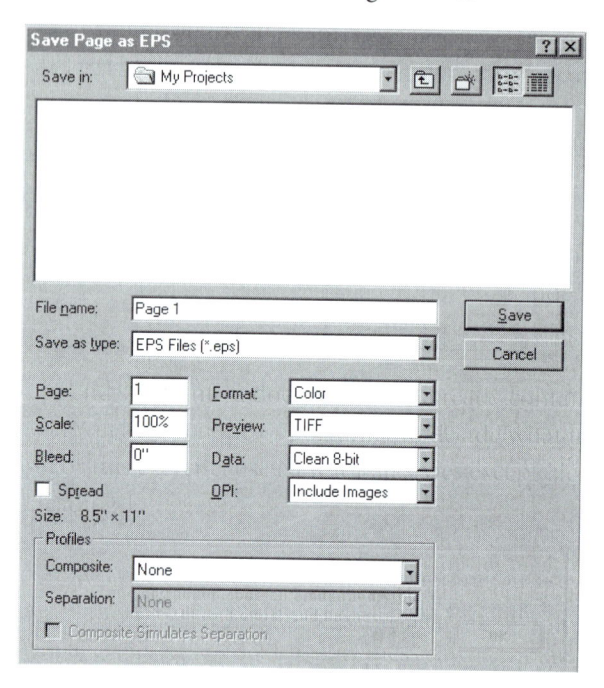

The Save Page as EPS dialog box allows you to save an EPS file and specify its settings. In the Save Page as EPS dialog box you can:

- Choose which page to save as an EPS file.

- Enter a percentage value to specify the size of the EPS in comparison to the original page.

- Save an EPS with bleed. This saves image data that extends beyond the edge of the QuarkXPress page. Bleed is required whenever you have an image that extends to the edge of the page. The image must actually extend off the page to prevent problems when printed pages are trimmed.

- Save an EPS of the page spread where the page you have selected is located.

- Choose a format for your EPS file. You can select from Color, B&W, DCS, and DCS 2.0.

- Choose a preview from three options: PICT, TIFF, and None.

- Control how raster data is saved. Choose either Binary, ASCII, or Clean 8-bit. Note: Only use Clean 8-bit if you are experiencing problems printing over a parallel port. Select Binary if you are planning to output the file to an imagesetter or similar PostScript device.

- Separate high-resolution images from your EPS file by selecting the Open Prepress Interface (OPI) method. By using the Open Prepress Interface (OPI) system, QuarkXPress will substitute a low-resolution preview of the image into the EPS file that an OPI server or imagesetter can later substitute with the high-resolution image when film is being output. Consult your service provider about the capabilities of their OPI system (if they have one) before you attempt to use this feature.

Creating an Output Request Form

Before you give your completed documents to a service provider or printer you must complete an output request form. This form contains all the information a service provider needs before they can generate film or plates from your files. QuarkXPress provides a template that works in conjunction with the Collect for Output feature of QuarkXPress.

Most service providers will provide you with their own output request forms to fill out. You should always perform a Collect for Output, flow the report into the Output Request Template and include it with the job. Collect for Output provides information you may not even be aware of (such as "live" type in graphics).

Trapping

Proper trapping compensates for the imperfection of printing. Variables that make printing a less-than-perfect science include ink, paper, humidity, type of press, and even the press operator. Ink colors may print out of register, causing gaps or color shifts between colors that print adjacent to one another. Gaps that allow the paper to show through will occur when spot colors print out of register. Color shifts or leaks occur when process colors are not registered.

Documents must be trapped to compensate for misregistration on a press. As a general rule, the darker color will determine the direction of the trap. You will expand a light color into a dark background (spreading) or contract into a dark color on a light background (choking). The lighter color always expands in the direction of the darker color.

As a rule of thumb, it is best to discuss trapping in detail with your service provider. Many service providers use dedicated trapping programs, with which the trapping in QuarkXPress interferes. Dedicated programs trap based on values of the colors, as opposed to information about the object, such as QuarkXPress uses.

Trapping in QuarkXPress

QuarkXPress determines trapping using object colors and background colors. Object color is the color applied to an item in front of another color. Background color is the color of an item behind another color. QuarkXPress determines the trapping of two colors by measuring the difference in luminance (brightness) between the two colors on an object-by-object basis.

Never argue with a service provider over what information you will provide to them or what form it will take. Many workflows are built around working with forms in a particular manner.

If a service provider is too inflexible for you to deal with, simply find another one.

QuarkXPress's trapping default of 0.144 pt. is generally considered to be far too small — about half what most printers would like to see for a trap.

You can trap object color in four different ways:

- Knockout an object color. The background color beneath the object will be erased so that there is no overlap of the two colors.

- Overprint a dark color on a light background. The darker color will print over the lighter ink without knocking it out.

- Choke a darker colored object. Choking reduces the size of the knockout area behind an object and creates a trap.

- Spread a lighter colored object into a background. Items that are spread enlarge to trap the darker color.

You can set default trapping for QuarkXPress under the Edit menu. Select Preferences>Document>Trapping. The default trapping value determines how QuarkXPress will automatically trap colors based on their luminance.

To edit the way a specific color traps within a document, use the Trap Specifications dialog box. Select Edit>Colors>Edit Trap; the Trap Specifications dialog box will appear. You can specify Overprint, Knockout, Spreads, and Choke values, or use the defaults set in the programs Application Preferences dialog box.

The Trap Information palette allows you to trap specific items (text, boxes, and so forth). Select View>Show Trap Information. Preferences set for your document will override your application defaults. Trapping set for Items will override all of your trapping preferences.

Trapping Text

You can trap text in QuarkXPress the same way you can trap other objects. Either set the color-specific defaults, or apply item-specific trapping. Small type is difficult to trap and still retain good readability. As a general rule you should select a dark color for small type and objects.

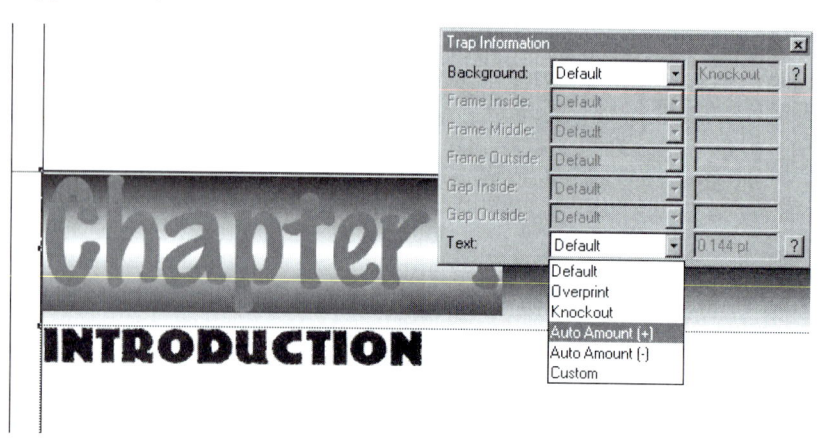

Unless you are fully confident that you know what you are doing when trapping in QuarkXPress, and have controlled the trapping for all imported EPS images, it is best to leave trapping to your service provider and dedicated trapping programs.

Trapping Frames

You can trap a picture or text box frame using the Trap Information palette. This allows you to trap the inside of the frame to a background or picture, the middle of a frame to colors beneath it, and the outside of a frame to adjacent background colors. QuarkXPress cannot apply a trap to a picture.

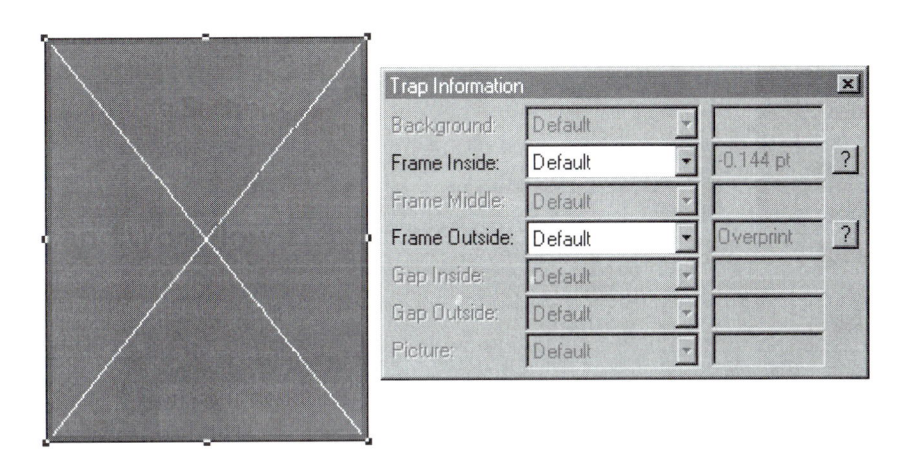

Due to the variables involved in trapping, you should always consult your service provider or printer before attempting to trap a file. Different press, paper and ink combinations require different traps and only your service provider will know what is best for their equipment. Ideally, you should let your printer or service provider do the trapping for you. Most service providers can trap your files using specialized trapping software.

Digital Imposition

Often, copies of small designs (cards, letterheads, and so forth) are printed on larger paper stock. They may be arranged so that when printed, the front and back line up correctly with the right pages. Large publications (like this book) may be run with as many as 16–32 pages imposed on one sheet. The resulting sheet is called a signature. Signatures are folded and trimmed to create the final bound book or magazine.

Imposition can be done by hand or digitally. Digitally imposing film can reduce the cost of a print job and increase the accuracy of color registration. Many service providers can digitally impose your film for you using high-end imposition software. Discuss the benefits of digital imposition with your service provider.

Output Tips

PostScript is a powerful language that gives output devices the ability to create accurate, high-resolution output from QuarkXPress documents. A service provider sends a PostScript file to a Raster Image Processor (RIP) that converts PostScript commands into color separated, screened, raster images. The imagesetter uses a laser to image the raster information onto film or paper. You give the resulting film separations to your printer and he or she uses the film to create printing plates.

The learning curve associated with creating and submitting files is high. You can avoid costly mistakes and missed deadlines by observing the following tips:

- Talk to your service provider before you begin a project. Find out how they require files to be prepared. Every imagesetter has slight differences, so make certain that you are aware of these in advance to avoid problems. Most service providers will be glad to assist you.

Contract proofs are so named because your acceptance of the proof and subsequent authorization for the printer to print the job constitutes a contract between you and the printer. It is the printer's responsibility to match the proof within the tolerances of accepted trade practices, and it is your responsibility to pay the bill. An error discovered after the proof has been agreed upon is considered your change, and it is chargeable.

- Supply all images, support art, and fonts used in your document. If you fail to do this, your service provider will be unable to output your file.

- Provide a final, to-size laser proof (color separated — especially if you are using spot color in your document) so that your service provider can check your film for errors.

- Always print separations of your document and check them before you give your file to a service provider. You will catch mistakes (such as extra color plates, incorrect colors, and so forth) before the printer creates film. This will save you time and money.

- Complete an output request form and provide it with your disk.

- Communicate any special requests or concerns and ask if you will be charged extra for them.

- Did we mention that you must communicate in advance?

Contract Proofing

Printers create laminate proofs by exposing your separated film onto proofing material and then laminating the layers together. The resulting proof is extremely accurate for color proofing. Laminate proofs are used as contract proofs because of their high quality. Discuss your printer's contract proofing requirements before supplying film.

Commercial printers require laminate proofs for process color printing (CMYK). After you have reviewed and signed a contract proof, your job will be printed.

Before signing a contract proof, carefully check the following:

- Color matching.
- Color balance.
- Registration.
- Trapping and overprinting.
- All art and copy correct and present on the proof.

Point out any problems with the proof and discuss them with your printer before proceeding.

Complete Project F: The GASP Newsletter

Review #2

Chapters 6 Through 9:

In Chapters 6 through 9, you learned how QuarkXPress controls the combination of text and graphics on a page. You also learned how to use imported art or other text boxes to define runarounds, wrap text, and color text and text boxes. You learned about the importance of Editorial Priority with the use of Paragraph and Character styles. You learned about first-level headlines and subheads. You should know how to properly create, edit, and manage long documents. You understand how to achieve a more superior design through consistency and continuity in your work. And finally, you have learned the proper method of preparing the necessary elements for an outside service provider. After completing the second half of this course you should :

- Know how to create transparent text boxes for placing text over imported art or another text box. You know how to create and use runarounds in your designs. You understand clipping paths; different types of runarounds; how to adjust hyphenation and justification of runarounds; kerning and tracking in runarounds; and you understand anchored objects.

- Know how to create a Default style document and how to append styles from one document to another. You understand the importance of Styles and Workflow; you understand widow controls. You have learned how to create and apply Character styles; and you have learned how to delete styles from the Default document.

- Realize the importance of creating a Document Master containing certain repeating attributes to enhance efficiency and consistency in a long document. You understand QuarkXPress's Book Creation feature. You have learned how to make global changes using the Master Document. You understand Lists, types of Lists, and you know how they work. You also understand the Index palette.

- Know how to work with Print styles. You have learned about Separations and Separation Proofs. You understand Tiling; halftoning; how to use the PPD Manager; how PostScript relates to QuarkXPress; and how to create an Output Request Form for an outside service provider. You have learned about Trapping and Digital Imposition. You have also learned output tips and Contract Proofing.

Project A: Gym Ad

Importing Graphics and Defining Colors

1. Create a new document (File>New).

2. Set the document to be 8.5″ × 11″ with 0.5″ Margin Guides for the top, bottom, left, and right sides. Set Columns to 2 with a Gutter Width of 0.5″. Turn Automatic Text Box On.

3. Set a Baseline Grid starting at 0.136″ and an Increment of 14.5 pt. (Edit>Preferences>Document>Paragraph). Save the document to your **Work in Progress** folder as "Gym Ad.QXD".

4. Drag a Horizontal Guide down to 7.5″, then drag the top of the automatic text box down to 7.5″. Draw a 7.5″ × 6.5″ rectangular picture box that fills the area above the text box within the margins. Make certain that the picture box is filled with White.

5. Select the picture box and choose File>Get Picture. Go to the **SF-Adv QuarkXPress** folder and open **Body Builders.TIF**.

6. With the Content tool, move the image around to focus on the couple.

7. We want to match the colors in the image as closely as possible. From Edit>Colors click New. Name the color ATC Purple, Model: CMYK. Spot color should not be checked. Assign values of Cyan: 70, Magenta: 100.

8. Click OK, then click New. Name the new color ATC Beige with CMYK values of Cyan: 0, Magenta: 25, Yellow: 50. Click OK.

9. Create one final process color: ATC Brown with CMYK values of Cyan: 50, Magenta: 85, Yellow: 100. Click OK, then click Save.

10. The image isn't as wide as the text box; there's some white showing around the left and right sides. Check your Document Prefs to make certain that Framing is set to Inside. Add a Frame of 6 pt. ATC Brown to the box to hide the thin, white edge. We could also enlarge the image slightly to Fill the box, but you should not get into the habit of doing this to compensate for incorrect image sizes.

Press Command-E (Macintosh) or Control-E (Windows) to Get Picture.

Press Shift-F12 to Edit Colors.

Press Command/Control-Y to open the Document Preferences dialog box. Click the General tab to set Framing.

PROJECT A/GYM AD **A-1**

Press Option/Alt-D to display the Step and Repeat dialog box.

The F5 key controls the arrangement of QuarkXPress layers.

F5
  Bring to Front.

Shift-F5
  Send to the Back.

Option/Alt-F5
  Bring Forward.

Shift-Option/Alt-F5
  Send Backward.

Creating Text Boxes and Importing Text

1. Draw a rectangular text box 1″ from the top of the page spanning the margins and is about 2″ High. Type "Give us your Body for a Week". Set the text to ATC Sea Breeze, 45 pt. on 50 pt. leading. Assign a Color of ATC Brown, tinted to 20%, Assign Tracking of +15. Align Centered. The Text Box Color and Runaround should be set to None.

2. With the text box selected, choose Item>Step and Repeat. Duplicate the text box once, with Offsets of 0.04″ for both Horizontal and Vertical. Set the Text Color to 100% ATC Brown.

3. Choose Item>Send Backward while holding down the Option/Alt key. This will create a shadow effect.

4. Draw a rectangular text box as described below. Type "and We'll Give You Back Your Mind." Make the font ATC Sea Breeze, 24 pt. with leading set to Auto. Color it ATC Purple and center it.
   X: 05″   W: 7.5″
   Y: 7.125″   H: 0.5″

5. Click in the two-column automatic text box, go to File>Get Text and select **Gym Ad.TXT** from **the SF-Adv QuarkXPress** folder.

6. Click in the text with the Content tool and press Command/Control-A to select all copy. Make the font ATC Sands, 11 pt. with leading set at 14.5 pt. Choose Style>Formats and select Lock to Baseline, then click OK.

7. Highlight the first two words, "Tropical Suites", and make the font ATC Sea Breeze, 13 pt. Color it ATC Purple.

8. At the end of the text, press the Return/Enter key, then type, line-for-line, Centered:
   "800/TROPICS. [Return]
   It's all a body can ask for."

   With the Content tool, select the telephone number. Make it ATC Sea Breeze, 24 pt. ATC Brown on 30 pt. leading. The bottom line bumps over into the next column. Why? Change the leading of the telephone number to 29 pt. (a multiple of the increment of the Baseline Grid). The bottom line moves back into the first column.

A-2 PROJECT A/GYM AD

The shortcut to access the Center command is Command/Control-Shift-C.

Press Command/Control-Shift-F to display the Paragraph Formats dialog box.

Press Command/Control-T to display the Runaround dialog box.

9. On the pasteboard, draw a rectangular picture box W: 2.5" × H: 1.35" and import the file named **Tropical Suites logo.EPS** from the **SF-Adv QuarkXPress** folder. Scale the logo to 80% (proportionately). Press Command/Control-Shift-M to place the logo in the middle of the picture box.

10. Select the Item tool, click on the picture box, and press Command/Control-X to cut it. Switch to the Content tool and click in the right column. You should see a blinking Insertion Point at the top. If not, press Return/Enter once. Paste the box into the column as an Anchored box.

11. Click on the anchored box with the Content tool. Look at the left side of the Measurements palette. The Lower icon adjusts the object relative to the *baseline* of the line to which it is anchored and is the default setting for newly anchored items. Click the Upper icon to adjust to the ascent of adjacent text. The In-line graphic acts just like text. With the Content tool on the same line as the graphic, click the Center icon to Center it on the line.

12. Draw a rectangular picture box W: 1.75" × H: 2.4". Press Command/Control-M to access the Modify dialog box. Select the Box tab and assign a Color of White, select the Runaround tab and assign a 5 pt. Offset on all sides. Click OK. Press Command/Control-E (Get Picture) to import **Aerobics.TIF** from the **SF-Adv QuarkXPress** folder.

13. Move the picture box to the lower left corner of the page, resting on the Margin Guides. The text will reflow to the next column and the logo will move down with it.

Finishing Up

1. Look closely at the body text.

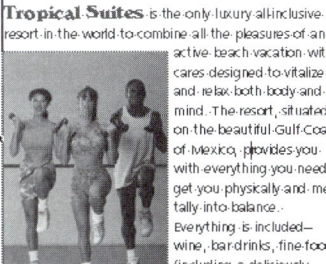

It's a fairly light typeface and looks somewhat jammed together. A heavier face might look better, but this is the typeface the client specified. Choose

Project A/Gym Ad   A-3

Edit>H&Js, and make a new H&J. Name the new H&J Body, and set the Hyphenation and Optimal Space values as shown below. (Min/Max aren't used, because this text is not justified). When you have set the values, click OK.

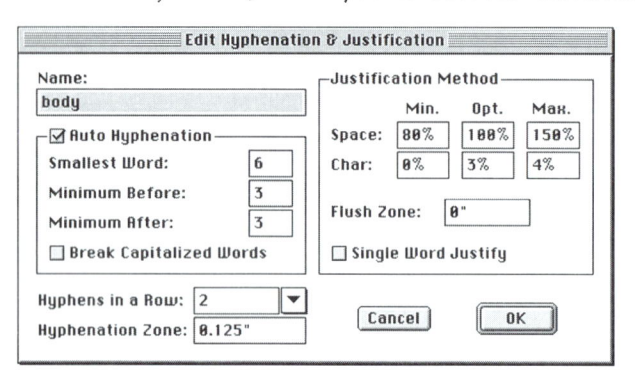

2. Click the cursor in the paragraph of running text. Press Command/Control-Shift-F to display the Formats tab of the Paragraph Attributes dialog box. Set the H&J to Body. Here's the new body text:

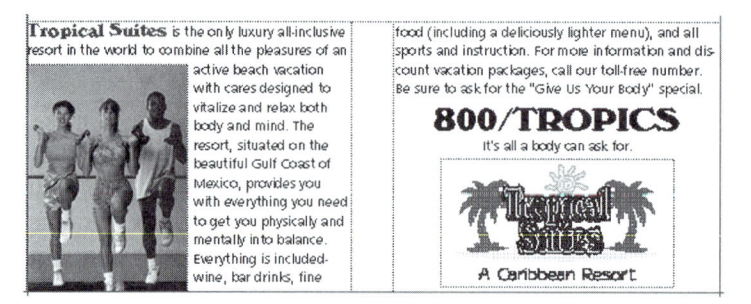

Notice the difference in the word spacing, and the Right Margins are less ragged.

3. Save and close the file.

Project B: Recipe Book

Create a New Document

1. Create a new document. In the New Document dialog box, set the dimensions of the page to 13″ Wide × 10″ High with .02″ margins on the Top and Bottom, a 0.5″ margin on the Inside, and a 0.2″ margin for the Outside, Facing Pages, one Column, Gutter Width 0.5″. Automatic Textbox should be unchecked. Click OK.

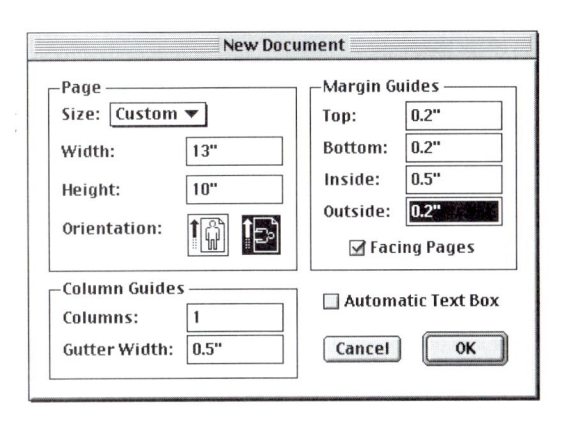

2. Save the document as "Recipe Book.QXD" into your **Work in Progress** folder.

3. Open the Document Layout and Colors palettes from the View menu. Double-click on the master page, A-Master A and rename it "Cover". Drag a New Facing Pages master page to the Master Page list. Double-click the name of the New master page and name it "Inside Spread".

4. Double-click the Inside Spread master to view it. Choose Page>Master Guides. Set up the Master Guides as 3 Columns with a 0.5″ Gutter Width. Keep the existing margin settings (0.5″ and 0.2″). Click OK.

5. Drag the Inside master to the Document Layout palette twice to add two pages. Drag the Cover master once to create the last page. Save the document.

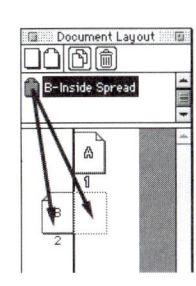

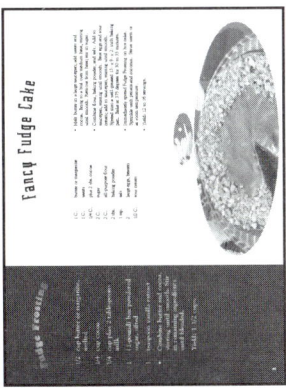

Double-click the Master Page icon in the Document Layout palette to view the master page, or select the master page from the pop-up menu at the bottom of the screen.

PROJECT B/RECIPE BOOK **B-1**

You can also add pages by choosing Page>Add Pages… and specifying how many new pages you want to add, and where.

Your Document Layout palette should look like this:

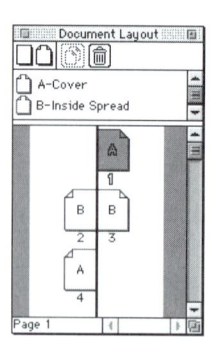

6. Create some new colors. Choose Edit>Colors>New. From the Model drop-down menu, select Pantone Solid-to-Process. Select Pantone Blue 072. Spot Color should be unchecked. Click OK.

We chose process simulations of solid (spot) Pantone colors because this project uses full-color images. Using spot colors would require extra time to convert them when the job is processed for printing, or might result in unwanted (and expensive) color separations.

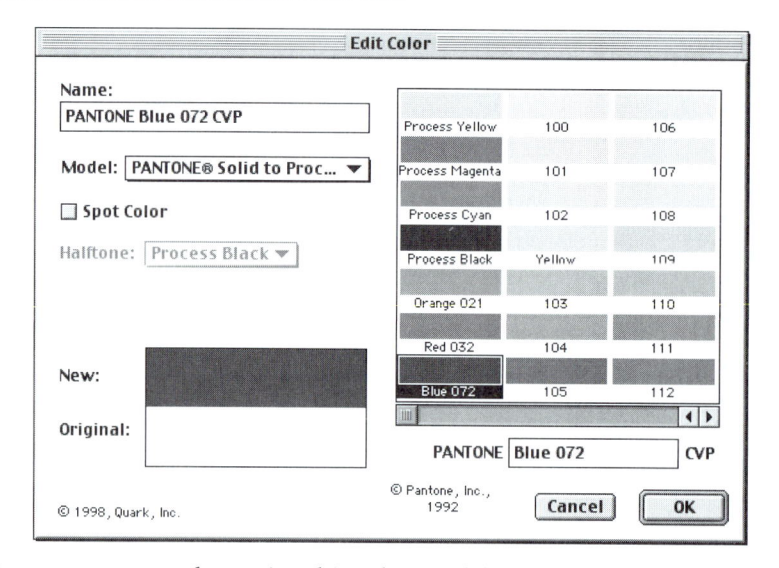

Create two more colors using this color model: Pantone 116 and Pantone 186. Click Save to return to the document.

Set the Design Parameters

1. Double-click the Inside Spread Master Page icon. On the left master page, draw a rectangular picture box to the size and coordinates shown below and fill it with Pantone Blue 072.

   X: −0.125″   W: 4.25″
   Y: −0.125″   H: 10.25″

Press Shift-F12 to display the Edit Colors dialog box.

B-2 PROJECT B/RECIPE BOOK

2. Draw a 3.767″ (the width of one column) × 0.3″ text box within the left column. Beginning with second sentence: Position it at X: 0.2″, Y: 9.5″. Color it Pantone Blue 072.

3. Click the Content tool in the text box and press Command/Control-3 to insert the automatic page number symbol <#>.
Style the page number ATC Cabana Normal, 12 pt. with left and right Indents of 0.267″, Aligned Left. Assign it a Color of White and turn the Color of the text box to Pantone Blue 072.

4. Using the Item tool, hold the Shift key and select both boxes. With both boxes selected, Step and Repeat with Horizontal and Vertical Offsets of 0″. Hold down the Shift key to constrain the movement to horizontal, and drag the boxes to the right column of the right master page. Position them at X: 8.875″, Y: –0.125″, so the right page mirrors the left.

5. Reposition the text box to fall between the Margin Guides and change the Alignment of the text to Right.

6. Should be: Drag four horizontal guides to 1″, 1.5″, 2″, and 2.5″ on each page. On the left page, drag a vertical guide to 2.056″. On the right page, drag a vertical guide to 10.917″.

7. Go to the Cover master page and draw two picture boxes big enough to cover each (left and right) page with a 0.125″ bleed.

8. Return to the document pages. Choose Edit>H&Js>New and create an H&J with hyphenation deselected (to turn off word breaks). Name it "NoBreaks".

Press Command-Option/Control-Altl-D to display the Step and Repeat dialog box.

PROJECT B/RECIPE BOOK B-3

Press Command/Control-Option/Alt-H to display the H&Js dialog box.

Press Shift-F11 to display the Edit Styles dialog box.

Command/Control-click a style or color in the Style Sheets or Color palette to quickly edit it.

Option/Alt-click a style to restore selected text to that style.

You can fine-tune your image by selecting the element and typing the desired dimensions in the Measurements palette.

9. Chose Edit>Style Sheets and create three new Paragraph styles as follows (the first word is the name you should assign to the style).

   Sidebar: Based on No Style, Next Style Self, ATC Cabana Bold, 17 pt., Pantone 116. Left and Right Indents 0.5″, leading 19 pt., Space Before and After 0.08″, Alignment Left, H&J NoBreaks.

   Ingredients: Based on No Style, Next Style Self, ATC Cabana Normal, 12 pt., Black. Left Indent 1.25″, leading 19 pt., Aligned Left, H&J NoBreaks. Set a Left-Aligned Tab at 2″.

   Body Copy: Based on No Style, Next Style Self, ATC Cabana Normal, 12 pt., Black. Left Indent 0.20″, First Line Indent of –0.20″, leading 14.4 pt., Space After 0.08″. Set a Left-Aligned tab at 0.2″.

10. Go to page 2. Select the Bézier Text-Path tool.

    Create a curved arch between the Horizontal Guides at 1″ and 1.5″ using the Guides as a reference.

    Type "Fudge Frosting" on the path. Style it as ATC Cabana Heavy 24 pt., +5 Tracking, Centered. Select all the text, then choose Style>Text to Box. Select the text on a path and delete it. Fill the new picture box with a circular blend of Pantone 186 (#1) and Pantone 116 (#2). Move the top of the box to the Upper Guide at 1″.

Add the Text

1. Repeat step 4 on page 3 in the far right column. Use "Raspberry Sauce" for the text.

2. On page 2, draw a rectangular text box to the following specifications:

   X: 0″   W: 4.0″
   Y: 2.5″ H: 5.5″

Press Command/Control-D to display the Text Attributes dialog box.

Press F11 to display or hide the Style Sheets palette.

Press Command/Control-T to display the Runaround dialog box.

Assign it a fill of PMS Blue 072. Import the file **Fudgesauce.TXT** from your **SF-Adv QuarkXPress** folder. Apply the Sidebar style to all the text.

3. Copy the text box to page 3. Position it at X: 9.0″, Y: 2.5″. Import the file **Raspsauce.TXT** from your **SF-Adv QuarkXPress** folder. Apply the Sidebar style to all the text.

4. Draw a Bézier text path between the two columns on page 2 between the horizontal guides at 1″ and 1.5″.

Type "Fancy Fudge Cake" and style it as ATC Tequila, 48 pt., Centered.

5. Select the text path and duplicate it across the first and second columns of page 3. Replace the text with "Meringues with Raspberry Sauce".

6. Draw a text box within the margins of the middle column of page 2, Fill of None, Runaround of None. The top of the box should be at the 2 Horizontal Guide; the bottom at the Lower Margin Guide. Type the text below; place a Tab between the amount and the ingredient, and apply the Ingredients style when finished.

1 C.	butter or margarine
1 C.	water
1/4 C.	plus 2 tbs. cocoa
2 C.	sugar
2 C.	all-purpose flour
2 tbs.	baking powder
1 tsp.	salt
2	large eggs, beaten
1/2 C.	sour cream

PROJECT B/RECIPE BOOK **B-5**

Press Command/Control-C to Center selected text.

7. Copy the text box to the Left Column of page 3 and type:

1/4 C.	chopped walnuts
5	large egg whites
1 tsp.	vanilla extract
1/4 tsp.	cream of tartar
1/8 tsp.	salt
1 C.	sugar
	chocolate ice cream
	raspberry sauce

8. Step and Repeat the text box to the middle column of page 3. Assign it a Horizontal Offset of 4.267″. Import **Meringue Recipe2.TXT** from the **SF-Adv QuarkXPress** folder. Apply the Body Text style.

9. Repeat the procedure with **Fudgecake.TXT** in the Right Column on page 2.

10. Across the two right columns of page 2, draw oval picture boxes to create a drawing of a big, happy person who gets to eat this dessert. Use a Bézier picture box to make the smiling mouth. Make it like this, or however you prefer, as long as all the boxes touch.

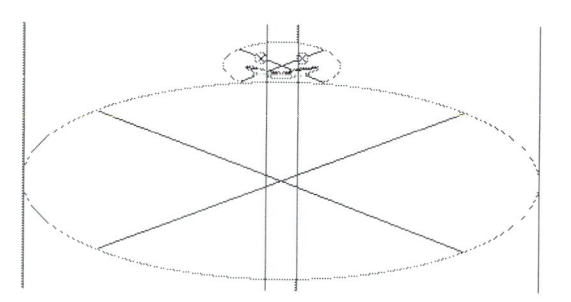

11. With the Item tool, select all of the boxes. Be careful not to select the text boxes in the columns. Choose Item>Merge>Combine to create a single picture box from the shapes.

12. Import the image **Fudge Cake.TIF**. Arrange the image within the box.

13. Copy the picture to page 3. Position it between the two left columns. Locate and place **Meringue.TIF**. Arrange the image within the box. You may need to adjust the box's Runaround.

14. Go to page 1. Color the picture box Pantone Blue 072. Draw a text box and type "DESSERTS". Set the type to ATC Cabana Heavy, 96 pt. with +15 Tracking, Centered. Rotate the box 90 degrees with the Measurements palette and place it against the Right Margin, Centered between the Top and Bottom Margins.

15. Select all the text and choose Style>Text to Box. Reposition the new picture box where the text was and delete the original text box. Import the file **Pie.TIF** and reposition the image within the letters to show off the pie crust.

16. Go to page 4 and place the same image (Pie.TIF) in the picture box.

That's it. This is what the completed pages should look like:

If you wish to print this document, select "Spreads" in the Print Setup dialog box to print the center spread on one page.

17. Save and close the file.

Project C: Tropical Suites Brochure

Creating a New Document, Colors, and Styles

1. Create a new document. In the New Document dialog box, set the parameters to a Custom 4″ × 8.75″ page, Portrait (Tall) Orientation, One Column, Facing Pages and Automatic Text Box Off. Set the Margins to 0.2″. Click OK.

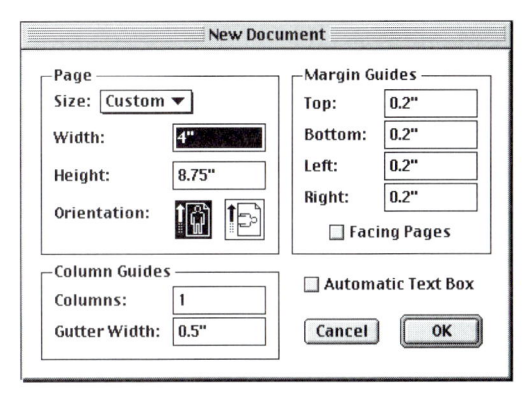

2. We're going to create this ten-panel brochure as two spreads of five pages each. This allows easy rearrangement of panels (pages) and is easier for a print shop to work with than if it were built as two single 20″ wide pages.

   Drag a new page next to the first one from the Master Page palette.

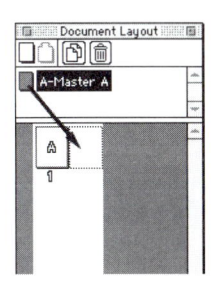

   Repeat three more times.

   Start a new spread by dragging a new page under page 1 and repeat four times. Your Document Layout panel should look like this:

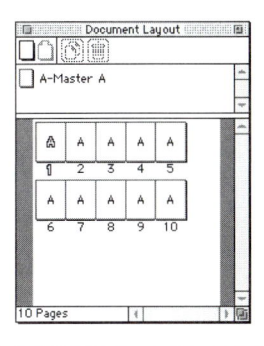

PROJECT C/TROPICAL SUITES BROCHURE C-1

This project is an example of a design that could be constructed in a variety of ways — all of them correct. Since QuarkXPress allows the use of adjacent panels, this method creates a single page for each panel. Printing a spread would result in only two pieces of film being output: pages 1 through 4 on one sheet and pages 5 through 8 on another. Whenever you're doing a job that requires extensive folding, be certain to speak with your output service provider before you begin your project.

You can rearrange pages in a spread simply by dragging them to a new location. Everything on the page will move with it, except items that overlap adjacent pages.

3. From Edit>Preferences>Document, select the Tool tab. Set the preferences for text boxes to Color: White, Runaround: None. Set the preferences for picture boxes to Color: White, Runaround: None. Save the document as **TropSuites.QXD** into your **Work in Progress** folder.

4. The client just called. The budget for this project has been reduced, so now its an eight-panel brochure. Click the proxy for page 5 in the Document Layout palette; hold down the Command/Control key and select page 10, then click the Delete button at the top of the panel. Confirm the deletion. Your Document Layout palette should now look like this:

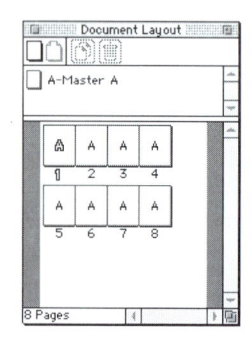

   If you had built the document as one large page with Guides for delineating the panels, instead of as spreads, you'd have to start all over again. Imagine getting a call like this *after* you finish a project!

5. Choose Edit>Colors and click New. Select the Pantone Solid to Process model and type 186 into the Pantone Color Number box.

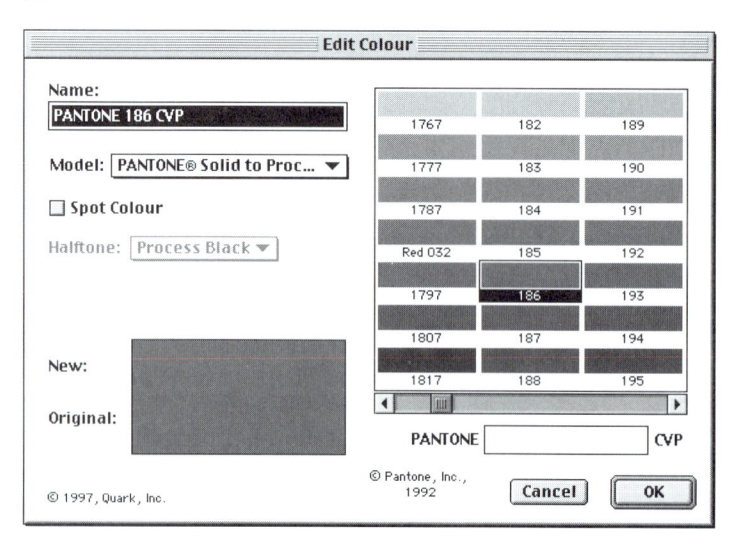

   Repeat for two new colors: Pantone 158 and 196. Save the colors.

6. Create and save a new H&J that turns off Hyphenation. Call it "No Breaks."

7. Choose Edit>Style Sheets to display the Style Sheets dialog box. Create three paragraph styles as follows:

Choose Edit>Preferences> Document to make your box changes, or press Command/Control-Y and choose the Box and Runaround tabs. Or you can double-click the appropriate tool to display its preferences.

Body Text: Based on No Style with Next Style as Self. Select ATC Cabana Normal, 12 pt., Black at 100%. Set the Left and Right Indents to 0.5″, Auto Leading, Aligned Left, with an H&J of No Breaks.

Subhead: Based on No Style with Next Style as Self. Select ATC Cabana Bold, 20 pt., Pantone 186 at 100%. Set the leading to Auto, Space After to 0.2″, Aligned Left with an H&J of No Breaks. Set a Rule Below, Length: Indents, Width: 2 pt.

Headline: Based on No Style with Next Style as Self. Select ATC Tradewinds Ultra, 36 pt., Pantone 186, 100%, Tracked +15. Set the leading to Auto, Aligned Centered with an H&J of No Breaks.

Click Save in the Style Sheets dialog box to finish.

8. Go to the master page and drag a Horizontal Guide down to the 1.25″ mark and return to the document pages.

Importing Text and Assigning Styles

1. Draw a text box within the margins of page 1, 1.25″ from the top, then import **Tropical Suites1-1.TXT**.

2. Apply the Subhead style to "The Resort" and set the rest of the text to Body Text.

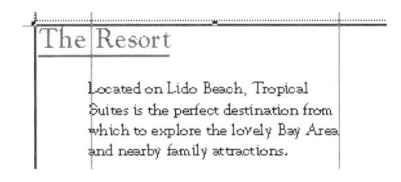

3. Draw a text box 1″ high at the top of page 1 that extends from the Left Margin on page 1 to the Right Margin of page 2. Type the words, "Your Tropical Island". Apply the Headline style. Center the text Vertically (use Item>Modify>Text Tab and set Vertical Alignment to Centered).

4. Step and Repeat the Body text box on page 1 as: Repeat Count: 1, Horizontal Offset: 8″ and Vertical Offset: 0. This will place it into position on page 3. With the Content tool, click in the new text box and press Command/Control-A to select all the text. Replace the text with the file **Tropical Suites1-3.TXT**. Apply Body Text.

5. Drag the bottom of the text box up to 6.75″. Create another text box in the remaining space and import the file **Tropical Suites1-4.TXT**. Apply Body Text to all the text. Select all the text and assign it a size of 9 pt. with Auto Leading. From

We chose process simulations of solid (spot) Pantone colors because this project uses full-color images. Using spot colors would require extra time to convert them when the job is processed for printing, or may result in unwanted (and expensive) color separations.

Double-click the Master Page icon in the Document Layout palette to view the master page, or select the master page from the pop-up menu at the bottom of the screen.

Press Command/Control-M and click the Text tab to modify the Vertical justification.

Press Command/Control-Option/Alt-D to display the Step and Repeat dialog box.

the Formats dialog box, assign Left and Right indents of 0.20″. Click the Content tool in the first paragraph, and, from the Formats dialog box, assign Space Before and Space After to 0.08″. Change the size to 9 pt., Auto Leading. Do the same for the rest of the New text, but do not assign Space Before or After. Highlight "Tropical Suites and Resorts" in the address, and change it to 16 pt.

6. Press Command/Control-B to access the Modify dialog box. Change the Color of the text box to Pantone 196. Click on the Text tab and set the Vertical Alignment Type to Centered.

7. On the same page, draw a text box 1″ in height between the margins at the top of the page and type the words, "Lido Beach." Apply the Headline style.

Select the headline text with the Content tool and convert it to a picture box (Style>Text to Box). Delete the original text box and move the picture box so that the bottom is 1″ from the top. Apply a circular blend as follows: #1 Yellow, #2 Pantone 186. Save the file.

This is what your first spread should look like so far:

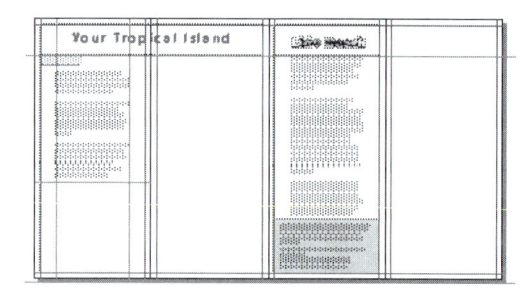

Importing Images

1. Go to page 1. Drag Horizontal Guides down to 5.5″ and 8.825″ (for Bleed), and Vertical Guides to 0.75″, 2″, and 3.25″. You will use these to help draw a half-oval Bézier picture box at the bottom of page 1. Click the Bézier Picture Box tool, then click once at the intersection of the Guides at 0.75″ and 8.825″. Click and hold the intersection at 2″ and 5.5″. Hold the Shift key and drag the mouse to create a curve. Release the mouse button and click at the intersection of the Guides at 3.25″ and 8.825″. Click on the original point to close the path.

Your picture box should look like the following image.

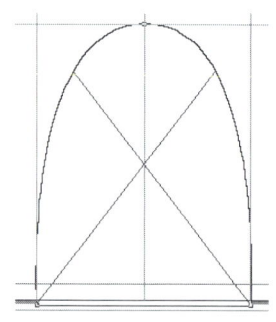

You can fine-tune your image by selecting the element and typing the desired dimensions in the Measurements palette.

Press Command/Control-Option/Alt-T to display the Clipping dialog box.

Remember that QuarkXPress's Clipping Path functions are rather limited; never rely on them to create clipping paths. Instead, create clipping paths in Photoshop, Freehand, or Illustrator before creating your layout.

Import **Kid on beach.TIF** from the **SF-Adv QuarkXPress** folder and move the image around as desired.

2. Draw a 3″ square picture box at the bottom of page 2, Centered between the Margins. Locate and import **Long Beach Walk.TIF** into the box. Move the picture around as desired for effect. Drag the bottom of the box down past the edge of the page to create a Bleed.

3. Draw a tall rectangular picture box above the one you just made, 1.4″ × 3.5″. Locate and place **Bike woman.TIF**. Draw a similar box and import **Bike dude.TIF**. Both images have clipping paths created in Photoshop. For each image, turn off QuarkXPress's Automatic Clipping Paths by selecting each and choosing Item>Modify>Clipping Path. Set the Path Type to Item. Arrange the contents and boxes to effectively fill the remaining space on the page, which should be similar to the following image:

4. Go to page 4. Draw a 3.6″ × 2″ picture box and Place the file **Tropical Suites logo.EPS**. Position the box against the bottom margin of the page. Press Command/Control-Shift-M to position the logo in the middle of the box.

PROJECT C/TROPICAL SUITES BROCHURE C-5

Other image modifier keystrokes:

To force an object to fit in a picture box, press Command/Control-Shift-F. To force an object to fit while maintaining the image's proportions, press Command/Control-Option/Alt-Shift-F.

5. Draw another picture box 3.6″ Square above the logo. Place the image **Hotel Photo.TIF**. Set the background color of the picture box to Pantone 158. Press Command/Control-Shift-M to center the image within the box, and move the box up or down to center it more or less Vertically.

6. Draw a text box above the hotel image and type "Sun<line return>&<line return>Service". Style the text as Headline. Size the box to fit the text and set the top against the top margin.

7. Select the "Lido Beach" picture box on page 3 (the one you converted from text) and duplicate it. Move the copy to page 4, between the hotel image and the logo, Centered in the column.

Congratulations. You have finished the front side of the brochure. This is what it should look like. Save the document.

Importing More Text and Graphics

1. Go to page 5 and press Command/Option-0 (Macintosh) or Control/Alt-0 (Windows) to make the entire spread visible. Beginning at the left margin of page 6, draw a text box 1″ in height across the spread to the right margin of page 8. Type "Sunshine, Gourmet Cuisine and 4-Star Service". Apply the Headline style. Adjust the tracking to fit the type in the box. Set the Vertical Alignment to Centered.

2. Draw a text box on page 8 between the margins. Import the file **Tropical Suites-2-5.TXT**. Apply the Body Copy style. Move the box so that the bottom is on the bottom margin and resize the top down to fit the text in the box.

C-6 PROJECT C/TROPICAL SUITES BROCHURE

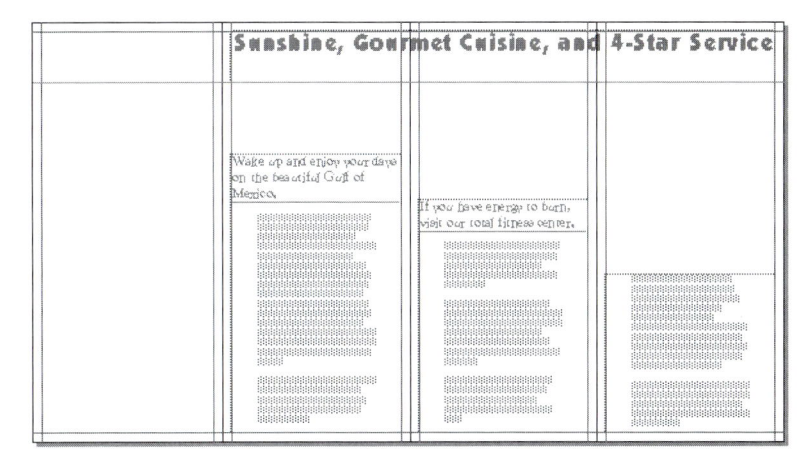

Press Command/Control-T to display the Runaround dialog box.

3. Draw a text box on page 7 between the margins. Import **Tropical Suites 2-3.TXT**. Apply the Subhead style to the first paragraph and the Body Text style to the rest of the text. Move the box so that the bottom is on the Bottom Margin and resize the top down to fit the text in the box.

4. Draw a text box on page 6 between the Margins. Import **Tropical Suites 2-2.TXT**. Select the first sentence and apply the Subhead style. Highlight the remaining text and apply Body Text. Adjust the box as you did above.

If the Overset Text Warning appears at the bottom of these text boxes, check for an extra Return character at the end of the story and delete it.

With the text placed, your spread should look like this:

5. Draw a picture box within the left and right margins of page 5, extending 0.125″ below the page, to allow for bleed. Import **Chef Silo.TIF**. Be sure the image bleeds off the page. Set Clipping to use the Embedded Path. Set the Runaround as Type: Non-White Areas, Outset: 15 pt.

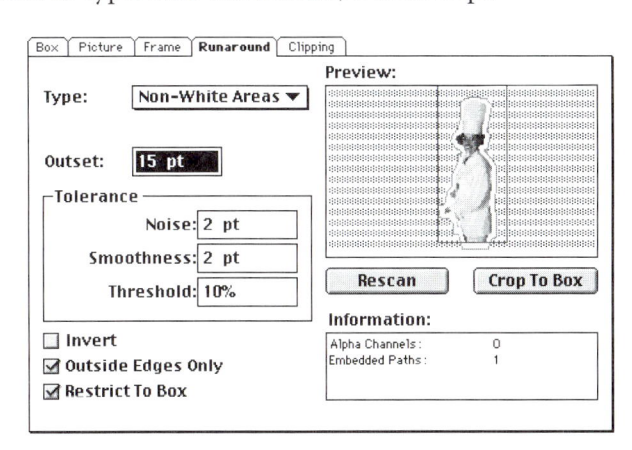

PROJECT C/TROPICAL SUITES BROCHURE C-7

6. Move the text box on page 6 to the left so that the left edge is about halfway onto page 5. Adjust the box's placement to achieve a pleasing Runaround. Change the left and right indents to 0.05".

It's OK to use a Runaround derived from an embedded clipping path or any other kind of Runaround because these will not affect the image, unlike a clipping path created in QuarkXPress.

7. On the left pasteboard, draw a picture box and import **Dining Couple.TIF**. Resize the box to crop the image slightly on the sides and bottom. Move the picture box to page 5, positioning it against the top margin, and overhanging the Page by 0.125" to allow for bleed. Press Shift-F5 to send to Back.

C-8   PROJECT C/TROPICAL SUITES BROCHURE

If you wish to print this document, be certain to select "Spreads" in the Print Setup dialog box to print each side of the brochure on one page, rather than each document page on eight separate pages.

In most cases, it's better to build documents such as this multi-panel brochure as page spreads rather than as large pages.

8. On page 6, draw a 2.5″ × 7.6″ picture box at X: 1.3″ and Y: 1.25″. Import **Bartender.TIF**. Adjust the image to feature the bartender's smile.

9. Draw a 7.6″ × 2.3″ picture box at X: 7.2″ and Y: 1.25″, crossing pages 2 and 3. Import **Fun at the Beach.TIF** and move it around to a pleasing position.

10. On page 8 draw a picture box between the Beach image and the text box within the Right and Left Margin Guides. Import **Hammock.TIF** and position the image as you like.

    This is what your finished second page should look like:

11. Save and close your document.

Notes:

Project D: Staying Alive Newsletter

Setting up the New Document

1. Create a new document, letter-size, 0.5″ Margins all around, Facing Pages Off and Automatic Text Box Off.

2. Double-click the master page. Rename it "Cover". Choose Page>Master Guides and set up the Guides as shown below.

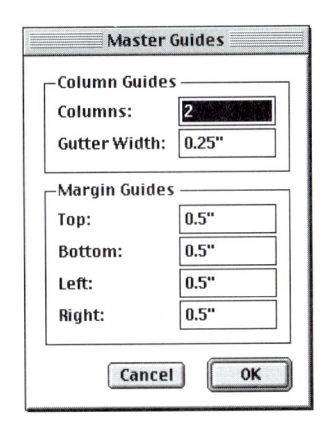

Click OK. Here's the master page with the Guides applied:

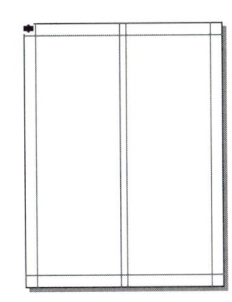

3. Create a new master page by dragging a Single Page New Master to the Master Pages section of the Document Layout palette. Name it "Inside". Double-click on it to view the page.

Double-click the Master Page icon in the Document Layout palette to view the master page, or select the master page from the pop-up menu at the bottom of the screen.

PROJECT D/STAYING ALIVE NEWSLETTER D-1

4. Choose Page>Master Guides and set up the Guides as shown below.

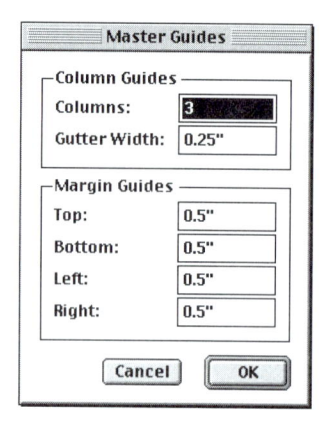

5. Click OK. Draw a large text box that fits within the Page Margins. Choose Item>Modify>Text and set up the text box as shown below.

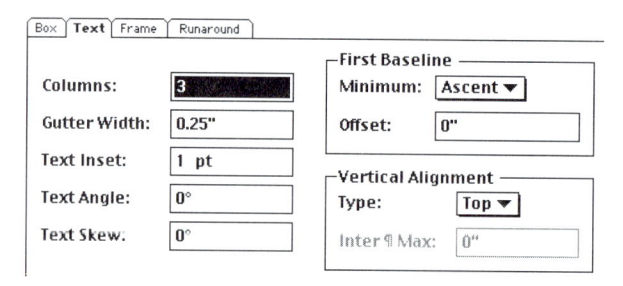

6. Choose Edit>Preferences>Document>Paragraph and set a Baseline Grid starting at 0.5″ from the Top, 14 pt. Increment.

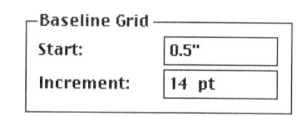

7. Draw a small text box across the Left Column within the Top Margin 0.25″ from the top of the page and type "Staying Alive". Style it as ATC Cabana Bold, 12 pt. with 14 pt. of leading.

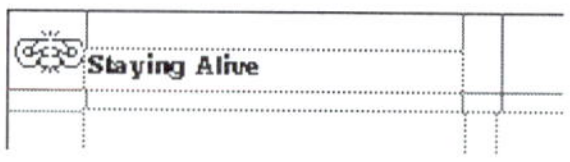

8. Draw a text box with the following specifications:
   X: 5.667   W: 2.333
   Y: 10.5   H: 0.375
   Press Command/Control-3 to type an automatic page number symbol. Style it as ATC Cabana Normal, 12 pt. on 14 pt. leading, right aligned, and centered vertically.

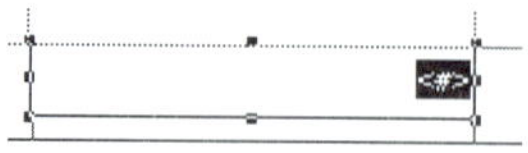

9. Here's the Inside master page:

10. Drag three copies of the Inside master page to the Document Pages area of the Document Layout palette after the First page. (Hold down the Option/Alt key as you drag them into the palette and type "3" into the dialog box that appears.) Save to your **Work in Progress** folder as "Staying Alive.QXD".

11. Your client's standard colors are Pantone 5483, 116, and 186, but we'll be using full-color images in this document, so you must use process color derivations of the client's colors. Define new colors by choosing Edit>Colors. If Red, Green and Blue are present in the list of colors, delete them. You can't delete Black, Cyan, Magenta, Yellow, or Registration.

    Click New and choose the Pantone Solid to Process library from the Model: pop-up menu and type "5483" into the Color Number field. Make certain that the Spot Color check box remains unchecked. Click OK.

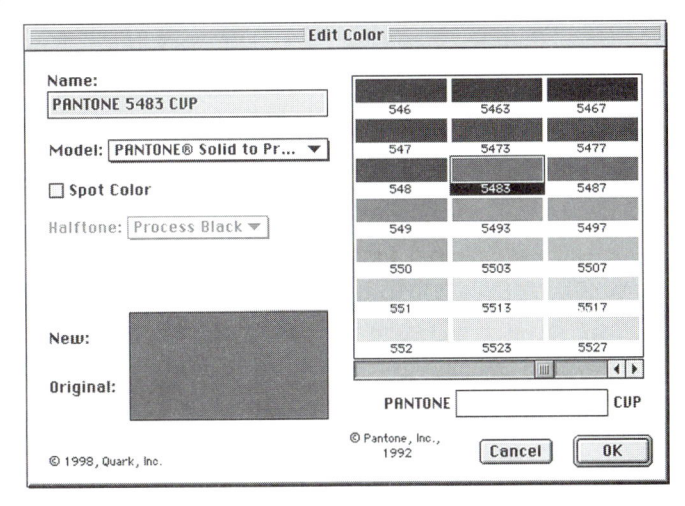

Press Shift-F12 to display the Edit Colors dialog box.

We chose process simulations of solid (spot) Pantone colors because this project uses full-color images. Using spot colors would require extra time to convert them when the job is processed for printing, or may result in unwanted (and expensive) color separations.

PROJECT D/STAYING ALIVE NEWSLETTER **D-3**

Create two more colors: Pantone 116 and Pantone 186. Your color list should look like this:

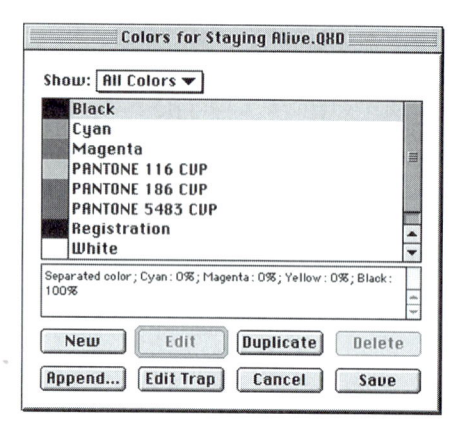

Click Save and return to the document.

12. Create a new H&J that turns off Automatic Hyphenation. Name it "No Hyphens". We'll use this when setting up style sheets.

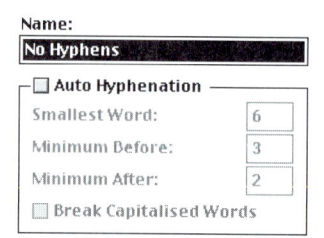

13. Now create the style sheets to use in the document. Choose Edit>Style Sheets to display the Style Sheets dialog box. Click New to create the first style, Body Text, as a Paragraph style. Press Tab to select the Keyboard Equivalent field, then press Numeric Keypad-1 to assign this keystroke to the style.

Set the Character Attributes as shown below.

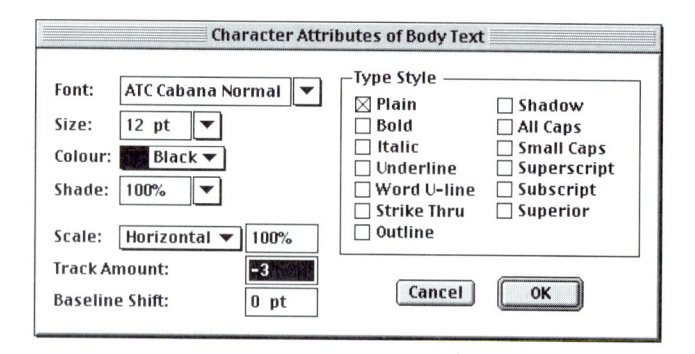

Press Command-Option-H (Macintosh) Control-Alt-H (Windows) to display the Hyphenation dialog box.

Press Shift-F11 to display the Edit Styles dialog box.

Command/Control-click a style or color in the palette to quickly edit it.

Opt/Alt-click a style to strip all formatting from the selected text and apply that style.

You can fine-tune your image by selecting the element and typing the desired dimensions in the Measurements palette.

Choose the Formats tab and modify the settings as shown (don't forget the Lock to Baseline Grid check box), then click OK.

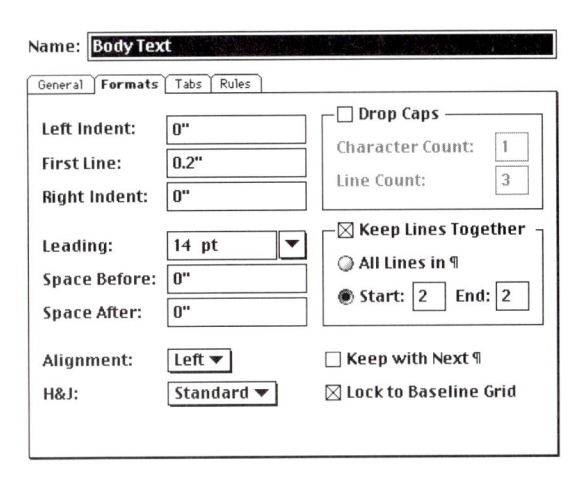

Press Command/Control-D to display the Character Attributes dialog box.

14. Create another style, Body Text w/Drop Cap, Based On Body Text. Give this style a keyboard equivalent of Numeric Keypad-2. Choose the Formats tab and set up a drop cap for this style as shown below (you must change the Left Indent to zero):

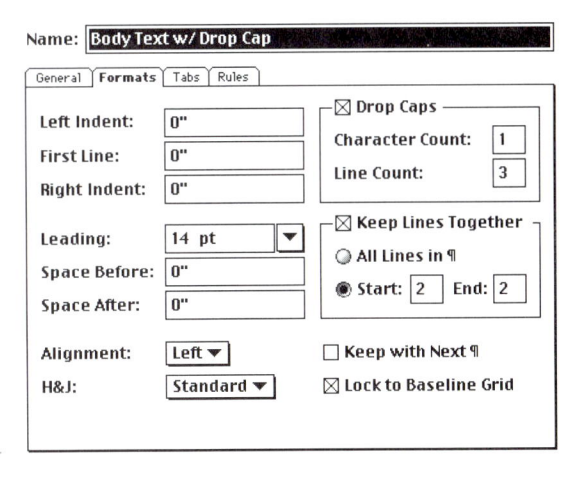

Keyboard equivalents use one of the 15 function (F) keys at the top of the keyboard in conjunction with the Control, Shift and Alt keys (Windows) or the Command, Control, Option, and Shift keys (Macintosh). Be careful not to define an existing QuarkXPress keystroke, such as Shift-F12 to a style because it will be overridden until the document is closed.

15. We're going to create more Paragraph style sheets, so just set them up as shown in the following specifications. Most of these will be based on Body Text, so you only need to make the changes shown.

    Chart Head: Based on Body Text, Next Style Self, ATC Cabana Normal, 14 pt. No Indents, leading 18 pt., Space Before 0.194″ and Space After 0.125″, not locked to Baseline Grid. Left Tab Stops at 1.75″ and 2.75″. Rule Below to Length of Indents, All Dots, a Width of 2 pt., Pantone 186.

    Chart Text: Based on Body Text, Next Style Self, ATC Cabana Normal, 12 pt. No Indents, leading 14 pt., Space After 0.05″, not locked to Baseline Grid. Left Tab Stops at 1.75″ and 2.75″.

    Heading 1: Based on No Style, Next Style Self, ATC Coconuts Extra Bold, 48 pt., Pantone 5483. No Indents, leading 60 pt., Aligned Centered, H&J of

PROJECT D/STAYING ALIVE NEWSLETTER D-5

Get in the habit of writing type specifications as you see them here — consistent and progressive from menu to menu. Otherwise you'll be flipping from Character to Format to Rules and back again.

No Hyphens, not locked to Baseline Grid. Rule Below indented 1″ from Left and Right with a Width of 1 pt., Pantone 186.

Heading 2: Based on Heading 1, Next Style Body Text, ATC Coconuts Extra Bold 28 pt., leading 32 pt. with no rule.

Heading 3: Based on No Style, Next Style Self, ATC Coconuts Extra Bold, 28 pt., Tracking of –4. No Indents, leading 32 pt., Space Before and After 0.25″, Aligned Left, H&J of No Hyphens, Keep All Lines in Paragraph Together, Keep With Next Paragraph. Rule Below to Length of Indents, All Dots, with a Width of 3 pt., Pantone 5483.

Pull Quote: Based on Body Text, Next Style Self, ATC Cabana Normal, 12 pt., Indent Left and Right 0.25, No First Line Indent, Drop Cap with a Character Count of 2, 2 Lines Deep, Keep All Lines in Paragraph Together, not locked to Baseline Grid.

16. Create the following character styles as specified:

    Body Italic: Keyboard equivalent of Numeric Keypad-3, ATC Cabana Italic, 12 pt.

    Heading 1-186: ATC Coconuts Extra Bold, 48 pt., Pantone 186.

    Drop Cap 5483: ATC Coconuts Extra Bold, 12 pt., Pantone 5483.

17. Save the file.

Importing Images

1. Draw a rectangular picture box 5.25″ × 3.85″ and place it against the Right and Bottom Margins of page 1. Give it a 2 pt. Frame of Pantone 116. Import the image **Foot in Boot.TIF** from the **SF-Adv QuarkXPress** folder. Position the image in the middle of the box by pressing Command/Control-Shift-M.

2. On page 2 draw a picture box with the following dimensions and coordinates, with a Frame of 2 pt., Pantone 5483. Import the image **Tent-cooking.TIF** and center it in the box.

    X: 3.5″   W: 4″
    Y: 0.625″ H: 5.5″

3. Go to page 3 and draw an oval picture box with a Frame of 2 pt., Pantone 5483. Assign it a Runaround Offset of 10 pt. Import the image **Backpackers.TIF** and center the two people in the box.

    X: 2.75″ W: 3″
    Y: 7.0″ H: 3.5″

4. Go to page 4 and draw a 3.4″ tall rectangular picture box at the top of the Middle Column with a Frame of 2 pt., Pantone 116. Import the image **Backpacker II.TIF** and center it in the box.

Importing Text

1. Go to page 1 and Draw a textbox with the following parameters:

   X: 0.5″   W: 7.5″
   Y: 2.25″   H: 8.5″

   From Item>Modify, select the Text tab, and assign 2 Columns with a Gutter Width of 0.25″. Import the text file **Staying Alive text1.TXT** from the **SF-Adv QuarkXPress** folder. Press Command/Control-A to select all of the text, then press Numeric Keypad-1 to style it as Body Text.

2. Select the first line that reads "Staying Alive in the Woods" and cut it. Create a new text box with the following parameters:

   X: 0.5″   W: 7.5″
   Y: 0.5″   H: 1.7″

   Give the text box a 2 pt. frame of Pantone 5483 and a background of 30% Pantone 116. Paste the text you cut. Remove the hyphens and their spaces from around the text. From Item>Modify>Text, choose a Vertical Alignment of Centered.

3. Click an Insertion Point before "Staying". Type "Staying Alive" and press Return. Style the first line as Heading 1. Style the second line as Heading 2. Select the word "Alive" in the first line and apply the Character style Heading 1–186.

4. If there is a blank line at the top of the body text delete it. In the large text box, select the first line, "Every Necessity is Free," and apply the Heading 3 style.

5. Click anywhere in the first paragraph and apply the style Body Text w/Drop Cap. Select the drop cap "A" in "any" and apply the Character style Drop Cap 5483.

6. Page 1 should now look like this. Save the file.

7. Go to page 2 and click an Insertion Point in the First Column. Import the text file **Staying Alive text 2.TXT** from the **SF-Adv QuarkXPress** folder. Select All, and style it as Body Text. Select the First Line and style it as Heading 3. Click anywhere in the first paragraph and apply the style Body Text w/Drop Cap. Select the drop cap "S" in "starvation" and apply the Character style Drop Cap 5483.

Press Command/Control-T to display the Runaround dialog box.

The Next Column character can be used to force copy to jump to the next column or the next text block in a linked chain of text boxes. This is very useful for formatting repetitive material such as a corporate phone directory.

8. Click an Insertion Point before the "W" at the beginning of the fourth paragraph and press the Enter key on the Numeric Keypad. The rest of the story jumps to the next column. Click the picture box and give it a Bottom Runaround of 25 pt.

9. Go to the end of this story and press Enter again to move the insertion point to the next column (it may jump to the top, next to the image, but that's OK). Import **Staying Alive text 3.TXT** into the third column. Select the first line and style it as Heading 3. Format the first paragraph as you did previously with the colored drop cap. Click in the second paragraph and style it as Body Text. You should see the small red overset text warning symbol at the bottom of the column.

10. At the bottom of the right column, draw a new text box over the column to hold a "continued on page x" notation. Make it the width of the column and 0.25″ in height with an runaround of 1 pt. Type "continued on page " and then type Command/Control-4 to insert the Next Box Page Number character. This will appear as <none>, but will change to the correct page number after you link the overset text to another text box on a different page. Select the entire line and style it as ATC Cabana Italic, 10 pt., Pantone 5483, Aligned Right. Position the box on the bottom margin.

11. Save the document. Here's what page 2 should look like:

12. Switch your View to 50% or less, so you can see both pages 2 and 3. Click the Link tool once on the last column of text on page 2, then click the text box on page 3.

13. Select the text on page 3 and style it as Body Text. Click in the line "Letting Predators Hunt For Us," and style it as Heading 3. Apply the usual Drop Cap settings to the first paragraph. Apply the same Subhead/Drop Cap styling with the other sections starting with "A Spaghetti That Grows On Trees" and "How To Test For Edibility".

14. Zoom in on the drop cap "T". It is overlapping the characters to the right.

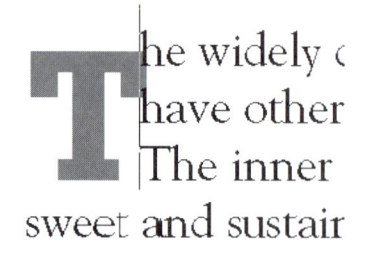

Click between the "T" and the following "h" and type a non-breaking flex space. Create a Line Return (Command-Return [Macintosh] or Control-Enter [Windows]); do the same for the "h" on the Second Line. This will move the two "h" letters over. It is a matter of taste and preference whether to space the "T" in the Third Line over any more, and we have left it alone.

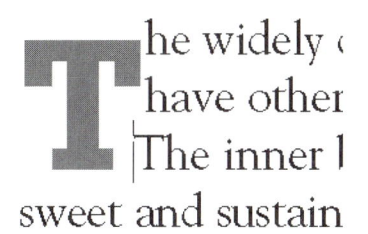

15. Add another "continued on…" box at the bottom of the Right Column. Copy and Paste the one from page 2 with the Item tool. The number will change automatically. Adjust the box position to fit in the remaining space.

16. This is what page 3 should look like:

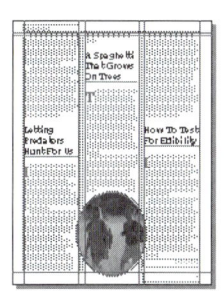

17. Link the large text box on page 3 to the box on page 4. With the Item tool selected, Paste the "continued on…" box at the top of the column. The page number will change to <none>. Select <none> and type Command/Control-2 to insert the Previous Text Box character, which will show as 3. Change "on" to "from".

18. Select the large text box on page 4 and change it to a single column (Item> Modify>Text>Columns). Resize the box to fit within the left column guides.

19. Draw a new text box within the guides of the two right columns. Fill it with 30% Pantone 116 and give it a 2 pt. Frame of Pantone 186. Send the box to the back. Import the file **Staying Alive text 4.TXT** from the **SF-Adv QuarkXPress** folder into the box. The default runaround of the image (Item, 1 pt. Outset) will cause the text to flow around it. Select all of the text and style it as Body Text. From Item>Modify>Runaround, set Bottom to 10 pt. and Right to 20 pt. Select the first line and style it as Heading 3. Assign the first paragraph style and treat the drop cap appropriately. Remove all extra spaces between paragraphs.

20. Select the line "Item Quantity Purpose," and style it as Chart Head. Select the rest of the text below this line and style it as Chart Text.

21. Draw a text box 5.125″ Tall with the bottom against the Bottom Margin Guide. Fill it with 30% Pantone 116 and give it a 2 pt. Frame of Pantone 5483. Import the file **Masthead.TXT** and make certain that Include Style Sheets is checked. Center the text Vertically (Item>Modify>Text). If an Overset Text Warning appears, delete the extra Return character after the phone number.

22. Here's what page 4 should look like:

23. Go to page 2 and draw a text box 2.25″ Tall within the Left Column with the bottom against the Bottom Margin Guide. Fill it with 30% Pantone 116 and give it a 2 pt. Frame of Pantone 5483. In the first paragraph of the Second Column, Select and Copy the sentence that starts with "When regular rations …" and Paste it into this box. Style it as Pull Quote. Select the "W" drop cap and color it Pantone 5483. Center the text Vertically, then position the box within the column to fill the space.

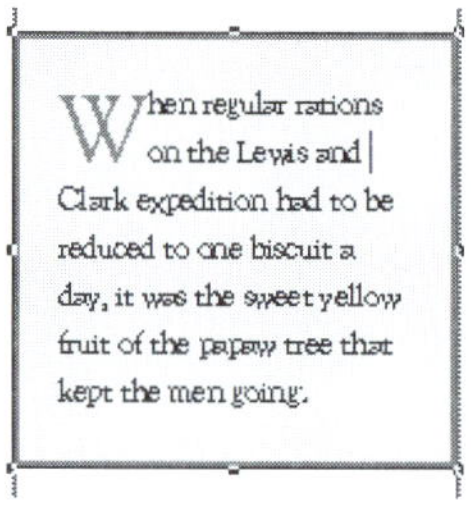

24. Save and close the file. You're done.

To type a non-breaking flex space character, press Command/Control-Option/Alt-Shift-<Space bar>. A flex space is a special variable-width space character; you can specify the width in the Document Preferences>Text dialog box as a percentage of the width of an en space.

Project E: Automation Booklet

Setting up the New Document

1. Create a new document, letter-size, 1″ Margins all around, 3 Columns, 0.25″ Gutter Width, Facing Pages On and Automatic Text Box Off, as shown below.

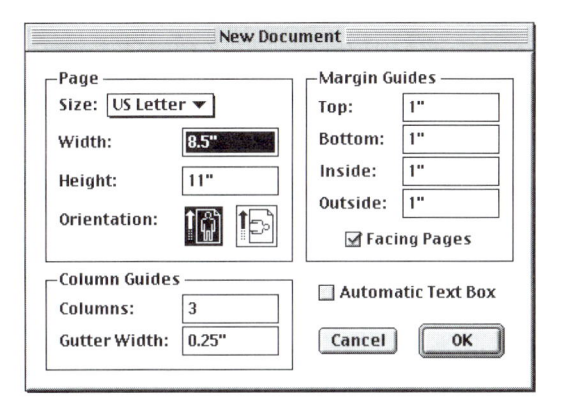

2. Go to the master page, A-Master A, and fit the Left Page in the window. Draw a rectangular picture box as described below, with no Frame and White as the Fill Color.
   X: 0.725   W: 7.4″
   Y: 0.6″   H: 9.5″

3. Import the file **Notes.EPS** from the **SF-Adv QuarkXPress** folder. Set a Uniform Scale of 95% to accommodate the drawing's left and right rules.

4. Draw a 1″ Square text box anywhere on the Left Page. Give it a Fill of None. Make it an automatic text box: Select the Link tool from the Tool palette, click the Link icon at the upper left corner of the (Left) Page, then click the new text box. This might seem like an odd thing to do, but there's a reason for it which we'll explain in a few steps.

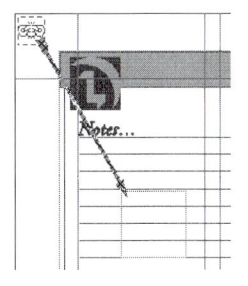

5. Fit the right-hand page of the spread in your window. Drag Vertical Guides to 2.375″ and 2.5″; drag Horizontal Guides down to 10.125″ and 10.25″.

6. Draw a text box as described below, filled with a Color of None. Link this box to the smaller left-hand text box by selecting the Link tool, clicking the Link icon at

---

We don't make a habit out of telling you to save your work every four or five steps, although that doesn't mean that you shouldn't. Since this is an advanced course, we assume that you've worked on machines long enough to have lost important files more than once. Saving often is a good idea, especially when you're working on long documents.

If you draw your rule from the bottom upward, you can use the Measurements palette to accurately and easily position it.

Double-click the Master Page icon in the Document Layout palette to view the master page, or select the master page from the pop-up menu at the bottom of the screen.

the top left of the Right Page, then clicking the text box.

X:	2.5″	W:	5″
Y:	1″	H:	9″

7. Draw a picture box: Width: 1.375″ and Height: 1.8″. Position it against the Upper Left Margins of the Left Column on the Right Page.

8. Draw a 1 pt. vertical rule 7.5″ in length, beginning at X: 1″, Y: 10.125″. (See the sidebar for a quick tip.)

9. Draw a text box to hold the Page footer, starting at X: 1″, Y: 10.25″ and stretching across the three columns, 0.2″ in Height. Type the following: "Automation, press Option/Shift-<tab> to insert a Right-aligned tab, Page " (put a space after "Page") then press Command/Control-3 to add an automatic page number character, which appears as <#>. Press Command/Control-A to select all, and style the text ATC Cabana Normal, 11 pt. auto leading. The footer should look like this:

Automation   Page <#>

10. Copy the text box and paste it to X: 1″, Y: 10.125″ on the left page. Delete everything in front of "Page <#>". Click the insertion point after "<#>" and press Option/Shift-<tab>. Type "Notes." The Left Footer should look like this:

Page <#>   Notes

11. Save the document as "Automation Booklet.QXD" into your **Work in Progress** folder.

Create Styles

1. Now create the style sheets to use in the document. Choose Edit>Style Sheets to show the Style Sheets dialog box. Click New to create the first style, Body Text, as a Paragraph style, Based on: No Style, Next Style: Self. Set the Character Attributes as shown below.

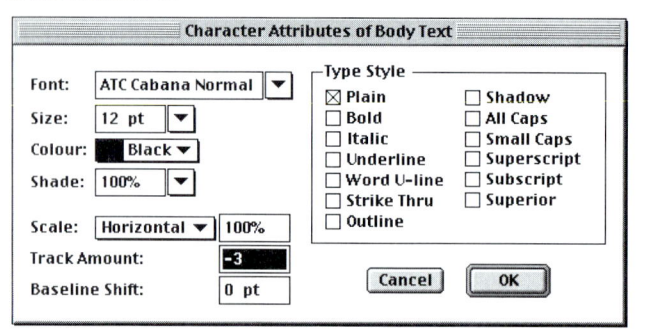

E-2   PROJECT E/AUTOMATION BOOKLET

Click OK, then click the Formats tab. Set the Left Indent: 0.333″, leading 16.5 pt., Space After 0.155″, Alignment Left. Keep Start 2 and End 2 Lines Together. Click OK to close the Edit Style dialog box.

2. Create the following styles:

Heading 1 — Based on: No Style, Next Style: Body Text. Font ATC Margarita Bold, 18 pt., Track Amount: –2, no Indents, leading: 22 pt., Space After: 0.35″ Keep with Next ¶; Rule Below: Length of Indents, 6 pt. from Left and Right, Offset: 0.15″, Style: Solid, Width: 2 pt., Color: Black.

Heading 2 — Based on: Heading 1, Next Style: Body Text, Font ATC Margarita Bold, 12 pt., Track Amount: –2, Left Indent 0.25″, leading 16.5 pt., Space After: 0.15″, no Rule Below.

Bullets — Based on: Body Text, Next Style: Self, Left Indent 0.813″, First Line Indent –0.25″, Tabs at Left, 0.813″.

3. Save the document.

Add Text and Pages

1. Go to the document page (double-click in the Document Layout palette to jump to the page).

2. Insert some extra pages for the Cover and Table of Contents. Choose Page>Insert… and add four pages to the end of the document, based on A-Master A.

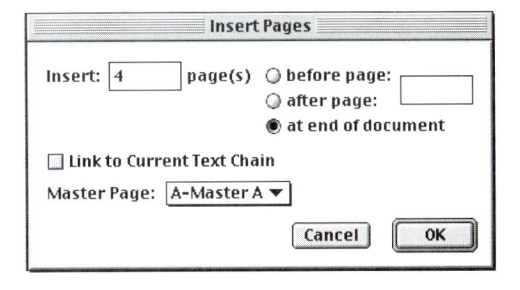

3. Delete all of the Master Page items on pages 1 through 3 except for the Master Page Guides.

4. Press Command/Control-Y to show the Document>General preferences. Make certain that Auto Page Insertion is set to End of Document.

5. Go to page 5, select the Content tool, then click an Insertion Point in the large text box. Import the file **Booklet.TXT** from the **SF-Adv QuarkXPress** folder. Make certain that the Include Style Sheets box is checked. The imported text will automatically flow and add pages until all the text is placed.

Don't use the Horizontal or Vertical scale to stretch, condense, bloat up or otherwise modify the shapes of the typeface. If you want a condensed typeface, use a condensed typeface such as ITC Garamond Condensed or Futura Condensed. Don't artificially create a condensed (or expanded or tall) typeface because it will look terrible; the letters lose all of their proportions and often look malformed. Just because a feature is there doesn't mean you have to use it!

With the Item tool, draw a Selection box around the entire page to select the contents. Be certain to Shift-click on any items you don't want to select. Using the Select All command on spread pages will select everything on both pages.

6. Remember the funny, seemingly orphaned picture box you drew on the left side of the master page? QuarkXPress won't flow text automatically on just one side of a two-page spread; you have to fool it into thinking there's an automatic text box on each page of the spread. Hence the small mystery box — it's there to guide the text flow. We don't want any text to actually appear in it; we need to alter it so that no text appears in it. We can do this the hard way by inserting Next Box characters (typed by pressing the Enter key on the far right of the keyboard) in the text, or the easy way by setting a Text Inset that is bigger than the text box. This will force all the text to the Right Pages. Go to the master page, select this Text-Traffic-Controller box, and give it a Text Inset (Item>Modify>Text) of 35 pt.

7. The text will now flow only through the boxes on the right-hand pages.

Add the Artwork

1. Go to page 5 and select the rectangular picture box in the upper left corner by the heading "Can workflow be automated?" Import the file, **Guy on the Raft.EPS** from the **SF-Adv QuarkXPress** folder. Press Command/Control-Opt/Alt-Shift-F to automatically scale the artwork proportionally to the picture box bounds.

2. Go to page 7 and import **Leader of People.EPS** into the picture box next to the header. Scale the image as you did in Step 22.

3. The following pages get their own images. Follow the guide on the next page to determine what pages get which images placed into the box next to the header (and be certain to save your document frequently). Scale each image to proportionally fit within the picture box:

Page   Image File

11   **Students with Questions.EPS**

15   **Counting Money.EPS**

17   **Students around Computer.EPS**

19   **File Repair Mechanic.EPS**

23   **Counting Money.EPS**

33	**Flatten the Learning Curve.EPS**
37	**Output Person.EPS**
43	**Trade Salesperson.EPS**
45	**Customer Service Rep.EPS**
47	**Leader of People.EPS**

4. You may need to link some of the text boxes. Save the document.

Adding Final Text

1. Add a final page 48 if there isn't one, based on the master page. Remove all Master Page items from page 48, because this will be a blank Back Cover.

2. Go to page 1. Draw a 1.5″ Square picture box in the middle of the Center Column, 1.25″ from the top of the page. Import the file **Fulfillment/Distribution.EPS** and scale it the same way as the other images you just placed.

3. Draw a text box to the following specifications:

   X: 1″   W: 6.5″
   Y: 3.3 ″   H: 0.5″

   Type "Automation in a Prepress Environment" and apply the Heading 1 style. Center the text. Here's what you should have:

4. Duplicate the text box and Center it between the columns 9.7″ from the top of the page. Select all the text, delete it, and type "Prepared for:" and then type Shift+Return (new line, not new paragraph). Type "Luminous Corporation" and style all of the text as Heading 2, Centered.

5. Go to page 2. Draw a 1.5″ or so Tall text box across the Columns 8.5″ from the top. Type "The materials contained in this document cannot be reproduced or distributed by any means, electronic or otherwise, without the express written permission of the authors." Style the text as Body Text. At the end of paragraph, press Return and type the following: "Copyright © 1998" and press Shift+Return for a New Line. Continue with "Against the Clock" <new line> "All Rights Reserved."

This artwork is all EPS vector art and can be scaled up or down without any loss of image quality. Do not scale TIFF or other bitmap/raster images; this can cause the image quality to degrade.

Type the © symbol as: Option-G (Macintosh) or Alt-G (Windows).

6. Select all the text, Center it, and remove the Indents (Style>Formats>Indents: 0).

7. Save the document.

Creating a Table of Contents

1. Go to page 3 and apply the master page to it. Delete the Footer text box. Import the image **Graduate.EPS** into the picture box, scaling it automatically.

2. Click an Insertion Point in the Main text box. Choose Edit>Lists… .

3. In the Edit Lists dialog box, click New.

4. Name the new list "Table of Contents".

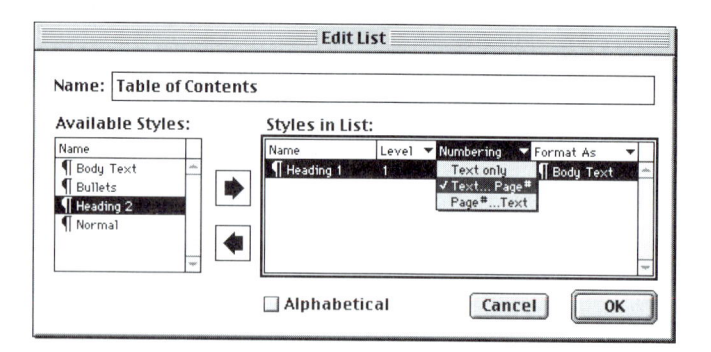

We want all of the Page headers to be the reference for the Table of Contents. Luckily, all of the headers use the same style, Heading 1. Click Heading 1 in the Available Styles list, then click the Right Arrow in the dialog box to define the list around the Page headers. Select Level 1, Numbering of Text… Page #, and format it as Body Text. Click OK, then click Save in the Lists dialog box.

5. Choose View>Show Lists; the list appears. If the box is empty, click the Update button to collect all of the List items.

6. Make certain that the Insertion Point is in the text box on page 3, then click the Build button on the Lists palette. The Table of Contents is automatically built and placed in the text box. The formatting isn't so great, but all the ingredients are there. Select all of the text and assign a right-hand Tab at 4.5″. Delete the first line, because the Title doesn't need to be in the Table of Contents.

7. Click an Insertion Point before the First Line and type "Lesson Plan". Style it as Heading 1. Here's what page 3 should look like:

8. Save the document. You're done!

If you change the text that's assigned to be included in the table of contents or any other type of list, click the Update button to refresh the contents of the list.

Notes:

Project F: GASP Newsletter

Setting up the Document

1. Choose File>New and create a letter-sized document with Facing Pages. Set the Inside Margin to 0.5", the Outside and Top to 0.375" and the Bottom Margin to 0.625" with Three Columns, 0.25" Gutter Width, and Automatic Text Box Off.

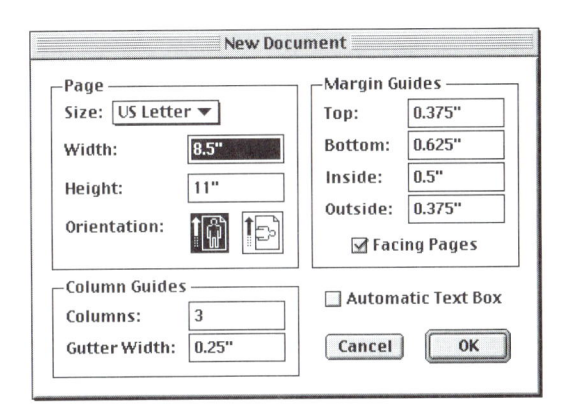

2. Choose Edit>Colors and click New. Select Pantone Coated from the Model: pop-up menu. Type "876" to select Pantone 876 and click OK. Click Save.

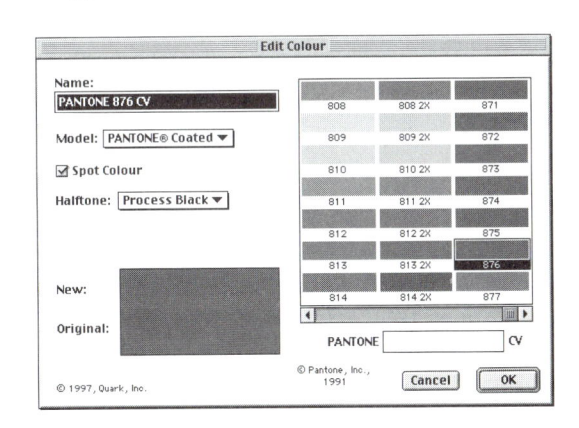

3. Double-click the Master Page name and rename it "3 columns". Go to the left side of the master page. With the Oval Text Box tool, draw a circle that is 0.25" in diameter. Fill the circle with None, and give it a Frame of 1 pt. Pantone 876.

4. In the round text "box," type a page number marker (Command/Control-3); make it 12 pt. ATC Tequila, Centered. Position the "box" at the bottom center of the page at the 10.5" mark. Uh oh, the page number marker <#> won't fit in a round box. Change the content type to None (Item>Content>None) with a Runaround of None, draw a rectangular text box, 0.25" Square, with a Fill of

PLEASE EXCUSE US!

Incorrect text files were inadvertently included on your Student CD. Corrected files for this project may be found on our Web site: AgainstTheClock.com.

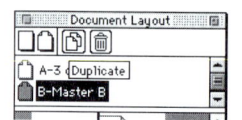

Pantone 876 is a metallic copper-colored ink — it has had a small amount of very fine metal powder (typically aluminum or bronze) mixed with the base ink to give it a metallic sheen. Large areas of metallic ink on the page should be varnished to prevent fingerprints and tarnishing over time. Metallic inks are also quite expensive, so use them only after presenting a printing estimate to your client.

White, then type the page number marker in the text box, Centered Horizontally and Vertically. Group both items, with the text box Behind. Position the group at X: 4.125, Y: 10.5.

5. Step and Repeat the box 8.5″ Horizontally, Zero Vertically to make a copy Centered at the bottom of the Right Page.

6. With the Orthogonal Line tool, draw a Vertical 10″ line. Change the line specifications as shown below.

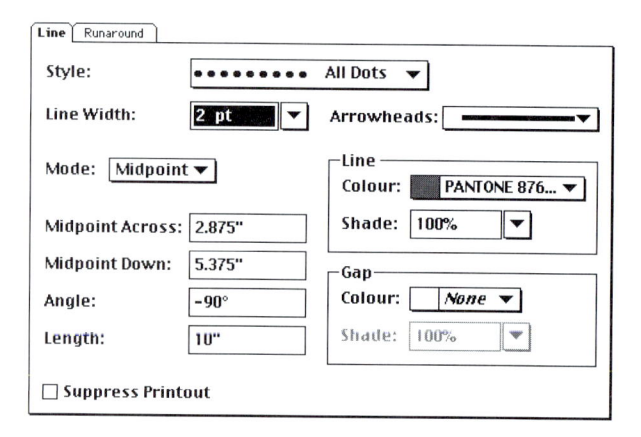

These setting will set the rule precisely within the Left Gutter, between Columns One and Two.

7. Step and Repeat the rule once Horizontally 2.625″ and Zero Vertically to place a copy in the Second Gutter. Select both rules and Step and Repeat them 8.625″ (not 8.5″ because of the differing Inner and Outer Margins) Horizontally across the spread to place them in the gutters of the right-hand page.

8. Draw a text box with a background of White on each page within the margins, with three columns and a Gutter of 0.25″. Do not Link or Auto link them. Send them to the Back.

9. In the Document Layout palette, duplicate the 3 Column master and rename the duplicate "3 columns-header".

Get into the habit of positioning objects numerically rather than by eye. With simple math, you can precisely position objects such as these rules rather than trying to "eyeball" them. Using Step and Repeat ensures that multiple copies will also be precisely positioned on the page.

Select the 3 columns-header master page. Choose Page>Master Guides and change the Top Margin to 1″ then select one of the Dotted Line rules. Click the Top Endpoint and Shift-drag it down to the 1″ Top Margin; repeat for the other three rules. The text boxes will be automatically resized. Add a Horizontal Ruler Guide across the spread at 0.375″.

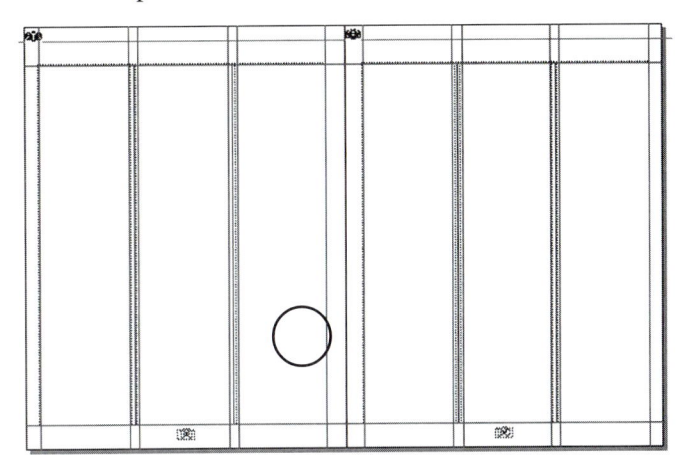

Press Command/Control-Option/Alt-D to display the Step and Repeat dialog box.

10. Drag a new one-page master to the Master Page palette. Name it "Masthead".

11. With the Masthead master page selected, choose Page>Master Guides… and set the page as shown below.

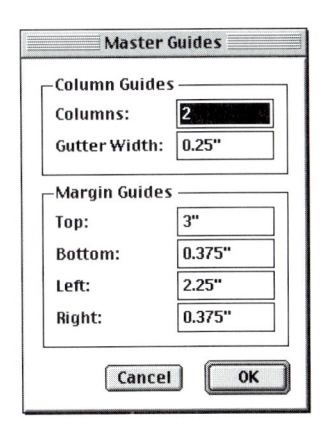

12. Draw four rectangular boxes to the specifications below. Set the Fill as specified and Frame with None. The box contents are in the Last Column. All measurements are in inches:

X: −0.125	Y: −0.125	W: 8.75	H: 2.375	Fill: 100% Black,	Picture
X: −0.125	Y: 2.25	W: 2	H: 8.875	Fill: 10% Black,	Picture
X: −0.125	Y: 2.125	W: 8.75	H: 0.125	Fill: 50% Pantone 876,	Text
X: 1.875	Y: 2.25	W: 0.125	H: 8.875	Fill: 70% Pantone 876,	None

The image is a duotone created in Photoshop. A duotone is a grayscale image that is converted to an image that uses Black (or any spot color) and a second ink color to produced a tinted effect in the printed image. Usually, the Black (or darkest ink) is used in the shadow and midtone areas of the image, and the second ink is used in the midtone and highlight areas of the image. This particular duotone uses Black and the Metallic Copper Pantone 876 inks.

13. Select the top Black box and Step and Repeat it once with Zero Offset. Choose Item>Content>Text to change it to a text box. Type "GASP". Make it 150 pt. ATC Coconuts Extra Bold, Centered Vertically and Horizontally, and Color it White. Select all the text and choose Style>Text to Box. The new box appears below the text box. Select the text box and delete it, then Center the new picture box within the Black Rectangle. Import the image **Press guy2.EPS** into the box and position it as desired.

14. Draw a transparent text box and type "THE". Make it 60 pt. ATC Cabana Normal; Align Left and Color it White. Position the box at X: 0.5″, Y: 0.25″. Step and Repeat the text box. Select the word "THE" and replace it with "REPORT". Resize the text box as necessary and position it at X: 4.5″, Y: 1.25″.

15. Draw a Transparent text box and type "In This Issue:" Make the text 18 pt. ATC Colada with 18 pt. leading and Small Caps, Centered. Position it at X: 0 and Y: 2.5″. Adjust the Width to 1.87″ to fit within the Gray box between the Left Edge and the Narrow Vertical Bar.

16. Draw a text box as follows:
    X: 0.25″   W: 1.5″
    Y: 9.825″ H: 0.8″
    with a Fill of 100% Pantone 876. Type the following into the box:

    "For subscription information <New Line>
    visit our Web site at <New Line>
    www.gaspnet.com or call <New Line>
    800/256-4282 <New Line>"

Highlight the text and make it ATC Tequila, 11 pt. 20% Pantone 876, 12 pt. leading, Centered Vertically and Horizontally.

17. This is what the finished Masthead page looks like:

18. Save the document to your **Work in Progress** folder and name it "GASP Report.QXD".

Building the Document

1. Go to page 1 and apply the Masthead master.

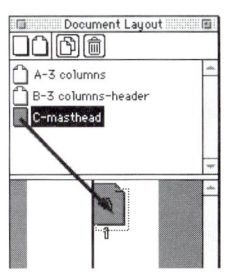

2. Drag the 3 columns master four times to create pages 2–5 as spreads.

3. Drag the 3 columns-header master to the left of the spine for pages 6, 8, and 10, and drag it to the right of the spine for page 11. Drag the 3 columns master to the right of the spine for pages 7, 8, and 9, and to the left of the spine for page 12.

Your Document Layout palette should look like this:

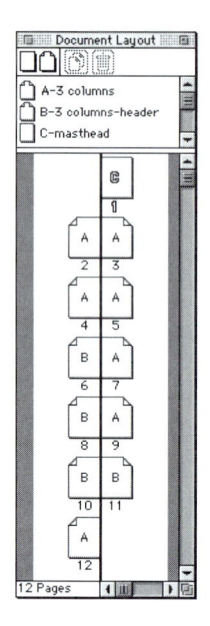

Creating Styles

1. Create a new H&J that turns off Automatic Hyphenation. Name it "No Hyphens".

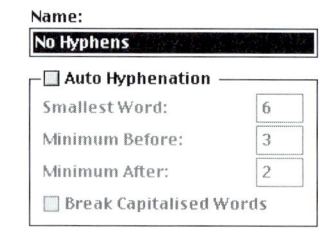

Create two more H&Js, "Tighter" and "Looser" based upon the following settings.

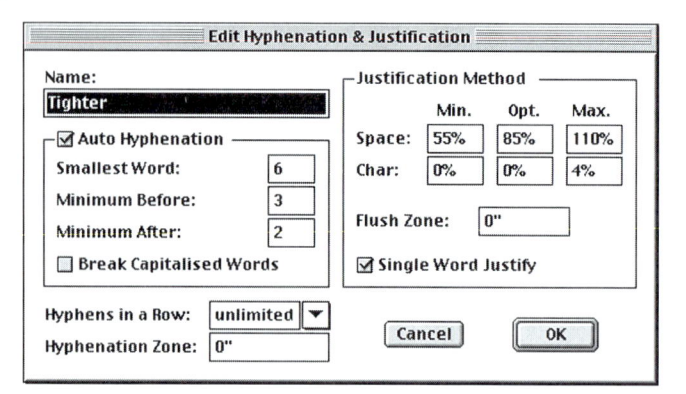

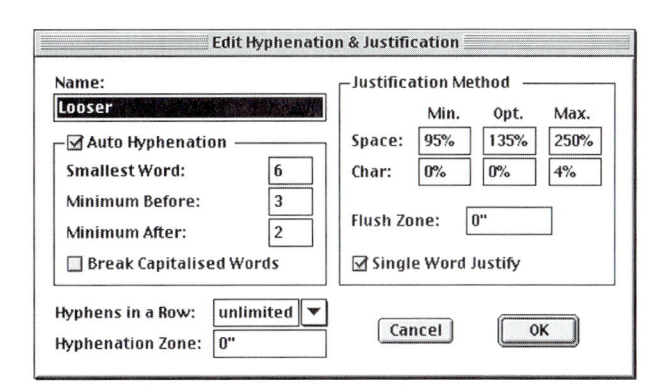

We'll use these H&Js when setting up the style sheets.

2. Choose Edit>Preferences>Document>Paragraph and set a Baseline Grid starting at 0.5″ from the top, 14 pt. Increment.

3. Create the style sheets to use in the document. Choose Edit>Style Sheets to display the Styles dialog box. Click New to create the First style, Body Text, as a Paragraph style, Based on: No Style, Next Style: self. Set the Character Attributes as shown.

Press Command/Control-Option/Alt-H to display the Edit H&Js dialog box.

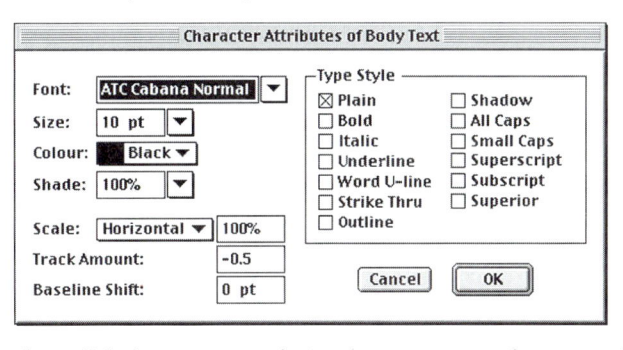

Click OK, then click the Formats tab. Set the Formats as shown on the next page.

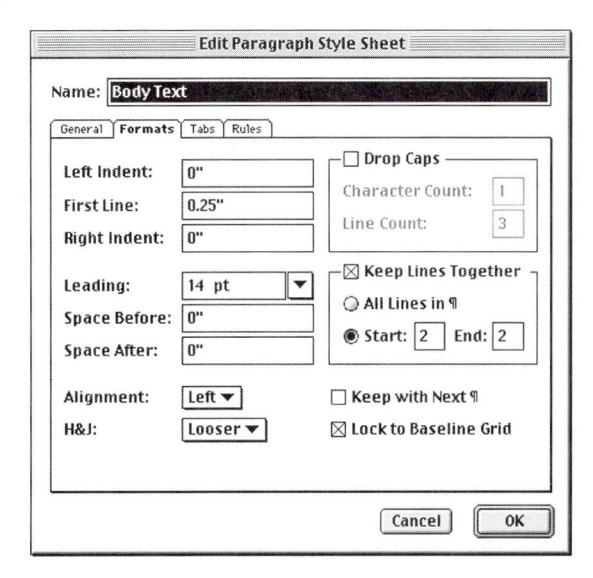

PROJECT F/GASP NEWSLETTER F-7

Sometimes, as in the case of Content Head and Content Text, which reference one another, you simply have to create one, then go back after you've created the Referenced style to create the "Next Style" feature.

4. Click OK to close the Edit Style dialog box.
5. Create the following Paragraph styles:

    Body Text Tighter: Based on: Body Text, Next Style: self, H&J: Tighter.

    Bullets: Based on: Body Text Tighter, Next Style: self, Left Indent: 0.25″, First Line: –0.25″, Space Before/After: 0.05″, Lock to Baseline Grid Off, Left Tab: 0.25″.

    Content Head: Based on: No Style, Next Style: Content Text, Font/Leading: ATC Tequila 15/15, Color: White, Track Amount: –2, All Caps, Right Indent: 0.04″, Alignment: Right, H&J: No Hyphens.

    Content Text: Based on: No style, Next Style: Content Head, Font/Leading: ATC Cabana Normal 7.5/8, Left Indent: 0.125″, Right Indent: 0.04″, Space Before and After: 0.04″, Alignment: Right, H&J: No Hyphens.

    First Para: Based on: Body Text, Next Style: Body Text, First Line Indent: 0″.

    First Para Drop Cap: Based on: First Para, Next Style: Body Text, Drop Cap of Char Count: 1, Lines: 3.

    First Para Tighter: Based on: First Para, Next Style: Body Text Tighter, H&J: Tighter.

    First Para Drop Cap Tighter: Based on: First Para Drop Cap, Next Style: Body Text Tighter, H&J: Tighter.

    Heading 1: Based on: No Style, Next Style: self, Font/Leading: ATC Tequila 36/36, Track Amount: –4, Left Indent: 0.15″, H&J: No Hyphens, Rule Above: Length of Indents, Solid, 24 pt., Color: 50% Pantone 876, Offset: 0.2″.

    Heading 2: Based on: Heading 1, Next Style: Body Text, Font/Leading: ATC Tequila 18/18, Track Amount: –2, No Indents, Space Before: 0.2″, Keep All Lines Together, Keep with Next ¶, Rule Above: Length of Indents, Solid, 2 pt., Color: Pantone 876, Offset: 0.2″, Rule Below: Width of Text, 2 pt., Solid, Color: Pantone 876, Offset: 0.05″.

    Last Para: Based on: Body Text, Next Style: self, Space After: 0.05″, and set a Right Tab at 2.375″.

    Last Para Tighter: Based on: Last Para, Next Style: self, H&J: Tighter.

    Pull Quote: Based on: No Style, Next Style: self, Font/Leading: ATC Cabana Italic 14/16, Track Amount: –2, No Indents, Space Before: 0.3″, Space After: 0.3″, H&J: No Hyphens, Tab at Left, 0.25″, Rule Above: Length of Indents, 4 pt., Solid, Color: Pantone 876, Offset: 0.25″, Rule Below: Width of Text, Solid, 4 pt., Color: Pantone 876, Offset: 0.15″.

    Sidebar: Based on: No Style, Next Style: self, Font/Leading: ATC Cabana 9/12.5, Track Amount: –1.5, Left Indent: 0.30″, First Indent: 0″, Right Indent: 0.30″, Space Before: 0″, Space After: 0.06″, H&J: Tighter.

Masthead Text: Based on No Style, Next Style: self, Font/Leading: ATC Cabana Normal 8/9, Color: Black, Track Amount: 0, Alignment: Centered, H&J Looser.

Masthead Titles: Based on No Style, Next Style: self, Font/Leading: ATC Tequila 12/12, Color: Pantone 876, Track Amount: –0.5, 0.1″ Before, Alignment Centered, H&J: Tighter.

Table Text: Based on No Style, Next Style: self, Font/Leading: ATC Cabana Normal 12/18, Color: Black, Alignment Left, Centered Tabs at 1″, 2.25″, 3.5″, 4.75″, and 6″.

Table Head 3: Based on Table Text, Next Style Table Text, Font/Leading: ATC Cabana Bold 12/13. Space Before and After 0.05″, Rule Above: Length of Indents, 1 pt., Solid, Color: Pantone 876, Offset: 0.167″, Rule Below: Length of Indents, Solid, 1 pt., Color: Pantone 876, Offset: 0.042″.

Table Head 2: Based on Table Text, Next Style Table Head 3, Space Before and After 0″, Centered Tabs at 2.75″ and 5.375″.

Table Head 1: Based on No Style, Next Style Table Head 2, Font/Leading: ATC Tequila, 28/Auto, Pantone 876, Space After: 0.1″.

Table Footnote: Based on Table Text, Next Style: self, Character Attributes: Style: Body Text Italic, Alignment: Centered. (You will have to wait until you style the Body Text Italic Character Style to complete this one.)

6. Create the following Character styles:

Body Text Italic: Font: ATC Cabana Italic 10, Track Amount: –0.5.

Pantone Drop Cap: Font: ATC Cabana Normal 10, Track Amount: –0.5, Color: Pantone 876.

Placing Images

1. Images are located in **SF-Adv QuarkXPress** folder. Create rectangular, white-filled picture boxes and import the following graphics; resize the boxes to fit the images:

Page 1 — **Row Master.TIF**
Scale 100%; position it against the Bottom Margin, Centered between the Columns; set a Runaround of type Auto Image with a 10 pt. Outset, Outside Edges Only.

Page 2 — **GASP Logo.TIF**
Scale 50%; place it anywhere on the page.

Page 3 — **Billboard.TIF**
Place the box against the Bottom Margin, between the two Right Columns. Drag the top of the box down to 7.5″ then press Command/Control-Option/Alt-Shift-F to force-fit the image in the

You must type the Rule Offset as 0.2″ including the inch mark. If you don't, QuarkXPress assumes you mean 0.2%.

box while maintaining the proportions.

Page 4 — **Figure Box.TIF**
Scale 100%; position it against the Top Margin, Centered across all Columns. Color the image (not the picture box) Pantone 876.

Page 5 — **Tall Box.TIF**
Position it in the two Right-hand Columns so it fits within the margins of the two columns. Press Command/Control-Option/Alt-Shift-F to force-fit the image in the box while maintaining the proportions. Color it Pantone 876.

Page 11 — **Row Smarter.TIF**
Scale 113%; place the box against the Bottom Margin Centered across the columns; set a Runaround of type Item with a 1 pt. Outset all around.

Creating Text Elements

1. Go to Page 1. Select the thin, Horizontal Bar below "The GASP Report" and type <tab> "Volume 1", then <tab> "August 1998". The text will probably disappear, so select all of it (even though you can't see it) and make it 7 pt. ATC Cabana Bold with auto leading. Select the text and set a Left Tab at 0.5″ and a Right Tab at 8.25″. Color the text White.

2. Draw a transparent text box as described below, then import the file **Content.XTG**.
   X: 0.5″   W: 1.35″
   Y: 3″   H: 6″

3. Using the Bézier Picture Box tool, draw a shape like the one below, filled with Pantone 876 and no Frame, on the pasteboard.

Make the box 1.3″ Wide at its widest point and 0.42″ High. Move the box over the text box you just made so the top of the picture box is against the 3″ Horizontal Guide (click and drag the box quickly to show just the outline of the box) and the Right Edge is slightly overlapping the thin, Vertical Bar.

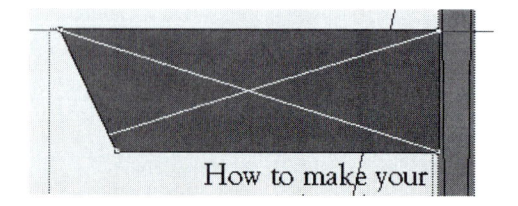

Since the Content Text style hasn't been created yet, you'll have to go back to the Content Head style and change the Next Style setting from None or Self to Content Text.

4. Step and Repeat the box 0″ Horizontally and 0.827″ Vertically. Repeat five more times to cover all the Content Head items.

5. Select the text box and choose Item>Bring to Front. Select the thin, Vertical Bar to the right of the text box and bring it to the Front.

6. Turn Invisibles On (Command/Control-I). Convert inappropriate paragraph returns to line returns, and remove extra spaces between lines, as appropriate. Apply the Content Head and Content Text styles to the appropriate text.

   Here's what the top of the Contents area should look like:

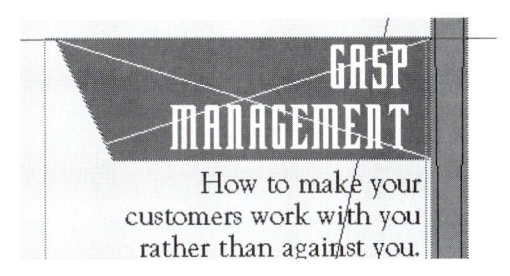

7. Draw a small, Transparent text box with a Runaround of None as described below. With the Text tool, type the number "1"; make it 36 pt. ATC Tequila, Pantone 876, and Align it Right.
   X: 0″   W: 0.5″
   Y: 3″   H: 0.55″

8. Step and Repeat the box with the same Vertical Offset, six times.

9. Renumber the remaining text blocks from top to bottom, as follows: 5, 6, 8, 9, 10, and 12. The finished Contents section should look as shown on the next page.

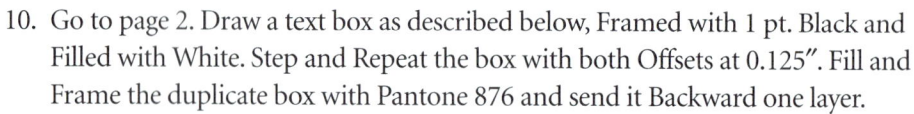

10. Go to page 2. Draw a text box as described below, Framed with 1 pt. Black and Filled with White. Step and Repeat the box with both Offsets at 0.125″. Fill and Frame the duplicate box with Pantone 876 and send it Backward one layer.
    X: 0.375″   W: 2.25″
    Y: 5″   H: 5.25″

11. Select the box with the GASP logo and resize it to 1.6″ by 0.9″. Place the box 5.1″ from the top of the page, Centered at the top of the box you just created. Position the logo in the middle of the box, and give it a Runaround type of Item, 1 pt. Offsets.

12. Import the file **Pub-Info.TXT** into the White text box. Apply the Masthead Titles style to "Editors", "Managing Editor", "Production Staff", "Illustrations", and "Legal Stuff". Apply the Masthead Text style to the balance of the text. Convert paragraph returns to line returns where appropriate. Remove extra spaces between paragraphs. (Leave the spaces in the Legal Stuff area, except for the one following the copyright line.) You might need to move the bottom of the GASP logo picture box up somewhat. The masthead should look like the one below when you're finished.

Press F5 to bring selected items to the front. Press Shift-F5 to send items to the back.

13. Look closely at the copyright line. The author simply used a "c" instead of the copyright symbol. Change it to the correct character — Option-G (Macintosh) or Alt-0169 (Windows).

14. Select the last two paragraphs at the bottom of the text block ("annual subscriptions…" and the phone number) and Copy them to the clipboard. Draw a text box in the Billboard graphic on page 3 and Paste. Resize the text box to 4″ Wide, Select the first paragraph and make it 20 pt. ATC Coconuts Extra Bold with auto leading. Select the telephone number and change it to 48 pt. ATC Tequila and Color it Pantone 876. Add a hard return before the word "for" and Center the text box within the billboard.

15. Go to page 8. Draw a text box as described below 7.625″ Wide and 0.5″ Tall, spanning all three columns. Type "For Consulting Information, call: 1.800.256.4282". Make the type 28 pt. ATC Tequila, Centered on the line and Vertically Centered in the box. Fill the text box with a Diamond Blend of White–#1 and Pantone 876–#2. Position it at X: 0.375″, Y: 3.625″.

    X: 0.375″ W: 7.625″
    Y: 3.625″ H: 0.5″

    For Consulting Information, call: 1.800.555.4282

16. Go to page 4 and draw a Transparent text box roughly within the border of the image. Type the following text, line for line. Insert tabs at the → character, line returns at the ↵, and full (paragraph) returns where you see the ¶ symbol. Assign the Paragraph styles before typing each line of text.

    Style: Table Head 1
    Appropriate Scan Resolution¶

    Style: Table Head 2
    →Good Quality→   Best Quality¶

    Style: Table Head 3
    →→   →   File Size→   →   File Size↵
    →Line Screen→ Resolution→ per Sq. Inch→ Resolution→ per Sq. Inch¶

    Style: Table Text
    →85 lpi→   130 ppi→   68k→   170 ppi→   116k¶
    →100 lpi→   150 ppi→   90k→   200 ppi→   160k¶
    →120 lpi→   180 ppi→   130k→   240 ppi→   230k¶
    →133 lpi→   200 ppi→   160k→   266 ppi→   283k¶
    →150 lpi→   225 ppi→   202k→   300 ppi→   360k¶
    →175 lpi→   265 ppi→   281k→   350 ppi→   490k¶
    →200 lpi→   300 ppi→   360k→   400 ppi→   640k¶

    Style: Table Footnote
    Supplying your customers with information such as this can save both of you time and money.

    Notice that except for the Table Footnote style, all styles were self-applying as you entered paragraph returns.

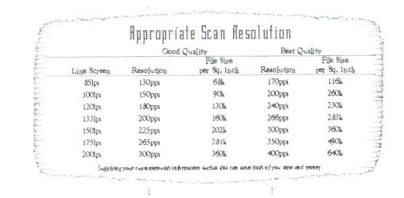

17. Drag a Horizontal Ruler Guide down to the 4.375" mark on page 4, then save your document.

Flowing the text

1. Go to page 1 and draw a new 2 column 5.875" × 7.625" text box with a Gutter of 0.25". Send it to the Back. On top of it draw a 5.875" × 0.68" one column text box. Give it a Runaround Type of Item, 1 pt. Outset. Import `Customers.XTG` into the small box. Link the box to the 2 column box.

2. Link the text through pages 2, 3, 4, and 5. Check to be certain that images and other text boxes have Runarounds, or you might lose text behind them.

3. Draw a small picture box on the pasteboard and import `Ender.EPS`. Scale it to 25%. Select the Item tool, Copy the box, select the Content tool and Paste the box as an Anchored Image at the beginning of the first line of each of the paragraphs to which the Bullets style was applied. Type a Tab between the In-line graphic and the first character of each line.

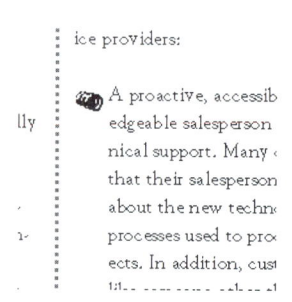

4. Go to page 5. Select the text box and choose Item>Modify>Text. Change the number of columns to 1. Resize the text box to fit in the Left Column. Paste the Ender after the last word of the story, not the author's comments or biographical information.

5. Save the file.

Press Command/Control-Shift-F to show the Formats dialog box.

This project made extensive use of tagged text. We've deliberately pre-tagged all text to show the power of the QuarkXPress Tags feature. If all this text had been unformatted plain text, or an unstyled Microsoft Word document, you would have spent a lot more time applying the styles you created to the text. Actually, all of the styles are coded into the tagged text, so you really didn't need to create all those styles, but if a style with the same name already exists in the document, that style will override any style in the tagged text. This is an important feature that lets you change styles and not worry about them reverting back to their old forms when you import the text to a new version of the document.

6. Draw a new Transparent text box within the two right columns of page 5. Import **Peas.TXT**. Style it as Sidebar.

7. Format the head "Peas" as Heading 1.

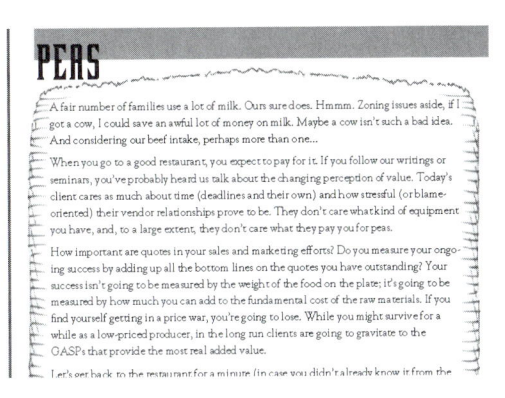

8. Paste **Ender.EPS** as an anchor after "more" in the last paragraph.

9. Go to page 6 and draw a new text box as described below. Import **Mission.XTG**, making certain that Include Style Sheets is checked. Link the text box to the three column boxes on pages 6 and 7.
   X: 0.375"   W: 7.625"
   Y: 0.25"   H: 0.75"

10. Apply the First Paragraph style to the first paragraph and to each paragraph after each Heading 2. Apply the Last Paragraph style to the last paragraph on page 7.

11. For each bullet item on page 7, style the first sentence or phrase (the part that poses the problem) as Body Text Italic.

12. You're going to have to use some skill and judgment here; the text has most likely overset the box. You should be able to, by losing widows using the Body Text Tighter Paragraph style, perhaps combined with some judicious Tracking, make the entire article fit.

13. Go to page 8 and draw a new text box as described below. Import **Paper or Plastic.XTG**, making certain that Include Style Sheets is checked. Link the text box to the three column boxes on pages 8 and 9. Change the text box on page 9 to a Single Column and resize to fit the Left Column.
    X: 0.375"   W: 7.625"
    Y: 0.25"   H: 0.75"

14. On page 9, draw a white-filled text box as described below, positioned in the Second and Third Columns. Import **Drawing.XTG**, making certain that Include Style Sheets is checked.

    X: 3.125″ W: 5″
    Y: 0.375″ H: 10″

15. Find "A Picture's Worth" in the fourth paragraph and italicize. Add a <tab> at the end of the last paragraph.

16. Save the file.

17. Go to page 10 and draw a new text box as described below. Import **Rowing.XTG**, making certain that Include Style Sheets is checked. Link the text box to the three column boxes on pages 10 and 11. Set a Top Runaround for the image on page 11 to 20 pt.

    X: 0.375″ W: 7.625″
    Y: 0.25″   H: 0.75″

18. Save the file.

19. Select Find and Replace and do a document-wide search for double hyphens -- and replace them with an em dash — (Option/Alt Shift-Hyphen). Do a search for double spaces and replace any with single spaces.

20. Go to page 12 and draw a new text box as described below. Import **Telecommunications.XTG** making certain that Include Style Sheets is checked. Link the text box to the three column box on page 10.

    X: 0.375″ W: 7.625″
    Y: 0.25″   H: 0.75″

21. Copy the first sentence in the second paragraph as a separate paragraph following the paragraph in column 3 that ends with the word "plan." Assign it the Pull Quote style. Track all Body Text Paragraphs in the story +1, to fill out the page.

22. Save the file.

Article Enders

1. Paste an Ender at the end of each story in the newsletter.

2. Go back to each article and check for widows and orphans. Clean up the articles using H&Js and Tracking to eliminate widows and orphans, and check carefully for lines and paragraphs that have deep rags, creating holes in the overall look of the document.

   If this were an actual document, we'd go into articles that ran short and add a pull quote, a small graphic, or a short blurb at the end to fill the space.

3. Save and close.

Congratulations! This is an accomplishment — a real-world experience.

Notes:

Glossary

Achromatic
By definition, having no color; therefore, completely black or white or some shade of gray.

Acrobat
This program by Adobe Systems, Inc. allows the conversion (using Acrobat Distiller) of any document from any Macintosh or Windows application to PDF format, which retains the page layout, graphics, color, and typography of the original document. It is widely used for distributing documents online because it is independent of computer hardware. The only software needed is a copy of Acrobat Reader, which can be downloaded free.

Adaptive Palette
A sampling of colors taken from an image, and used in a special compression process usually used to prepare images for the world wide web.

Additive Color Process
The additive color process is the process of mixing red, green, and blue light to achieve a wide range of colors, as on a color television screen. See Subtractive Color.

Adjacent Color
The eye will respond to a strong adjacent color in such a way as to affect the perception of the particular color in question. That is, a color having different adjacent colors may look different than it does in isolation. Also referred to as metamarism.

Adobe Systems Incorporated
A major software developer responsible for the creation of the PostScript page description language (see PostScript), used in almost all graphic arts environments. PostScript resides in a printer or Raster Image Processor (see Raster Image Processor) and is used to convert graphics from the screen to high-resolution output. Adobe also develops the highly popular Photoshop, Illustrator, PageMaker, and Premiere graphics and video applications, in addition to a range of others.

Algorithm
A specific sequence of mathematical steps to process data. A portion of a computer program that calculates a specific result.

All signature folding dummy
A folding dummy in which all of the signatures that make up the job are used to determine the page arrangement for each signature. Also known as a Job Worksheet.

Alpha Channel
An 8-bit channel of data that provides additional graphic information, such as colors or masking. Alpha channels are found in some illustration or graphics programs, and are used in video production.

Anti-Aliasing
A graphics software feature that eliminates or softens the jaggedness of low-resolution curved edges.

Archival storage
The process of storing data in a totally secure and safe manner. Archiving differs from backup in that it's meant to be used to restore entire systems or networks, rather than providing quick and easy access to specific files or folders.

Art
Illustrations and photographs in general; that is, all matter other than text that appears in a mechanical.

Artifact
By definition, something that is artificial, or not meant to be there. An artifact can be a blemish or dust spot on a piece of film, or unsightly pixels in a digital image.

Ascender
Parts of a lower-case letter that exceed the height of the letter "x". The letters b, d, f, h, k, l, and t have ascenders.

ASCII
The American Standard Code for Information Interchange, which defines each character, symbol, or special code as a number from 0 to 255 (8 bits in binary). An ASCII text file can be read by any computer, and is the basic mode of data transmission on the Internet.

ATM (Adobe Type Manager)
A utility program which causes fonts to appear smooth on screen at any point size. It's also used to manage font libraries.

Backing Up
The process of making copies of current work or work-in-progress as a safety measure against file corruption, drive or system failure, or accidental deletion. Backing up work-in-progress differs from creating an archive (see Archiving) for long-term storage or system restoration.

Banding
A visible stair-stepping of shades in a gradient.

Banner
A large headline or title extending across the full page width, or across a double-page spread.

Baseline
The implied reference line on which the bases of capital letters sit.

Bézier Curves
Curves that are defined mathematically (vectors), in contrast to those drawn as a collection of dots or pixels (raster). The advantage of these curves is that they can be scaled without the "jaggies" inherent in enlarging bitmapped fonts or graphics.

Bindery marks
Marks that appear on a press sheet to indicate how the sheet should be cropped, folded, collated, or bound.

Binding
In general, the various methods used to secure signatures or leaves in a book. Examples include saddle-stitching (the use of staples in a folded spine), and perfect-bound (multiple sets of folded pages sewn or glued into a flat spine).

Bit (Binary Digit)
A computer's smallest unit of information. Bits can have only two values: 0 or 1. This can represent the black and white (1-bit) pixel values in a line art image. Or in combination with other bits, it can represent 16 tones or colors (4-bit), 256 tones or colors (8-bit), 16.8 million colors (24-bit), or a billion colors (30-bit). These numbers derive from counting all the possible combinations (permutations) of 0 or 1 settings of each bit: $2 \times 2 \times 2 = 16$ colors; $2 \times 2 \times 2 \times 2 \times 2 \times 2 \times 2 \times 2 = 256$ colors; $2 \times 2 = 16.8$ million colors.

Bitmap image

An image constructed from individual dots or pixels set to a grid-like mosaic. Each pixel can be represented by more than one bit. A 1-bit image is black and white because each bit can have only two values (for example, 0 for white and 1 for black). For 256 colors, each pixel needs eight bits (2^8). A 24-bit image refers to an image with 24 bits per pixel (2^{24}), so it may contain as many as 16,777,216 colors. Because the file must contain information about the color and position of each pixel, the disk space needed for bitmap images is usually quite significant. Most digital photographs and screen captures are bitmap images.

Bitmapped

Forming an image by a grid of pixels whose curved edges have discrete steps because of the approximation of the curve by a finite number of pixels.

Black

The absence of color; an ink that absorbs all wavelengths of light.

Blanket

The blanket, a fabric coated with natural or synthetic rubber wrapped around the cylinder of an offset press, transfers the inked image from the plate to the paper.

Bleed

Page data that extends beyond the trim marks on a page. Illustrations that spread to the edge of the paper without margins are referred to as "bled off."

Blend

See Graduated fill.

Blind Emboss

A raised impression in paper made by a die, but without being inked. It is visible only by its relief characteristic.

Blow up

An enlargement, usually of a graphic element such as a photograph.

Body Copy

The text portion of the copy on a page, as distinguished from headlines.

Border

A continuous line that extends around text; or a rectangular, oval, or irregularly-shaped visual in an ad.

Bounding Box

The imaginary rectangle that encloses all sides of a graphic, necessary for a page layout specification.

Brightness

1. A measure of the amount of light reflected from a surface. 2. A paper property, defined as the percentage reflection of 457-nanometer (nm) radiation. 3. The intensity of a light source. 4. The overall percentage of lightness in an image.

Bullet

A marker preceding text, usually a solid dot, used to add emphasis; generally indicates that the text is part of a list.

Burn

1. To expose an image onto a plate. 2. To make copies of ROM chips or CD-ROMs. 3. To darken a specific portion of an image through photographic exposure.

Byte

A unit of measure equal to eight bits (decimal 256) of digital information, sufficient to represent one text character. It is the standard unit measure of file size. (See also Megabyte, Kilobyte, and Gigabyte).

Cab

See Flat.

Calibration

Making adjustments to a color monitor and other hardware and software to make the monitor represent as closely as possible the colors of the final printed piece.

Calibration Bars

A strip of reference blocks of color or tonal values on film, proofs, and press sheets, used to check the accuracy of color registration, quality, density, and ink coverage during a print run.

Callout

A descriptive label referenced to a visual element, such as several words connected to the element by an arrow.

Camera Ready

A completely finished mechanical, ready to be photographed to produce a negative from which a printing plate will be made.

Cap Line

The theoretical line to which the tops of capital letters are aligned.

Caps

An abbreviation for capital letters.

Caps and Small Caps

A style of typesetting in which capital letters are used in the normal way, while the type that would normally be in lower case has been changed to capital letters of a smaller point size. A true small-caps typeface does not contain any lower-case letters.

Caption

The line or lines of text that identify a picture or illustration, usually placed beneath it or otherwise in close proximity.

CD-ROM

A device used to store approximately 600MB of data. Files are permanently stored on the device and can be copied to a disk but not altered directly. ROM stands for Read-Only Memory. Equipment is now available on the consumer market for copying computer files to blank CD-ROMs.

Center marks

Press marks that appear on the center of all sides of a press sheet to aid in positioning the print area on the paper.

Character Count

The number of characters (letters, figures, signs or spaces) in a selected block of copy. Once used to calculate the amount of text that would fit on a given line or region when physically setting type.

Choke

See Trapping

Chooser

A part of the Macintosh operating system that permits selection of a printer or other peripheral device. Chooser is also used to access resources on a network.

Chroma

The degree of saturation of a surface color in the Munsell color space model.

Cromalin

A single-sheet color proofing system introduced by DuPont in 1971 and still quite popular in the industry. It uses a series of overlaid colorants and varnish to simulate the results of a press run.

Chromaticity Diagram

A graphical representation of two of the three dimensions of color. Intended for plotting light sources rather than surface colors. Often called the CIE diagram.

Cicero/Didot Point

The cicero is a unit of horizontal distance slightly larger than the pica, used widely in continental Europe. A cicero equals 0.178 inches, or 12 Didot points.

Clipboard

The portion of computer memory that holds data that has been cut or copied. The next item cut or copied replaces the data already in the clipboard.

Cloning

Duplication of pixels from one part of an image to another.

CMS

See Color Management System

CMYK

Acronym for cyan, magenta, yellow, and black, the four process color inks which, when properly overprinted, can simulate a subset of the visible spectrum. See also color separation. Also refers to digital artwork that contains information necessary for creating color separations.

CMYK (Cyan, Magenta, Yellow, Black)

Acronym for the process colors cyan, magenta, yellow, and black (subtractive primaries) used in color printing. The letter K stands for "Key," although it is commonly used to refer to the Black ink that is added to the three colors when necessary. When printing black text as part of a four-color process, only the black ink is used. A normal four-color separation will have a plate for each of the four colors. When combined on the printed piece, the half-tone dots of each color give the impression of the desired color to the eye.

Coated

Printing papers having a surface coating (of clay or other material) to provide a smoother, more even finish with greater opacity.

Cold type

Type produced by photographic or digital methods, as opposed to the use of molten metal as in the old Linotype machine.

Collate

To gather separate sections or leaves of a publication together in the correct order for binding.

Collate and cut

Multiple signatures that are stacked then cut to be later placed in sequential order, drilled, and placed in three-ring binders.

Color Balance

The combination of yellow, magenta, and cyan needed to produce a neutral gray. Determined through a gray balance analysis.

Color Cast

The modification of a hue by the addition of a trace of another hue, such as yellowish green, pinkish blue, etc. Normally, an unwanted effect that can be corrected.

Color Chart

A printed chart of various combinations of CMYK colors used as an aid for the selection of "legal" colors during the design phase of a project.

Color Control Strip

A printed strip of various reference colors used to control printing quality. This strip is normally placed outside the "trim" area of a project, as a guide and visual aid for the pressman.

Color Conversion

Changing the color "mode" of an image. Converting an image from RGB to CMYK for purposes of preparing the image for conventional printing.

Color Correction

The process of removing casts or unwanted tints in a scanned image, in an effort to improve the appearance of the scan or to correct obvious deficiencies, such as green skies or yellowish skin tones.

Color Gamut

The range of colors that can be formed by all possible combinations of the colorants of a given reproduction system (printing press) on a given type of paper.

Color Key

An overlay color proof of acetate sheets, one for each of the four primary printing inks. The method was developed by 3M Corporation and remains a copyrighted term.

Color Management System

A process or utility that attempts to manage color of input and output devices in such a way that the monitor will match the output of any CMS-managed printer.

Color Model

A system for describing color, such as RGB, HLS, CIELAB, or CMYK.

Color overlay

A sheet of film or paper whose text and art correspond to one spot color or process color. Each color overlay becomes the basis for a single printing plate that will apply that color to paper.

Color Picker

A function within a graphics application that assists in selecting a color.

Color Proof

A printed or simulated printed image of the color separations intended to produce a close visual representation of the final reproduction for approval purposes and as a guide to the press operator.

Color Separation

The process of transforming color artwork into four components corresponding to the four process colors. If spot colors are used, additional components may be created containing only those items that will appear in the corresponding spot color layer. Each component is imaged to film or paper in preparation for making printing plates that correspond to each ink.

Color Sequence

The color order of printing the cyan, magenta, yellow, and black inks on a printing press. Sometimes called rotation or color rotation.

Color Space – Desktop Publishing

Color Space
Because a color must be represented by three basic characteristics depending on the color model, the color space is a three-dimensional coordinate system in which any color can be represented as a point.

Color Temperature
The temperature, in degrees Kelvin, to which a blackbody would have to be heated to produce a certain color radiation. (A "blackbody" is an ideal body or surface that completely absorbs or radiates energy.) The graphic arts viewing standard is 5,000 K. The degree symbol is not used in the Kelvin scale. The higher the color temperature, the bluer the light.

Color Transparency
A positive color photographic image on a clear film base that must be viewed by transmitted light. It is preferred for original photographic art because it has higher resolution than a color print. Transparency sizes range from 35mm color slides up to 8x10in. (203x254mm).

Colorimeter
An optical measuring instrument designed to measure and quantify color. They are often used to match digital image values to those of cloth and other physical samples.

Column rule
A thin vertical rule used to separate columns of type.

Combination signatures
Signatures of different sizes inserted at any position in a layout.

Comp
Comprehensive artwork used to present the general color and layout of a page.

Compose
To set copy into type, or lay out a page.

Composite proof
A version of an illustration or page in which the process colors appear together to represent full color. When produced on a monochrome output device, colors are represented as shades of gray.

Compression
A digital technique used to reduce the size of a file by analyzing occurrences of similar data. Compressed files occupy less physical space, and their use improves digital transmission speeds. Compression can sometimes result in a loss of image quality and/or resolution.

Condensed Type
A typeface in which the width of the letters has been reduced. Condensed type can be a specific font, or the result of applying a percentage of normal width by a formatting command.

Continuous Tone
An image such as an original photograph in which the subject has continuous shades of color or gray tones through the use of an emulsion process. Continuous tone images must be screened to create halftone images in order to be printed.

Contrast
The relationship between the dark and light areas of an image.

Copyright
Ownership of a work by the originator, such as an author, publisher, artist, or photographer. The right of copyright permits the originator of material to prevent its use without express permission or acknowledgment of the originator. Copyright may be sold, transferred, or given up contractually.

CorelDRAW
A popular drawing program originally designed for the Windows environment, but now available as a Macintosh program. CorelDRAW is known to create files that can cause printing and/or output problems in many prepress environments.

Creep
The progressive extension of interior pages of the folded signature beyond the image area of the outside pages. Shingling is applied to correct for creep.

Crop Marks
Printed short, fine lines used as guides for final trimming of the pages within a press sheet.

Cropping
The elimination of parts of a photograph or other original that are not required to be printed.

Crossover
An element in a book (text, line art, or other graphic) that appears on both pages of a reader spread crossing over the gutter.

Custom printer description file
A file containing information specific to a type of output device; used in conjunction with a standard PPD file to customize the printing process.

DCS (Desktop Color Separation)
Acronym for Desktop Color Separation, a version of the EPS file format. DCS 1.0 files are composed of five PostScript files for each color image: cyan, magenta, yellow, and black file, plus a separate low-resolution FPO image to place in a digital file. In contrast, DCS 2.0 files have one file that stores process color and spot color information.

Default
A specification for a mode of computer operation that operates if no other is selected. The default font size might be 12 point, or a default color for an object might be white with a black border.

Densitometer
An electronic instrument used to measure optical density. Reflective (for paper) and transmissive (for film).

Descender
The part of a lower-case letter that extends below the baseline (lower edge of the x-height) of the letter. The letters y, p, g, and j contain descenders.

Desktop
1. The area on a monitor screen on which the icons appear, before an application is launched. 2. A reference to the size of computer equipment (system unit, monitor, printer) that can fit on a normal desk; thus, desktop publishing.

Desktop Publishing (DTP)
Use of a personal computer, software applications, and a high-quality printer to produce fully composed printed documents. DTP is, in reality,

an incorrect term these days. In the early days of Macintosh and PostScript technology, the term Desktop Publishing inferred that the materials produced from these systems was somehow inferior (as opposed to professional publishing). Now, the overwhelming majority of all printed materials - regardless of the quality - are produced on these systems, up to and including nationally famous magazines, catalogs, posters, and newspapers

Die line

In a digital file, the outline used to mark where cutting, stamping, or embossing the finished printed piece will occur. Uses to create a particular shape, such as a rolodex card.

Digital

The use of a series of discrete electronic pulses to represent data. In digital imaging systems, 256 steps (8 bits, or 1 byte) are normally used to characterize the gray scale or the properties of one color. For text, see ASCII.

Digital Camera

A camera which produces images directly into an electronic file format for transfer to a computer.

Digital Proofs

Digital proofs are representations of what a specific mechanical will look like when output and reproduced on a specific type of printing press. The difference with a digital proof is that it is created without the use of conventional film processes and output directly from computer files.

Dingbat

A font character that displays a picture instead of a letter, number or punctuation mark. There are entire font families of pictographic dingbats; the most commonly used dingbat font is Zapf Dingbats. There are dingbats for everything from the little airplanes used to represent airports on a map, to telephones, swashes, fish, stars, balloons - just about anything.

Direct-to-plate

Producing printing plates directly from computer output without going through the film process.

Disk Operating System (DOS)

Software for computer systems that supervises and controls the running of programs. The operating system is loaded into memory from disk by a small program which permanently resides in the firmware within the computer. The major operating systems in use today are Windows95 and WindowsNT from Microsoft, the Macintosh OS from Apple Computer, and a wide range of UNIX systems, such as those from Silicon Graphics, SUN Microsystems, and other vendors.

Dithering

A technique used in images wherein a color is represented using dots of two different colors displayed or printed very close together. Dithering is often used to compress digital images, in special screening algorithms (see Stochastic Screening) and to produce higher quality output on low-end color printers.

Document

The general term for a computer file containing text and/or graphics.

Dongle

A security device that usually plugs into your keyboard or printer port, that allows copy-protected software to run on your system. Such protected software will only run on systems with the dongle present. This prevents a single copy of software from running on any but one machine at a time.

Dot Gain

The growth of a halftone dot that occurs whenever ink soaks into paper. This growth can vary from being very small (on a high-speed press with fast-drying ink and very non-porous paper) to quite dramatic, as is the case in newspaper printing, where a dot can expand 30% from its size on the film to the size at which it dries. Failure to compensate for this gain in the generation of digital images can result in very poor results on press. Generally speaking, the finer the screen (and therefore, the smaller the dot) the more noticeable dot gain will be.

Double-page Spread

A design that spans the two pages visible to the reader at any open spot in a magazine, periodical, or book.

Downloadable Fonts

Typefaces that can be stored on disk and then downloaded to the printer when required for printing.

DPI (Dots Per Inch)

The measurement of resolution for page printers, phototypesetting machines and graphics screens. Currently graphics screens use resolutions of 60 to 100 dpi, standard desktop laser printers work at 600 dpi, and imagesetters operate at more than 1,500 dpi.

Drop Shadow

A duplicate of a graphic element or type placed behind and slightly offset from it, giving the effect of a shadow.

Drum Scanner

A color scanner on which the original is wrapped around a rotary scanning drum. See Scanner.

DSC

Acronym for the Adobe Document Structure Conventions, designed to provide a standard order and format for information so applications that process PostScript, such as PressWise, can easily find information about a document's structure and imaging requirements. These conventions allow specially formatted PostScript comments to be added to the page description; applications can search for these comments, but PostScript interpreters usually ignore them. TrapWise requires that the PostScript in incoming files is formatted using conventional DSC comments, so certain functions may not work properly if the file is not DSC-conforming.

Duotone

The separation of a black-and-white photograph into black and a second color having different tonal values and screen angles. Duotones are used to enhance photographic reproduction in two-three-or sometimes four-color work. Often the second, third, and fourth colors are not standard CMYK inks.

Dye

A soluble coloring material, normally used as the colorant in color photographs.

Dye Transfer

A photographic color print using special coated papers to produce a full color image. Can serve as an inexpensive proof.

Electrostatic

The method by which dry toner is transferred to paper in a copier or laser printer, and liquid toners are bonded to paper on some large-format color plotters.

Element

The smallest unit of a graphic, or a component of a page layout or design. Any object, text block, or graphic might be referred to as an element of the design.

Elliptical Dot Screen

A halftone screen having an elliptical dot structure.

Embedding

1. Placing control codes in the body of a document. 2. Including a complete copy of a text file or image within a desktop publishing document, with or without a link (see Linking).

Emulsion

The coating of light-sensitive material (silver halide) on a piece of film or photographic paper.

En Dash

A dash - often used in hyphenated word pairs - that is usually half the width of an em dash.

En Space

A space that is usually equal to half the width of an em space.

EPS

Acronym for encapsulated PostScript, a single-page PostScript file that contains grayscale or color information and can be imported into many electronic layout and design applications.

EPS (Encapsulated PostScript)

Acronym for file format used to transfer PostScript data within compatible applications. An EPS file normally contains a small preview image that displays in position within a mechanical or used by another program. EPS files can contain text, vector artwork, and images.

Expanded Type

Also called extended, a widened version of a typeface design. Type may be extended artificially within a DTP application, or designed as such by the typeface designer. See also Condensed Type.

Export

To save a file generated in one application in a format that is readable in another application.

Extension

A modular software program that extends or expands the functions of a larger program. A folder of Extensions is found in the Macintosh System Folder.

Fill

To add a tone or color to the area inside a closed object in a graphic illustration program.

Film

Non-paper output of an imagesetter or phototypesetter.

Film assembly

See Stripping.

Filter

In image editing applications, a small program that creates a special effect or performs some other function within an image.

First signature folding dummy

A folding dummy that determines the page arrangement for a single signature layout template. This template can then be applied to a job that requires multiple signatures, and PressWise will correctly impose all the pages based on the numbering sequence and binding method specified by the first signature.

Flat

Individual film assembled onto a carrier readied for contacting or platemaking. Referred to as a cab in gravure printing.

Flat Color

Color that lacks contrast or tonal variation. Also, flat tint.

Flatbed Scanner

A scanner on which the original is mounted on a flat scanning glass. See Scanner.

Flexographic printing

A rotary letterpress process printing on a press using a rubber plate that stretches around a cylinder making it necessary to compensate by distorting the plate image. Flexography is used most often in label printing, often on metal or other non-paper material.

Floating Accent

A separate accent mark that can be placed under or over another character. Complex accented characters such as in foreign languages are usually available in a font as a single character.

Flood

A user-defined screened or solid box that prints on and completely covers a PressWise blank page. Can be used to print a flat tint on the page, or to produce a mask for manual stripping in existing film-based pages.

Flop

To make a mirror image of visuals such as photographs or clip art.

Folder

1. The digital equivalent of a paper file folder, used to organize files in the Macintosh and Windows operating systems. The icon of a folder looks like a paper file folder. Double-clicking it opens it to reveal the files stored inside. 2. A mechanical device which folds preprinted pages into various formats, such as a tri-fold brochure.

Folding dummy

A template used for determining the page arrangement on a form to meet folding and binding requirements. See also All signature folding dummy and First signature folding dummy.

Font

A font is the complete collection of all the characters (numbers, uppercase and lowercase letters and, in some cases, small caps and symbols) of a given typeface in a specific style; for example, Helvetica Bold.

Force Justify

A type alignment command which causes the space between letters and words in a line of type to expand to fit within a line. Often used in headlines, and sometimes used to force the last line of a justified paragraph, which is normally set flush left, to justify.

Form – Halftone

Form
In PressWise, the front or back of a signature.

Four-color Process
See Process Colors

FPO
Acronym for For Position Only, a term applied to low-quality art reproductions or simple shapes used to indicate placement and scaling of an art element on mechanicals or camera-ready artwork. In digital publishing, an FPO can be low-resolution TIFF files that are later replaced with high-resolution versions. An FPO is not intended for reproduction but only as a guide and placeholder for the prepress service provider.

Frame
In desktop publishing, (1.) an area or block into which text or graphics can be placed; (2.) a border on .

FreeHand
A popular vector-based illustration program available from Macromedia.

Full Measure
A line set to the entire line length.

G (Gigabyte)
One billion (1,073,741,824) bytes (230) or 1,048,576 kilobytes.

Galley Proof
Proofs, usually of type, taken before the type is made up into pages. Before desktop publishing, galley proofs were hand-assembled into pages.

Gamma
A measure of the contrast, or range of tonal variation, of the midtones in a photographic image.

Gamma Correction
1. Adjusting the contrast of the midtones in an image. 2. Calibrating a monitor so that midtones are correctly displayed on screen.

Gamut
See Color Gamut

GASP
Acronym for Graphic Arts Service Provider, a firm that provides a range of services somewhere on the continuum from design to fulfillment.

GCR (Gray component replacement)
A technique for adding detail by reducing the amount of cyan, magenta, and yellow in chromatic or colored areas, replacing them with black.

GIF - Graphics Interface File
A CompuServe graphics file format that is used widely for graphic elements in Web pages.

Global Preferences
Preference settings which affect all newly created files within an application.

Gradient fill
See Graduated fill.

Graduated fill
An area in which two colors (or shades of gray or the same color) are blended to create a gradual change from one to the other. Graduated fills are also known as blends, gradations, gradient fills, and vignettes.

Grain
Silver salts clumped together in differing amounts in different types of photographic emulsions. Generally speaking, faster emulsions have larger grain sizes.

Graininess
Visual impression of the irregularly distributed silver grain clumps in a photographic image, or the ink film in a printed image.

Gray Balance
The values for the yellow, magenta, and cyan inks that are needed to produce a neutral gray when printed at a normal density.

Gray Component Replacement
See GCR

Grayscale
1. An image composed in grays ranging from black to white, usually using 256 different tones of gray. 2. A tint ramp used to measure and control the accuracy of screen percentages on press. 3. An accessory used to define neutral density in a photographic image.

Greeking
1. A software technique by which areas of gray are used to simulate lines of text below a certain point size. 2. Nonsense text use to define a layout before copy is available.

Grid
A division of a page by horizontal and vertical guides into areas into which text or graphics may be placed accurately.

Grind-off
The roughing up at the back (or spine) of a folded signature, or of two or more gathered signatures, in preparation for perfect binding.

Gripper edge
The leading edge of a sheet of paper, which the grippers on the press grab to carry the paper through a press.

Group
To collect graphic elements together so that an operation may be applied to all of them simultaneously.

GUI
Acronym for Graphical User Interface, the basis of the Macintosh and Windows operating systems.

Gutter
Extra space between pages in a layout. Sometimes used interchangeably with Alley to describe the space between columns on a page. Gutters can appear either between the top and bottom of two adjacent pages or between two sides of adjacent pages. Gutters are often used because of the binding or layout requirements of a job — for example, to add space at the top or bottom of each page or to allow for the grind-off taken when a book is perfect bound.

Hairline Rule
The thinnest rule that can be printed on a given device. A hairline rule on a 1200 dpi imagesetter is 1/1200 of an inch; on a 300 dpi laser printer, the same rule would print at 1/300 of an inch.

Halftone
An image generated for use in printing in which a range of continuous tones is simulated by an array of dots that create the illusion of continuous tone when seen at a distance.

GLOSSARY

Halftone Tint
An area covered with a uniform halftone dot size to produce an even tone or color. Also called flat tint or screen tint.

Hard Drive
A rigid disk sealed inside an airtight transport mechanism that is the basic storage mechanism in a computer. Information stored may be accessed more rapidly than on floppy disks and far greater amounts of data may be stored.

High Key
A photographic or printed image in which the main interest area lies in the highlight end of the scale.

High Resolution File
An image file that typically contains four pixels for every dot in the printed reproduction. High-resolution files are often linked to a page layout file, but not actually embedded in it, due to their large size.

Highlights
The lightest areas in a photograph or illustration.

HLS
Color model based on three coordinates: hue, lightness (or luminance), and saturation.

HSV
A color model based on three coordinates: hue, saturation and value (or luminance).

HTML (HyperText Markup Language)
The language, written in plain (ASCII) text using simple tags, that is used to create Web pages, and which Web browsers are designed to read and display. HTML focuses more on the logical structure of a page than its appearance.

Hue
The wavelength of light of a color in its purest state (without adding white or black).

Hyperlink
An HTML tag directs the computer to a different Anchor or URL (Uniform Resource Locator). The linked data may be on the same page, or on a computer anywhere in the world.

Hyphenation Zone
The space at the end of a line of text in which the hyphenation function will examine the word to determine whether or not it should be hyphenated and wrapped to the next line.

Icon
A small graphic symbol used on the screen to indicate files or folders, activated by clicking with the mouse or pointing device.

Illustrator
A vector editing application owned by Adobe Systems, Inc.

Imaging
The process of producing a film or paper copy of a digital file from an output device.

Imagesetter
A raster-based device used to output a computer page-layout file or composition at high resolution (usually 1000 - 3000 dpi) onto photographic paper or film, from which to make printing plates.

Import
To bring a file generated within one application into another application.

Imposition
The arrangement of pages on a printed sheet, which, when the sheet is finally printed, folded and trimmed, will place the pages in their correct order.

Indexed Color Image
An image which uses a limited, predetermined number of colors; often used in Web images. See also GIF.

Indexing
In DTP, marking certain words within a document with hidden codes so that an index may be automatically generated.

Initial Caps
Text in which the first letter of each word (except articles, etc.) is capitalized.

Inline Graphic
A graphic that is inserted within a body of text, and may be formatted using normal text commands for justification and leading; inline graphics will move with the body of text in which they are placed.

Intensity
Synonym for degree of color saturation.

International Paper Sizes
The International Standards Organization (ISO) system of paper sizes is based on a series of three sizes A, B and C. Series A is used for general printing and stationery, Series B for posters, and Series C for envelopes. Each size has the same proportion of length to width as the others. The nearest ISO paper size to conventional 8-1/2 x 11 paper is A4.

ISO
The International Standards Organization.

Jaggies
Visible steps in the curved edge of a graphic or text character that results from enlarging a bitmapped image.

Job state
The state of working in PressWise while one or more jobs are open. Opposite of no-job state.

JPG or JPEG
A compression algorithm that reduces the file size of bitmapped images, named for the Joint Photographic Experts Group, an industry organization that created the standard; JPEG is a "lossy" compression method, and image quality will be reduced in direct proportion to the amount of compression.

Justification
The alignment of text along a margin or both margins..

Kelvin (K)
Unit of temperature measurement based on Celsius degrees, starting from absolute zero, which is equivalent to -273 Celsius (centigrade); used to indicate the color temperature of a light source.

Kerning
Moving a pair of letters closer together or farther apart, to achieve a better fit or appearance.

Key (Black Plate)
In early four-color printing, the black plate was printed first and the other three colors were aligned (or registered) to it. Thus, the black plate was the "key" to the result.

Keyline
A thin, often black border around a picture or a box indicating where to place pictures. In digital files, the keylines are often vector objects while photographs are usually bitmap images.

Kilobyte (K, KB)
1,024 (210) bytes, the nearest binary equivalent to decimal 1,000 bytes. Abbreviated and referred to as K.

Knockout
A printing technique that represents overlapping objects without mixing inks. The ink for the underlying element does not print (knocks out) in the area where the objects overlap. Opposite of overprinting.

L*a*b
The lightness, red-green attribute, and yellow-blue attribute in the CIE Color Space, a three-dimensional color mapping system.

Landscape
Printing from the left to right across the wider side of the page. A landscape orientation treats a page as 11 inches wide and 8.5 inches long.

Laser printer
A high quality image printing system using a laser beam to produce an image on a photosensitive drum. The image is transferred to paper by a conventional xerographic printing process. Current laser printers used for desktop publishing have a resolution of 600 dpi. Imagesetters are also laser printers, but with higher resolution and tight mechanical controls to produce final film separations for commercial printing.

Layer
A function of graphics applications in which elements may be isolated from each other, so that a group of elements may be hidden from view, locked, reordered or otherwise manipulated as a unit, without affecting other elements on the page.

Layout
The arrangement of text and graphics on a page, usually produced in the preliminary design stage.

Leaders
A line of periods or other symbols connecting the end of a group of words with another element separated by some space. For example, a table of contents may consist of a series of phrases on separate lines, each associated with a page number. Promotes readability in long lists of tabular text.

Leading ("ledding")
Space added between lines of type. Usually measured in points or fractions of points. Named after the strips of lead which used to be inserted between lines of metal type. In specifying type, lines of 12-pt. type separated by a 14-pt. space is abbreviated "12/14," or "twelve over fourteen."

Letterspacing
The insertion or addition of white space between the letters of words.

Library
In the computer world, a collection of files having a similar purpose or function.

Ligature
Letters that are joined together as a single unit of type such as oe and fi.

Lightness
The property that distinguishes white from gray or black, and light from dark color tones on a surface.

Line Art
A drawing or piece of black and white artwork, with no screens. Line art can be represented by a graphic file having only one-bit resolution.

Line Screen
The number of lines per inch used when converting a photograph to a halftone. Typical values range from 85 for newspaper work to 150 or higher for high-quality reproduction on smooth or coated paper.

Linking
An association through software of a graphic or text file on disk with its location in a document. That location may be represented by a "placeholder" rectangle, or a low-resolution copy of the graphic.

Linotype-Hell
The manufacturer of imagesetters such as the Linotronic that process PostScript data through an external Raster Image Processor (RIP) to produce high resolution film for printing.

Lithography
A mechanical printing process used for centuries based on the principle of the natural aversion of water (in this case, ink) to grease. In modern offset lithography, the image on a photosensitive plate is first transferred to the blanket of a rotating drum, and then to the paper.

Lossy
A data compression method characterized by the loss of some data.

Loupe
A small free-standing magnifier used to see fine detail on a page. See Linen Tester.

LPI
Lines per inch. See Line Screen.

Luminosity
The amount of light, or brightness, in an image. Part of the HLS color model.

LZW
The acronym for the Lempel-Ziv-Welch lossless data- and image-compression algorithm.

M, MB (Megabyte)
One million (1,048,576) bytes (220) or 1,024 Kilobytes.

Macro
A set of keystrokes that is saved as a named computer file. When accessed, the keystrokes will be performed. Macros are used to perform repetitive tasks.

Margins
The non-printing areas of page, or the line at which text starts or stops.

Mask
To conform the shape of a photograph or illustration to another shape such as a circle or polygon.

Masking
A technique that blocks an area of an image from reproduction by superimposing an opaque object of any shape.

Match Print
A color proofing system used for the final quality check.

Mechanical
A pasted-up page of camera-ready art that is to be photographed to produce a plate for the press.

Mechanical Dot Gain
See Dot Gain

Medium
A physical carrier of data such as a CD-ROM, video cassette, or floppy disk, or a carrier of electronic data such as fiber optic cable or electric wires.

Megabyte (MB)
A unit of measure of stored data equaling 1,024 kilobytes, or 1,048,576 bytes (1020).

Megahertz
An analog signal frequency of one million cycles per second, or a data rate of one million bits per second. Used in specifying computer CPU speed.

Menu
A list of choices of functions, or of items such as fonts. In contemporary software design, there is often a fixed menu of basic functions at the top of the page that have pull-down menus associated with each of the fixed choices.

Metafile
A class of graphics that combines the characteristics of raster and vector graphics formats; not recommended for high-quality output.

Metallic Ink
Printing inks which produce an effect of gold, silver, bronze, or metallic colors.

Midtones or Middletones
The tonal range between highlights and shadows.

Misregistration
The unwanted result of incorrectly aligned process inks and spot colors on a finished printed piece. Misregistration can be caused by many factors, including paper stretch and improper plate alignment. Trapping can compensate for misregistration.

Modem
An electronic device for converting digital data into analog audio signals and back again (Modulator-DEModulator.) Primarily used for transmitting data between computers over analog (audio frequency) telephone lines.

Moiré
An interference pattern caused by the out-of-register overlap of two or more regular patterns such as dots or lines. In process-color printing, screen angles are selected to minimize this pattern.

Monochrome
An image or computer monitor in which all information is represented in black and white, or with a range of grays.

Monospace
A font in which all characters occupy the same amount of horizontal width regardless of the character. See also Proportional Spacing.

Montage
A single image formed by assembling or compositing several images.

Mottle
Uneven color or tone.

Multimedia
The combination of sound, video images, and text to create a "moving" presentation.

Nested signatures
Multiple signatures that are folded, gathered, and placed one inside another, and then saddle-stitched at the spine.

Network
Two or more computers that are linked to exchange data or share resources. The Internet is a network of networks.

Neutral
Any color that has no hue, such as white, gray, or black.

Neutral density
A measurement of the lightness or darkness of a color. A neutral density of zero (0.00) is the lightest value possible and is equivalent to pure white; 3.294 is roughly equivalent to 100% of each of the CMYK components.

Noise
Unwanted signals or data that may reduce the quality of the output.

Non-breaking Space
A typographic command that connects two words with a space, but prevents the words from being broken apart if the space occurs within the hyphenation zone. See Hyphenation Zone.

Non-reproducible Colors
Colors in an original scene or photograph that are impossible to reproduce using process inks. Also called out-of-gamut colors.

Normal Key
A description of an image in which the main interest area is in the middle range of the tone scale or distributed throughout the entire tonal range.

Nudge
To move a graphic or text element in small, preset increments, usually with the arrow keys.

Object-oriented art
Vector-based artwork composed of separate elements or shapes described mathematically rather than by specifying the color and position of every point. This contrasts to bitmap images, which are composed of individual pixels.

Oblique
A slanted character (sometimes backwards, or to the left), often used when referring to italic versions of sans-serif typefaces.

Offset
In graphics manipulation, to move a copy or clone of an image slightly to the side and/or back; used for a drop-shadow effect.

Offset Lithography
A printing method whereby the image is transferred from a plate onto a rubber covered cylinder from which the printing takes place (see Lithography).

Opacity
1. The degree to which paper will show print through it. 2. Settings in certain graphics applications that allow images or text below the object whose opacity has been adjusted, to show through.

OPI

Acronym for Open Prepress Interface. 1. A set of PostScript language comments originally developed by Aldus Corporation for defining and specifying the placement of high-resolution images in PostScript files on an electronic page layout. 2. Incorporation of a low resolution preview image within a graphic file format (TIF, EPS, DCS) that is intended for display only. 3. Software device that is an extension to PostScript that replaces low-resolution placeholder images in a document with their high-resolution sources for printing.

Optical Disks

Video disks that store large amounts of data used primarily for reference works such as dictionaries and encyclopedias.

Output device

Any hardware equipment, such as a monitor, laser printer, or imagesetter, that depicts text or graphics created on a computer.

Overlay

A transparent sheet used in the preparation of multicolor mechanical artwork showing the color breakdown.

Overprint

A printing technique that lays down one ink on top of another ink. The overprinted inks can combine to make a new color. The opposite of knock-out.

Overprint Color

A color made by overprinting any two or more of the primary yellow, magenta, and cyan process colors.

Overprinting

Allowing an element to print over the top of underlying elements, rather than knocking them out (see Knockout). Often used with black type.

Page Description Language (PDL)

A special form of programming language that describes both text and graphics (object or bit-image) in mathematical form. The main benefit of a PDL is that makes the application software independent of the physical printing device. PostScript is a PDL, for example.

Page Layout Software

Desktop publishing software such as PageMaker or QuarkXPress used to combine various source documents and images into a high quality publication.

Page Proofs

Proofs of the actual pages of a document, usually produced just before printing, for a final quality check.

PageMaker

A popular page-layout application produced by Adobe Systems.

Palette

1. As derived from the term in the traditional art world, a collection of selectable colors. 2. Another name for a dialog box or menu of choices.

Panose

A typeface matching system for font substitution based on a numeric classification of fonts according to visual characteristics.

Pantone Matching System

A system for specifying colors by number for both coated and uncoated paper; used by print services and in color desktop publishing to assure uniform color matching.

Parallel fold

A folding method in which folds of a signature are parallel.

Pasteboard

In a page layout program, the desktop area outside of the printing page area, on which elements can be placed for later positioning on any page.

PCX

Bitmap image format produced by paint programs.

PDF (Portable Document Format)

Developed by Adobe Systems, Inc. (and read by Adobe Acrobat Reader), this format has become a de facto standard for document transfer across platforms.

Perfect binding

A binding method in which signatures are "ground off" at the spine of the book and then bound with adhesive, so each page is glued individually to the spine.

Perspective

The effect of distance in an image achieved by aligning the edges of elements with imaginary lines directed toward one to three "vanishing points" on the horizon.

Photoshop

The Adobe Systems image editing program commonly used for color correction and special effects on both the Macintosh and PC platforms.

Pi Fonts

A collection of special characters such as timetable symbols and mathematical signs. Examples are Zapf Dingbats and Symbol. See also Dingbats.

Pica

A traditional typographic measurement of 12 points, or approximately 1/6 of an inch. Most DTP applications specify a pica as exactly 1/6 of an inch.

PICT/PICT2

A common format for defining bitmapped images on the Macintosh. The more recent PICT2 format supports 24-bit color.

Pixel

Abbreviation for picture element, one of the tiny rectangular areas or dots generated by a computer or output device to constitute images.

PMS

See Pantone Matching System

PMT

Photo Mechanical Transfer - positive prints of text or images used for paste-up to mechanicals.

Point

A unit of measurement used to specify type size and rule weight, equal to (approximately, in traditional typesetting) 1/72 inch.

Polygon

A geometric figure consisting of three or more straight lines enclosing an area. The triangle, square, rectangle, and star are all polygons.

Portrait

Printing from left to right across the narrow side of the page. Portrait orientation on a letter-size page uses a standard 8.5-inch width and 11-inch length.

Positive – Registration Color

Positive
A true photographic image of the original made on paper or film.

Posterize, Posterization
The deliberate constraint of a gradient or image into visible steps as a special effect; or the unintentional creation of steps in an image due to a high LPI value used with a low printer DPI.

Postprocessing Applications
Applications, such as trapping programs or imposition software, that perform their functions after the image has been printed to a file, rather than in the originating application.

PostScript
1. A page description language developed by Adobe Systems, Inc. that describes type and/or images and their positional relationships upon the page. 2. An interpreter or RIP (see Raster Image Processor) that can process the PostScript page description into a format for laser printer or imagesetter output. 3. A computer programming language.

PostScript Printer Description file
See PPD.

PPD
Acronym for PostScript Printer Description, a file format developed by Adobe Systems, Inc., that contains device-specific information enabling software to produce the best results possible for each type of designated printer.

PPI
Pixels per inch; used to denote the resolution of an image.

Preferences
A set of defaults for an application program that may be modified.

Prepress
All work done between writing and printing, such as typesetting, scanning, layout, and imposition.

Prepress Proof
A color proof made directly from electronic data or film images.

Press sheet
In sheet-fed printing, the paper stock of common sizes that is used in commercial printing.

Primary Colors
Colors that can be used to generate secondary colors. For the additive system (i.e., a computer monitor), these colors are red, green, and blue. For the subtractive system (i.e., the printing process), these colors are yellow, magenta, and cyan.

Printer Command Language
PCL — a language, that has graphics capability, developed by Hewlett Packard for use with its own range of printers.

Printer fonts
The image outlines for type in PostScript that are sent to the printer.

Process colors
The four transparent inks (cyan, magenta, yellow, and black) used in four-color process printing. See also Color separation; CMYK.

Profile
A file containing data representing the color reproduction characteristics of a device determined by a calibration of some sort.

Proof
A representation of the printed job that is made from plates (press proof), film, or electronic data (prepress proofs). It is generally used for customer inspection and approval before mass production begins.

Proportional Spacing
A method of spacing whereby each character is spaced to accommodate the varying widths of letters or figures, thus increasing readability. Books and magazines are set proportionally spaced, and most fonts in desktop publishing are proportional. With proportionally spaced fonts, each character is given a horizontal space proportional to its size. For example, a proportionally spaced "m" is wider than an "i."

Pt.
Abbreviation for point.

QuarkXPress
A popular page-layout application.

Queue
A set of files input to the printer, printed in the order received unless otherwise instructed.

QuickDraw
Graphic routines in the Macintosh used for outputting text and images to printers not compatible with PostScript.

RAM
Random Access Memory, the "working" memory of a computer that holds files in process. Files in RAM are lost when the computer is turned off, whereas files stored on the hard drive or floppy disks remain available.

Raster
A bitmapped representation of graphic data.

Raster Graphics
A class of graphics created and organized in a rectangular array of bitmaps. Often created by paint software, fax machines, or scanners for display and printing.

Raster Image Processor (RIP)
That part of a PostScript printer or imagesetting device that converts the page information from the PostScript Page Description Language into the bitmap pattern that is applied to the film or paper output.

Rasterize
The process of converting digital information into pixels at the resolution of the output device. For example, the process used by an imagesetter to translate PostScript files before they are imaged to film or paper. See also RIP.

Reflective Art
Artwork that is opaque, as opposed to transparent, that can be scanned for input to a computer.

Registration
Aligning plates on a multicolor printing press so that the images will superimpose properly to produce the required composite output.

Registration Color
A default color selection that can be applied to design elements so that they will print on every separation from a PostScript printer. "Registration" is often used to print identification text that will appear outside the page area on a set of separations.

Registration marks
Figures (often crossed lines and a circle) placed outside the trim page boundaries on all color separation overlays to provide a common element for proper alignment.

Resolution
The density of graphic information expressed in dots per inch (dpi) or pixels per inch (ppi).

Retouching
Making selective manual or electronic corrections to images.

Reverse Out
To reproduce an object as white, or paper, within a solid background, such as white letters in a black rectangle.

RGB
Acronym for red, green, blue, the colors of projected light from a computer monitor that, when combined, simulate a subset of the visual spectrum. When a color image is scanned, RGB data is collected by the scanner and then converted to CMYK data at some later step in the process. Also refers to the color model of most digital artwork. See also CMYK.

Rich Black
A process color consisting of sold black with one or more layers of cyan, magenta, or yellow.

Right Reading
A positive or negative image that is readable from top to bottom and from left to right.

Right-angle fold
A folding method in which any successive fold of a signature is at right angles to the previous fold.

RIP
See Raster Image Processor

ROM
Read Only Memory, a semiconductor chip in the computer that retains startup information for use the next time the computer is turned on.

Rosette
The pattern created when color halftone screens are printed at traditional screen angles.

Rotation
Turning an object at some angle to its original axis.

RTF
Rich Text Format, a text format that retains formatting information lost in pure ASCII text.

Rubylith
A two-layer acetate film having a red or amber emulsion on a clear base used in non-computer stripping and separation operations.

Saddle-stitching
A binding method in which each signature is folded and stapled at the spine.

Sans Serif
Sans Serif fonts are fonts that do not have the tiny lines that appear at the top of and bottom of letters.

Saturation
The intensity or purity of a particular color; a color with no saturation is gray.

Scaling
The means within a program to reduce or enlarge the amount of space an image will occupy by multiplying the data by a scale factor. Scaling can be proportional, or in one dimension only.

Scanner
A device that electronically digitizes images point by point through circuits that can correct color, manipulate tones, and enhance detail. Color scanners will usually produce a minimum of 24 bits for each pixel, with 8 bits each for red, green, and blue.

Screen
To create a halftone of a continuous tone image (See Halftone).

Screen Angle
The angle at which the rulings of a halftone screen are set when making screened images for halftone process-color printing. The equivalent effect can be obtained electronically through selection of the desired angle from a menu.

Screen Frequency
The number of lines per inch in a halftone screen, which may vary from 85 to 300.

Screen Printing
A technique for printing on practically any surface using a fine mesh (originally of silk) on which the image has been placed photographically. Preparation of art for screen printing requires consideration of the resolution of the screen printing process.

Screen Shot
A printed output or saved file that represents data from a computer monitor.

Screen Tint
A halftone screen pattern of all the same dot size that creates an even tone at some percentage of solid color.

SCSI
Small Computer Systems Interface, a standard software protocol for connecting peripheral devices to a computer for fast data transfer.

Selection
The act of placing the cursor on an object and clicking the mouse button to make the object active.

Self-Cover
A cover for a document in which the cover is of the same paper stock as the rest of the piece.

SEP
A PostScript file format created from PageMaker that can contain multiple pages as well as links in the form of OPI comments to high-resolution images, in color or in black and white.

Separation
See Color separation.

Serif
A line or curve projecting from the end of a letter form. Typefaces designed with such projections are called serif faces.

Service Bureau
A business that specializes in producing film for printing on a high-resolution imagesetter.

SGML
Standard Generalized Markup Language, a set of semantics and syntax that describes the structure of a document (the nature, content, or function of the data) as opposed to visual appearance. HTML is a subset of SGML (see HTML).

Sharpness
The subjective impression of the density difference between two tones at their boundary, interpreted as fineness of detail.

Shortcut
1. A quick method for accessing a menu item or command, usually through a series of keystrokes. 2. The icon that can be created in Windows95 to open an application without having to penetrate layers of various folders. The equivalent in the Macintosh is the "alias."

Silhouette
To remove part of the background of a photograph or illustration, leaving only the desired portion.

Skew
A transformation command that slants an object at an angle to the side from its initial fixed base.

Small caps
A type style in which lowercase letters are replaced by uppercase letters set in a smaller point size.

Smart Quotes
The curly quotation marks used by typographers, as opposed to the straight marks on the typewriter. Use of smart quotes is usually a setup option in a word processing program or page layout application

Snap-to (guides or rulers)
An optional feature in page layout programs that drives objects to line up with guides or margins if they are within a pixel range that can be set. This eliminates the need for very precise, manual placement of an object with the mouse.

Soft or Discretionary Hyphen
A hyphen coded for display and printing only when formatting of the text puts the hyphenated word at the end of a line.

Soft Return
A return command that ends a line but does not apply a paragraph mark that would end the continuity of the style for that paragraph.

Spectrophotometer
An instrument for measuring the relative intensity of radiation reflected or transmitted by a sample over the spectrum.

Specular Highlight
The lightest highlight area that does not carry any detail, such as reflections from glass or polished metal. Normally, these areas are reproduced as unprinted white paper.

Spine
The binding edge at the back of a book that contains title information and joins the front and back covers.

Spot Color
Any pre-mixed ink that is not one of or a combination of the four process color inks, often specified by a Pantone swatch number.

Spread
Two facing pages that can be worked on as a unit, and will be viewed side by side in the final publication.

Stacking Order
The order of the elements on a PostScript page, wherein the topmost item may obscure the items beneath it if they overlap.

Standard Viewing Conditions
A prescribed set of conditions under which the viewing of originals and reproductions are to take place, defining both the geometry of the illumination and the spectral power distribution of the light source.

Step-and-repeat
A layout in which two or more copies of the same piece are placed on a single plate. This is useful for printing several copies of a small layout, such as a business card, on a single sheet. Also called a multiple-up layout.

Stet
Used in proof correction work to cancel a previous correction. From the Latin; "let it stand."

Stochastic Screening
A method of creating halftones in which the size of the dots remains constant but their density is varied; also known as frequency-modulated (or FM) screening.

Stripping
The act of manually assembling individual film negatives into flats for printing. Also referred to as film assembly.

Stroke, Stroking
Manipulating the width or color of a line.

Stuffit
A file compression utility used in the Macintosh environment.

Style
A set of formatting instructions for font, paragraphing, tabs, and other properties of text.

Style Sheet
A file containing all of the tags and instructions for formatting all parts of a document; style sheets create consistency between similar documents.

Subhead
A second-level heading used to organize body text by topic.

Subscript
Small-size characters set below the normal letters or figures, usually to convey technical information.

Substitution
Using an existing font to simulate one that is not available to the printer.

Subtractive Color
Color which is observed when light strikes pigments or dyes, which absorb certain wavelengths of light; the light that is reflected back is perceived as a color. See CMYK and Process Color.

Superscript
Small characters set above the normal letters or figures, such as numbers referring to footnotes.

System Folder
The location of the operating system files on a Macintosh.

Tabloid
Paper 11 inches wide x 17 inches long.

Tagged Image File Format (TIFF)
A common format for used for scanned or computer-generated bitmapped images.

Tags
The various formats in a style sheet that indicate paragraph settings, margins and columns, page layouts, hyphenation and justification, widow and orphan control and other parameters.

Template

A document file containing layout and styles by which a series of documents can maintain the same look and feel.

Text

The characters and words that form the main body of a publication.

Text Attribute

A characteristic applied directly to a letter or letters in text, such as bold, italic, or underline.

Text wrap

See Wrap

Texture

1. A property of the surface of the substrate, such as the smoothness of paper. 2. Graphically, variation in tonal values to form image detail. 3. A class of fills in a graphics application that give various appearances, such as bricks, grass, etc.

Thin Space

A fixed space, equal to half an en space or the width of a period in most fonts.

Thumbnails

1. The preliminary sketches of a design. 2. Small images used to indicate the content of a computer file.

TIFF

See Tagged Image File Format

Tile

1. A type of repeating fill pattern. 2. Reproduce a number of pages of a document on one sheet. 3. Printing a large document overlapping on several smaller sheets of paper.

Tint

1. A halftone area that contains dots of uniform size; that is, no modeling or texture. 2. The mixture of a color with white.

Tip In

The separate insertion of a single page into a book either during or after binding by pasting one edge.

Toggle

A command that switches between either of two states at each application. Switching between Hide and Show is a toggle.

Tracking

Adjusting the spacing of letters in a line of text to achieve proper justification or general appearance.

Transfer Curve

A curve depicting the adjustment to be made to a particular printing plate when an image is printed.

Transparency

A full color photographically produced image on transparent film.

Transparent Ink

An ink that allows light to be transmitted through it.

Trapping

The process of creating an overlap between abutting inks to compensate for imprecise registration in the printing process.

Trim

After printing, mechanically cutting the publication to the correct final dimensions. The trim size is normally indicated by marks on the printing plate outside the page area.

Trim page size

Area of the finished page after the job is printed, folded, bound, and cut.

TrueType

An outline font format used in both Macintosh and Windows systems that can be used both on the screen and on a printer.

Type 1 Fonts

PostScript fonts based on Bézier curves encrypted for compactness that are compatible with Adobe Type Manager.

Type Family

A set of typefaces created from the same basic design but in different weights, such as bold, light, italic, book, and heavy.

Typesetting

The arrangement of individual characters of text into words, sentences, and paragraphs.

Typo

An abbreviation for typographical error. A keystroke error in the typeset copy.

UCR (undercolor removal)

A technique for reducing the amount of magenta, cyan, and yellow inks in neutral or shadow areas and replacing them with black.

Undertone

Color of ink printed in a thin film.

Unsharp Masking

A digital technique (based on a traditional photographic technique) performed after scanning that locates the edge between sections of differing lightness and alters the values of the adjoining pixels to exaggerate the difference across the edge, thereby increasing edge contrast.

Uppercase

The capital letters of a typeface as opposed to the lowercase, or small, letters. When type was hand composited, the capital letters resided in the upper part of the type case.

Utility

Software that performs ancillary tasks such as counting words, defragmenting a hard drive, or restoring a deleted file.

Varnish Plate

The plate on a printing press that applies varnish after the other colors have been applied.

Varnishing

A finishing process whereby a transparent varnish is applied over the printed sheet to produce a glossy or protective coating, either on the entire sheet or on selected areas.

Vector Graphics

Graphics defined using coordinate points, and mathematically drawn lines and curves, which may be freely scaled and rotated without image degradation in the final output. Fonts (such as PostScript and TrueType), and illustrations from drawing applications are common examples of vector objects. Two commonly used vector drawing programs are Illustrator and FreeHand. A class of graphics that overcomes the resolution limitation of bitmapped graphics.

Velox

Strictly, a Kodak chloride printing paper, but used to describe a high-quality black & white print of a halftone or line drawing.

Vertical Justification

The ability to automatically adjust the interline spacing (leading) to make columns and pages end at the same point on a page.

Vignette

An illustration in which the background gradually fades into the paper; that is, without a definite edge or border.

Visible Spectrum

The wavelengths of light between about 380 nm (violet) and 700 nm (red) that are visible to the human eye.

Watermark

An impression incorporated in paper during manufacturing showing the name of the paper and/or the company logo. A "watermark" can be applied digitally to printed output as a very light screened image.

Web Press

An offset printing press that prints from a roll of paper rather than single sheets.

White Light

Light containing all wavelengths of the visible spectrum.

White Space

Areas on the page which contain no images or type. Proper use of white space is critical to a well-balanced design.

Window Shade

A type of text block used in certain applications, such as PageMaker. Windowshades have handles at the top and bottom which, when dragged with the mouse, will reveal or conceal text.

Wizard

A utility attached to an application or operating system that aids you in setting up a piece of hardware, software, or document.

WYSIWYG

An acronym for "What You See Is What You Get," (pronounced "wizzywig") meaning that what you see on your computer screen bears a strong resemblance to what the job will look like when it is printed.

X-height

The height of the letter "x" in a given typeface, which represents the basic size of the bodies of all of the lowercase letters (excluding ascenders and descenders).

Xerography

A photocopying/printing process in which the image is formed using the electrostatic charge principle. The toner replaces ink and can be dry or liquid. Once formed, the image is sealed by heat. Most page printers currently use this method of printing.

Zero Point

The mathematical "origin" of the coordinates of the two-dimensional page. The zero point may be moved to any location on the page, and the ruler dimensions change accordingly.

Zip

1. To compress a file on a Windows-based system using a popular compression utility (PKZIP). 2. A removable disk made by Iomega (a Zip disk) or the device that reads and writes such disks (a Zip drive).

Zooming

The process of electronically enlarging or reducing an image on a monitor to facilitate detailed design or editing and navigation.

INDEX

SYMBOLS

16- and 32-bit 12
8-bit 12

A

accents for all caps 23
accurate blends 20
Adobe Illustrator 74
agates 18
alignment 109
alpha channel 141
anchoring 146
append styles 156
application preferences 10, 11
auto
   backup 16
   constrain 20
   hyphenation 65
   kern 22
auto leading 20
auto page insertion 18
auto picture import 19
auto save 16
auto-image
   for creating runarounds 134
automatic text boxes 18

B

background color 122
   setting defaults 23
baseline 109
baseline grid 53
   applying to style 58
baseline shift 53
bézier 26
bézier path picture box tool 138
bezier pen tools 86, 107, 110, 111
bezier text placeholder 95
binary
   as a save option for eps previews 206
bleed 30
bleed elements 46
blends *displaying accurately* 20
body text 153
book command
   using 174
book palette 176
border 10
boxes
   trapping 209
break above 23
break capitalized words 66
building a book 175
bulleted lists 53

C

captions 153
capture settings feature 194, 197
changing backgrounds 122
chapters 174
   preferences 21
character styles 152
choke 208
choking 207
circles
   placing type around 114
clipping path 11
clipping paths 124, 125
   importing from a drawing program 136
   potential problems 142
closed shapes 86
CMS 27
CMYK 27, 200
collect for output 207
color balance 210
color management system 27
color output 194
color picker 11
color tiffs 12
colors 10, 30
   stroke 10
complex text elements 98
composited type characters 98
condensed type 64
consistency 170
consistent styles 152
content
   of a placeholder 93
continuous tone art 203
contract proofing 210
converting text to paths 98
copy fitting 59
CopyDesk 59
copywriters 152
CorelDraw 98
corners
   creating with the pen tool 91
creating and editing chapters 174
curved or shaped lines 86
curved paths
   for text 110
custom angles 204
custom grids 47
custom placeholders 74
customizing tools 24
cut 15
cyan 200

D

decimal
   inches 18
decks 153
default
   screen 204
   changing 10
default style document 154
delayed item dragging 14
deleting a print style 199
digital imposition 209
dingbats 116
display
   blend accuracy 20
   full screen preference 11
display tab 11
dividing pages 47
document preferences 10, 17
dot
   screen 204
drag and drop text 15
dragging 14

E

edit styles 165
editorial priority 152
ellipse
   screen 204
em space 59
embedded path 136
encapsulated postscript 206
end of story 18
endpoints 94
EPS 20, 206
   saving a QuarkXPress document 206
expert set 22
exporting a print style 199

F

fade to white 126
fills 10
flex space 22
flush zone 66
fractional 18
frame 10
frame width 23
frames
   trapping 209
framing 18
FreeHand 98
freehand picture placeholder 95
freehand text placeholder 95
French 13
full-screen documents 11

INDEX 1

G

German 13
global style changes 177
graphics from type characters 99
greek below 20
greek pictures 20
greeked 13
grids 30, 46
   building 48
   color 11
guides 18, 46
   hiding and displaying 48
   snap distance 19
   color 11

H

H&J's 10, 30, 64
   creating custom 66
halftoning 196, 203
handle 90
headlines 60, 153
horizontal
   ruler settings 17
hscale
   of superscript type 22
hyphenation and justification 64
hyphenation zone 66
hyphens in a row 66

I

Illustrator 74, 98
images *greeking* 20
imagesetter 194
imported art 122
importing a print style 200
imposition 30, 209
in line graphics
   anchoring 146
inches decimal 18
index palette 186
inside 18
interactive tab 13
item 128

J

join endpoints 94
joining complex paths 93
justification 64
   method 66

K

keep changes 19
keep document settings 11

keep with next paragraph 165
kern 22
kerning 59
   pairs 59
kerning table edit 59
knockout 208

L

laser printer 194
layout fitting 59
leading 53
libraries 27
ligatures 23
line
   screen 204
line width
   setting defaults 23
lines per inch 204
list of illustrations 181
lists 10, 181
live area 46
long documents
   managing 170

M

Macromedia FreeHand 74
Magenta 200
magnify tool
   setting defaults 23
maintain leading 21
managing output 194
margin 46
mask
   creating a 125
masks 98
master documents 177
master page items 19
master pages 30, 170
matching
   colors in a proof 210
measurement system 17
measurements pallete 108
merge
   union 77
merged objects
   applying blends to 80
merging 75
metric 18
Microsoft Word 152, 154
minimum after 66
minimum before 65
misregistration
   trapping and 207
mode
   paragraph 21

modified type elements 98
modify 23
monitors
   using multiple 11
multiple merged objects
   applying blends 83

N

new print styles
   creating 199
next paragraph 165
next style 163
non-printing grids 46
non-white areas 135
numbered lists 53

O

off-screen draw 11
offset
   of superscript type 22
Open Prepress Interface 207
OPI 207
ordered dither
   screen 204
orphans
   controlling 164
orthogonal line tool 108
output
   managing 194
Output Request Form 207
outset value 139
outside 18
overflow 18
overprint 208
overriding existing styles 160

P

page margins 46
page numbering 179
paragraph 165
   preferences 20
paragraph styles 152
parent/child relationships 20
paste 15
paths
   for text 107
pen tool 86
photographs
   halftoning 203
Photoshop
   masks 141
PICT 206
points/inch 19
polygons 122
PostScript 205

PostScript printer 194, 198
PostScript printer description files 205
PPD manager 205
PPD's 200
preferences 122
    application 10
    general 17
preferences 10, 11
prepress equipment 27
preview
    in an eps file 206
print dialog box 195, 205
print styles
    editing existing 199
printing

profiles
    for color management 27, 197
proofing 210
properties 172
publications 170
pull-quotes 153
punctuation 59

Q

QuarkXPress 152
quotation marks 13
quotes 13

R

Raster Image Processor 209
read-only 30
registration 210
registration marks 36
restrict to box 140
RGB 27
RIP 209
rotation tool 109
rulers 46, 48, 83
    color 11
rules above or below 53
runaround 10, 11, 14, 26, 122, 124
    setting defaults 23
    type 128
    alternative methods for creating 141
    tracking and kerning with 133

S

save as
    with template files 171
save page as EPS 206
saving a preview with an eps file 206
screening 203
screens 204
    setting custom angles 204

scrolling 13
section breaks 180
sections 179
seeing hidden guides 19
select similar shape 26
select similar type 26
separations 210
setup tab 195
shapes 46, 74
show tool tips 15
signatures 209
silohuettes
    wrapping type around 125
smallest word value 65
smart quotes 14
snap distance 19
soft edges 126
space before or after 53
spreading 207
square
    screen 204
standard em space 22
stationery pad 171
straight quotes 13
stroke colors 10
structured documents 170
style
    tags in text files 162
style features 98
style sheets 30
styles 10, 152
    appending from other documents 156
styles 153
subheads 153
superscript 22
synchronize command 179

T

table of contents 181
tagged text files 162
template 154
template files 47
templates 10, 30, 170
text
    coloring 122
    trapping 208
text boxes 10
text containers 74
text inset
    setting defaults 23
text on circles or ovals 114
text on curved paths 110, 11
text on paths 107
text path tool 95

text placeholders 30
    transparent
text to box 105
text to paths 98
thickness
    of borders 10
TIFF 20, 141, 206
    displaying in color 12
    displaying in grayscale 12
    grayscale 204
tiling 201
tool
    preferences 23
toolbar
    customizing 26
tracking 59, 87
transparent text boxes 122
trapping 26, 207
trim 30
trim guides 46
type
    color of 63
    expert characters 22
    greeking 13, 20
type inside of character-based graphics
    103
type management functions 98
type size 53
typesetting mode 21
typographer's quotes 13
typographic controls 98
typographical effects 60

V

vertical
    ruler setting 17
vignettes 126
vscale
    of superscript type 22

W

widow controls 164
word and letter spacing
    in runarounds 133
workflow 10, 161, 194

X

XTensions manager 17

Y

yellow 200

Z

zoom 26